The Kennedy Center
American College Theater
Festival Presents:

Award-Winning Plays from
the Michael Kanin National
Playwriting Program

THE KENNEDY CENTER AMERICAN COLLEGE THEATER FESTIVAL PRESENTS:

Award-Winning Plays from the Michael Kanin National Playwriting Program

EDITED BY GARY GARRISON

BACKSTAGE BOOKS
An imprint of Watson-Guptill Publications/New York

Senior Editor: Mark Glubke
Project Editor: Gary Sunshine
Cover Design: Platinum Design
Interior Design: Cheryl Viker
Production Manager: Ellen Greene

First published in 2006 by Back Stage Books,
an imprint of Watson-Guptill Publications,
a division of VNU Business Media, Inc.
770 Broadway, New York, NY 10003
www.wgpub.com.com

Library of Congress Control Number: 2005934745

ISBN: 0-8230-8390-X

Manufactured in the United States of America

First printing 2006

1 2 3 4 5 6 7 / 12 11 10 09 08 07 06

Be yourself.
There is something that you can do
better than any other.
Listen to the inward voice
and bravely obey that.

AUTHOR UNKNOWN

Leap . . . and the net will appear.

JOHN BURROUGHS

Dedication

This inaugural anthology is dedicated to the following tireless supporters of new plays and playwrights: the regional and national playwriting chairs for the Kennedy Center American College Theater Festival for the year the plays included were originally produced.

Lauren Friesen

Tom Isbell

Patricia Riggin

Judith Royer

Adrienne Thompson

Elliot Wasserman

Connie Whitt-Lambert

Contents

Foreword

What you're about to read is a testament of faith. A collection of testaments, actually, written by young pioneers who exhibit the same kind of fearless, can-do spirit as our hearty forefathers (and mothers) did. I'm talking about the student playwrights collected in this volume, most of whom are experiencing the thrill of being published for the first time, and who represent the very front lines of our artistic community and the best hope for the survival of our species. Being a playwright is an absolute guarantee of absolutely nothing. One can toil and strive for years in this business and have nothing come out of the arrangement other than heartbreak and disappointment. If they are true playwrights, however, the only greater disappointment that exists is the prospect of not writing plays at all. They will find that this is not an acceptable option, and their work will continue as they fly in the face of convention and good common sense. God (or whatever deity it is you fancy) be praised.

David Rabe once told me that playwrights need to stick together because we are like buffalo, a dying breed. Like those sturdy animals, though, the writers represented in this book (because anyone who writes, who actually sits down and puts their thoughts on paper is a writer) have weathered the storm and been variously praised by being a part of the American College Theater Festival at the Kennedy Center, won awards for their work and enjoyed the ephemeral pleasure of seeing their writing staged in front of an audience. And here it is, all that hard work, collected in a single volume for your own enjoyment; if you've made it this far you are indeed a lucky reader because you will momentarily experience the best that the young collegiate playwright has to offer.

So sit back and relax, get comfortable, and enjoy yourself. Put your feet up and value what you have in your hands as you understand the power of your position—you are as important as any audience these authors will ever face. Tonight you are their audience, and we are in the audience business, make no mistake about that. Writers want to entertain you—not play up or down to you, not pander to you, but really entertain you—as we slip the message in through the cracks while you're not watching. Chekhov once encouraged Gorki to "Write, write, write!" It was the most valuable advice he could offer the young scribe and it still pertains today. To you the reader I suggest the same directive, only in the form of "Read, read, read!" In this case, I promise that you will not be disappointed.

NEIL LaBUTE

Introduction

Writing a play is as daunting as trying to push a fat horse through the eye of a needle. It feels—in a word—impossible. Despite all your years of training, or working in/around/through every no-name/lame theater you could get involved with, or even after having some remarkable professional productions in semi-reputable theaters, each time you sit down to write a new play, it's your first time; an unwilling virgin to the blank page. Your neurotic, internal monologue goes something like this: "Oh, for God's sake, what are you doing?! You're trying to write a play? Why don't you do a four-point tire rotation on your car because you're about as skilled at doing that as you are at writing a play. You can't write! You can't even pretend to be a writer. You have no good ideas, your dialogue sucks, your characters are thinner than your hairline, your plots are about as obvious as your lack of talent, and your last play was a horror—and not in a *I Know What You Did Last Summer* kinda way. Didn't you vow the last time you wrote a play it would be your last? So what the hell are you doing? Go make a meatloaf. At least you get to eat that."

And yet . . . you begin. Somehow, some way, your head clears out, your heart opens up, your soul engages, and you begin this almost transcendent flow of creative energy: feelings from the heart stimulate ideas in the head which race to the page through fingers tapping out dramatic rhythms on a keyboard. Time disappears. The sloppy room you're in disappears. The over-due bills you have to remember to pay are easily forgotten. The phone calls you're supposed to make—also forgotten. Body functions stop. Your boyfriend/girlfriend/husband/wife/mother/father/brother/sister/roommate ceases to be. You don't eat, sleep becomes a waste of time and you have to remind yourself to breathe. Suspended in your own creativity, the world around you stops while the world inside you spins like a tornado. And out of nowhere, or *everywhere* inside you, mother-love, father-hate, lost love, found anger, explosive joy, or throbbing injury finds its way to the surface and obstinately plants itself in the landscape of your play.

One day, after weeks, months, or even years of that heart-to-head-to-fingers exchange, you earn the right to say, "I'm done. I've finished. Lights down. The end." But the messed-up truth is it's really just the very, very beginning. How could that be? How could it not be over?! How could there be a single thing left to do after all that worry, work, thinking, creating, and conceiving? DAMN IT! MAKING A MEATLOAF WOULD HAVE BEEN SO MUCH EASIER!

But there are second drafts, third drafts, tenth drafts, readings, more readings, workshops, and drafts twelve, thirteen, and fourteen to hammer out. And even then it's not over. When you've done all that you're capable of doing to the world of your play, somebody has got to actually produce it or it's just literature, and not even published literature at that. Your play has to begin its life and play out its turbulent childhood in front of audience. That's where the playwrights in this book became incredibly smart parents and took a huge step forward: they (and their colleges and universities) mounted a production of their play and entered it in the Kennedy Center's American College Theater Festival (KCACTF).

Every year KCACTF showcases more than twenty-thousand college students in more than twelve hundred student productions from all across the country in a celebration of the finest college theater. Can you imagine the collective energy?! Student actors, designers, playwrights, and technicians from eight regions in the country compete for awards for their artistry. Only a handful of original student plays, performed by some of our country's best student actors, vie for a variety of writing awards and a production at the nation's center for the performing arts at the annual KCACTF National Festival.

To make it to D.C. and the National Festival, it works something like this: you write a play (see description of agonizing process above). Your college or university scrapes together some money and produces your play and enters it in KCACTF. A response team of two trained, critical observers comes to your university, watches your play and then (hopefully) recommends to the region's creative-administrative staff that they consider it (among the several other student original plays produced in your region), to be invited to and reproduced at your regional festival. In each region, there is a "decision" weekend, and after days of often contentious deliberation, the regional officers choose your play among all student plays written and produced in your region. Your production, then, is awarded an invitation to the regional festival.

At your regional festival, your play is showcased and sandwiched in between productions such as *Much Ado About Nothing, Proof, How I Learned to Drive, The Laramie Project, Fences,* and *West Side Story* from neighboring colleges and universities. A national response team of four—composed of Gregg Henry, Artistic Director of KCACTF, a theater artist of national prominence, an artist from academia, and the National Chair of KCACTF— visit all eight regions evaluating every invited production brought to each region. They, in turn, have their own "decision" weekend, and choose one full-length student original play to bring to D.C., (the *Michael Kanin National Student Playwriting Award*–winner), as well as the best short play (the *John Cauble Award for Best Short Play*) as part of the Michael Kanin Playwriting Awards Program.

But if your play isn't invited to D.C., you don't have to take out the razor blade because all is not lost. The Kennedy Center (through the Kanin program) recognizes excellence in student playwriting through a large variety of awards based solely on the written text. If your play is comic or has some comic element to it, it's eligible for the *Mark Twain Comedy Award.* If a play is written by a person of African heritage, and it deals with the African-American experience here or abroad, it could be awarded the *Lorraine Hansberry Award*. If your play deals with the human experience of living with a disability, it could win the *Jean Kennedy Smith Award*. If your play celebrates diversity and encourages tolerance while exploring issues of marginalized voices not traditionally considered mainstream (read: gay/lesbian/bisexual/transgendered/others), you might win the *Paula Vogel Award* (Vogel, by the way, was herself a student award winner in KCACTF). If you're a person of Latino heritage, your play could be considered for the *Latino/a Playwriting Award*. If you've written a ten-minute play (and really, who hasn't?!), you could snag the *National Ten Minute Play Award*. You can be a student or a working playwright and win the *David Mark Cohen National Playwriting Award*. And there are other awards for children's plays and musicals; cash prizes and residencies with Sundance Theater Lab, The O'Neill Theater Center, and Portland Stage, to name a few.

Why create another anthology of plays? Does the world really need another anthology? Resolutely, yes. You need to read these plays. These plays are remarkable for their dramatic scope, vision, and imagination. And each play in this inaugural anthology has won at least one award or garnered some sort of recognition in KCACTF, and several playwrights had the nerve to win multiple awards the year they were presented at the Kennedy Center, (Molly Metzler's gorgeous family comic-drama, *Training Wysteria*, was cited with the Michael Kanin National Student Playwriting Award, the Mark Twain Comedy Award, and the David Mark Cohen National Playwriting Award—not bad for her first full-length play). If they didn't win a named award, they were in contention and are included in this anthology just because they were too damned good to leave out (I almost defy you to find a more deftly written, painfully poignant one-act than Brian Tanen's *The Man of Infinite Sadness*). If the Kennedy Center hadn't recognized the excellence of, say, Rebecca Basham's *Lot's Daughters*—a heart-wrenching period-drama centered around the love relationship between two women—it was only a matter of time before some smart theater, some savvy producer, astute artistic director, or insightful literary manager found it. We're just happy that we found it first.

Look, cowboys and cowgirls, I've been teaching playwriting for twenty-five years and have worked with KCACTF for the last twelve. *Nothing* in the contemporary theater compares to the support and encouragement that the Kennedy Center doles out on an annual basis. It's a grueling, mind-numbing business to write a play, but it's even more of an effort to bring your play from the page to the stage. The Kennedy Center and KCACTF understands just what it takes to be a young artist in this day and age, and so it strives to make life better for every young playwright in this country. If you want to know more about this extraordinary program, check out www.kcactf.org.

As you read through these extraordinary plays, written by some of the country's best student playwrights, remember where it all started: with some young playwright, sitting at a desk, staring at a blank screen, pushing away all the naysayers (including themselves), and finding the courage to embrace a hope, a desire and a dream.

Given the choice between making a meatloaf or writing one page of any of these plays, I'd struggle with writing that page any day of the week.

GARY GARRISON
National Chair
National Playwriting Program,
KCACTF

Full-Length Plays

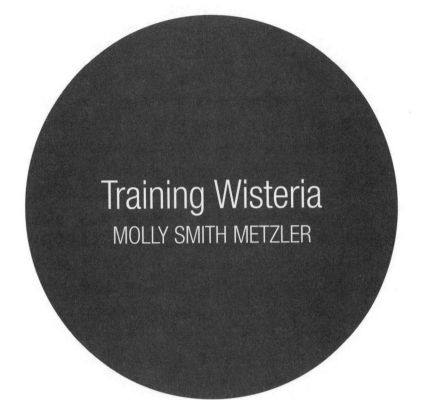

Training Wisteria
MOLLY SMITH METZLER

About the Playwright

As a playwright, **Molly Smith Metzler**'s work has been produced at The Kennedy Center, The Boston Playwrights Theater, The Cherry Lane Theatre (NY Fringe), and The American Globe Theater among others. She is an alumna of the graduate playwriting program at Boston University, where she wrote her first full-length play, *Training Wisteria,* the 2003 winner of the Michael Kanin National Student Playwriting Award, the David Mark Cohen National Playwriting Award and the Mark Twain Comedy Playwriting Award for the Kennedy Center's American College Theatre Festival. The play also earned Molly a fellowship at the Sundance Theater Lab. An earlier draft of *Training Wisteria* is published by Dramatic Publishing. Currently, Molly is a Rita and Burton Goldberg Playwriting Fellow at Tisch School of the Arts, NYU. She is a member of the Dramatists Guild.

Production History

Training Wisteria was first presented by the Boston Playwrights Theatre in Boston, MA (Artistic Director/Producer Kate Snodgrass) on October 3, 2002. It was directed by Sidney Freeman; it was assistant directed by Rebecca Mayer; the technical director was Marc Olivere; the scene designer was David Reynoso; the lighting designer was Jeff Brewer; the costume designer was Lisa Geiger; the audio designer was Martha Goode; the stage manager was Hannah Cohen; the assistant stage manager was Gregg Livoti; the assistant lighting designer was Steven McIntosh; the master electrician was Caleb Magoon; and the crew was Blake Metzler. The cast was as follows:

LYNN..Paula Langton

STEPHEN ....Kim H. Carrell

DYLAN..Ben Sands

RACHEL...Lisa Grossman

KACIE ....Mehera Blum

Characters

DYLAN, 18. About to graduate from high school. Primary interests include: heavy metal music, *Star Wars*, guitar, air guitar, the color black, ice cold Heinekens, and his Gameboy.

RACHEL, 20. Has just finished her freshman year at an Ivy League college, where she earned a 4.0 GPA and avoided boys, beer, and fun. Was a tennis champ in high school and aced the SATs.

KACIE, 13. An eighth grader at the local public school, where she is loved by teachers and considered cool by her peers. Spunky, wildly funny, easygoing, and wise beyond her years.

LYNN, 47. Their mother. Teaches third grade at the local elementary school, where she is thought to be the most coveted yet zaniest teacher. Passionate, messy, earthy, and very attractive.

STEPHEN, 50. Their father. A mathematics professor at an elite university. Earnest, brilliant in his field, devoted to his ideals, and a consummate gardener.

Time

A sunny Saturday in early June 1996.

Setting

The fenced-in backyard of a middle-class house. The back of the house is visible, with a stoop or steps leading to the back door. It's been a long and tough year for this family, and the lawn shows signs of neglect: the lawn furniture is weathered; garbage cans overflow; the fence has a broken board; the birdbath is tipped over; plants are dead; the compost pile is repugnant; and the light above the back door has a dead bulb. Center stage, there is an outdoor table with an umbrella and mismatched lawn chairs. Further away from the house is a badly painted shed in a bold color. Scattered on the ground are signs of recent but half-assed home improvement: paint cans, paintbrushes, shovels, rakes, brooms, and bins full of garbage. One might say this yard is on its way to "hell hole" status, but is merely unattended as of today.

ACT I
Scene 1

AT RISE: It is almost noon and very, very loud heavy metal music, which is rich in curse words, pumps out of the stereo. **DYLAN**, *who is dressed for high school commencement activities (cap and gown), plays his Gameboy to the unbearable thrashing of his music.* **DYLAN**'s *gown is on backwards and has paint (in the same shade as the shed) down the side of it. This is the scene until the music becomes absolutely irritating to us. Finally,* **RACHEL** *bursts onto the stage with her hands over her ears. She wears pajamas and searches for the stereo urgently.*

RACHEL: Dylan! Are you kidding me!?

DYLAN: Can't hear you! [*Screams, improv sings with lyrics:*] YEAH! YEAH!

RACHEL: The ground is trembling! [**RACHEL** *finds the stereo and shuts it off. She pants.*] Imbecile. Morning. We have neighbors!

DYLAN: Ifyourabigasscheesesaywhat.

RACHEL: What?

DYLAN: Hah!

RACHEL: What did you say?

DYLAN: [*Slower.*] Ifyourabigasscheesesaywhat.

RACHEL: I was sleeping, Dylan. It's bad enough that your mutant stuff is in my room and I'm stuck on the couch.

DYLAN: Correction: my mutant stuff is in my room.

RACHEL: A poster on the door does not make it your room.

DYLAN: No, the deadbolt does.

RACHEL: I had a six hour drive last night to get to Sofa City. It would be nice if you would show a little consideration—

DYLAN: Boo fucking hoo. I've been up since seven.

RACHEL: Yeah, mastering Gameboy.

DYLAN: Try painting the shed.

RACHEL: What do you mean you painted the . . . [**RACHEL** *turns to see the horribly, brightly painted shed. She gasps.*] Oh. My. God. What did you do! Your shed looks like a scene from Medea, Dylan.

DYLAN: [*At game.*] C'mon! Asswipe!

RACHEL: [*About shed:*] At least she offsets your landscaping aesthetic. [*Surveying yard.*] Impressive, Dyl. Sparse. Minimalist. Very PoMo. Very . . . high death toll. I take it you've been manning the garden all year . . . [*Suddenly, with alarm:*] Oh Sweet Jesus OhmyGod. That compost friggin' reeks. [**RACHEL** *runs away from the compost pile.* **DYLAN** *wafts the compost in her direction with his graduation cap.*]

RACHEL: Eh, Dylan don't!

DYLAN: "Eh, Dylan don't!" [**RACHEL** *turns to go.*]

RACHEL: It's too early for this. I'm going back to bed. [*Loudly.*] Keep the screaming boys in spandex below eight decibels this time! [**RACHEL** *is about to exit.*]

DYLAN: Ah, I can't let you do that there, scout. I have instructions for you from the big chief. She bid me wake your highness up and give you your chore. [**DYLAN** *points at the compost pile.*]

RACHEL: What?

DYLAN: Compost pile, baby. Look at her. Just waiting for you.

RACHEL: I don't get it.

DYLAN: You, shovel, bag. Go hard. Go strong. I'm on vacation and it works out good: you're home. [**DYLAN** *plays his game.*]

RACHEL: That's not funny, Dylan. I'm in college. You don't get chores in college!

DYLAN: Apparently you do. [*At game.*] D'oh! c'mon! BALL LICKER!

RACHEL: I don't DO compost. [*Holding nose.*] Seriously. Seriously, Dylan.

DYLAN: [*Mocking her.*] Seriously. Seriously, Dylan?

RACHEL: She clearly hasn't touched it all year! Why's this my problem? Where's Mom!

DYLAN: Try the basement.

RACHEL: What's she doing down there?

DYLAN: She's looking for rope or something. She bought some bush.

RACHEL: And she's tying it up?

DYLAN: Go ask her. I'll save you a cold one. [**RACHEL** *begins to exit, and then realizes what she's heard.*]

RACHEL: [*About beer:*] What did you say?

DYLAN: Brewsky. It dulls the pain. Cuts the odor too. Have one?

RACHEL: WHAT?!

DYLAN: Heine. Heineken. The nectar of the gods. The honey of the earth. The plentiful stash Madre has in a cooler in the shed.

RACHEL: Dylan, that's for the party!

DYLAN: And?

RACHEL: And! It's not even noon! The Cro-Magnon men in my dorm don't drink before noon!

DYLAN: I thought you were in college and are therefore supposed to be cool.

RACHEL: You're not even of age! You're going to develop bad habits!

DYLAN: Oh . . . that's so sweet. Are we gonna have one of those "not so fresh" douche moments? Where's the row boat? [**DYLAN** *gestures rowing a boat around* **RACHEL.**]

RACHEL: Give me the beer.

DYLAN: Okay, here. [**DYLAN** *holds it out for her and then yanks it away.*]

RACHEL: Dylan.

DYLAN: Yeah, you're right. Sorry. Here. [*He holds it out again, and takes it away when she reaches for it.*]

RACHEL: Dylan!

DYLAN: I'm such a jackass. Okay for real this time . . . Here 'go. [**DYLAN** *chugs the rest of the beer, crushes it with his foot, and then hands it to her.*]

RACHEL: Let me tell you what drinking before noon says to me. It says, "You know, Rache, I need to share my feelings." [**DYLAN** *belches as a response.* **RACHEL** *waits.*] Well, that's a shame. There'll be a lot of friends and family here tomorrow. I may have to get the sixth grade photos out. The ones where your blond bowl cut delicately brushes against the sailor shirt? The laser beam backdrop highlighting your orthodontia . . . [**DYLAN** *pauses his game.*]

DYLAN: Let the bonding begin.

[*Beat.*]

RACHEL: How many beers have you had today?

DYLAN: Just that one. And it stops here. Admitting you have a problem is the first step. I am through with the brew. Let's do a trust fall.

RACHEL: Should it strike me as odd that you're wearing your cap and gown a day early?

DYLAN: No.

RACHEL: Are you excited about tomorrow?

DYLAN: No.

RACHEL: Do you know who's giving the keynote address?

DYLAN: What?

RACHEL: Are you decided about college in the fall?

DYLAN: No.

RACHEL: Do you know who's coming tomorrow?

DYLAN: No.

RACHEL: You don't know who's coming to your own part—

DYLAN: No.

[*Beat.*]

RACHEL: Are you going to come visit me this summer?

DYLAN: No. Nerd. Camp.

RACHEL: It's not nerd camp! It's college summer session.

DYLAN: Weed league. Dorkville.

RACHEL: You don't know what you're talking about. There's nothing dorky about language seminars. [**DYLAN** *laughs as he goes back to the shed and reaches in for another beer.*]

DYLAN: Listen, Carpe DORKum, Rache. Enjoy not being here. [**DYLAN** *cracks his beer.* **RACHEL** *watches him with concern.*]

RACHEL: I thought admitting you had a problem was the first step?

DYLAN: Denial is the second. You try; stop denying your primal thirst. [**DYLAN** *holds the beer out to her.*]

RACHEL: Aren't you afraid of being caught?

DYLAN: By who? Captain Random? She's one spork short of take out.

RACHEL: Well Dad would die if he saw you. [**DYLAN** *chugs the rest of his beer hard. Beat. Awkward.*]

RACHEL: Is Dad coming tomorrow?

DYLAN: I'm not talking about Dad with you, Rachel.

[*Silence.*]

RACHEL: Have you seen him? How'd he tell you? [*Pause.*] Dylan. How'd he tell you?

DYLAN: Rache, I don't talk about Dad.

RACHEL: Well, I got the really classy and sensitive "I'm to Be Wed" e-mail. Did you hear me? [**DYLAN** *nods.*] So yes or no. Has he introduced you to that reptilian, adulterous woman?

DYLAN: In Anglese?

RACHEL: Helen of Troy. Have you met her or not?

DYLAN: Nope.

RACHEL: Has Kacie? Dylan, has Kacie—

DYLAN: Dunno.

[*Beat.* **RACHEL** *waits for* **DYLAN** *to expand.*]

RACHEL: That's it? You don't have eyes? You don't have ears? You don't have anything to say?

DYLAN: What do you want to hear?

RACHEL: What do you think? Your honest reaction. Feelings.

DYLAN: Okay. [*Clearly joking.*] I am burning inside with anger and fury. I can't sleep at night. I've had to turn to the bottle for comfort. Beer! Beer is my only friend.

RACHEL: How about Mom? You can at least attest to how she is.

DYLAN: You've seen her.

RACHEL: At Christmas. Before he got engaged to her.

DYLAN: I dunno. She's up these days—home improvement overdrive. I ask her how she's doing and she says, "Oh, I'm doing real good, feeling real real good. But I've been thinking . . . Let's build a spiral staircase and a garage today. We could make a waterfall that runs through both by mid-June!"

RACHEL: At least she's not on the couch. And she has plenty to keep her busy.

DYLAN: Keep me busy you mean. GIDDY. UP. [*"Whipping" himself.*] Y'AH!

RACHEL: I see Dad's rosebushes didn't survive the . . . spring. She's outdone herself. I didn't know you could kill a whole garden in only a year.

DYLAN: They're in a better place now, Rache. [**DYLAN** *crosses himself, indicates the compost.*]

RACHEL: The soil properties are all lost now. You think she'd remember to turn compost over once in a while. It's just ROT now.

DYLAN: Yep, I hate to see her go. [*To compost:*] We've gotten close, haven't we, punkin?

RACHEL: Dylan . . . [**DYLAN** *cuddles with the compost.*] Dylan, gross.

DYLAN: [*To compost:*] I don't care if you have soil properties or not . . .

RACHEL: If you're going to make out with the compost, at least take your gown off. [**RACHEL** *begins unzipping his gown.*] This is backwards, jackass. The zipper goes in front. Don't you know what these are supposed to look like? And you got paint on it! It's not a smock, Dyl. Turn around. [**DYLAN** *allows his sister to partially remove his gown. In doing so, his arm is revealed. A series of burns on his forearm catches* **RACHEL**'s *eye.*] Hey. Come back here. [*With alarm:*] What's all over your arm?

DYLAN: What.

RACHEL: On your arm. These pocks. What are they?

DYLAN: They're not pocks, dumb-ass.

RACHEL: They're burns!

DYLAN: No, they're bug bites. I have fleas.

RACHEL: They're burns! Terrible burns!

DYLAN: So? The fleas went marching on, okay? I caught 'em from the compost—

RACHEL: Why do the burns line up like that?

DYLAN: Well, while cleaning out gutters . . . cleaning up compost piles . . . mowing the balding spots of grass . . .

RACHEL: Dylan.

DYLAN: [*Continued:*] . . . turning this yard into *Better Homes and Gardens* . . . I started getting itchy and realized that a giant herd of fleas . . .

RACHEL: I know what this is.

DYLAN: Well, I take my work seriously. Rain or shine, fleas or—

RACHEL: Dylan! Answer my question.

DYLAN: What!

RACHEL: Why are the burns in a straight line?

DYLAN: A couple people bumped into me with cigarettes.

RACHEL: And a couple people methodically scorched your flesh with lit cigarettes?

DYLAN: I forget.

RACHEL: You've given yourself permanent scars. Permanent scars! Has anyone seen these?

DYLAN: It doesn't matter.

RACHEL: That's not an answer. Has Mom seen them or not?

DYLAN: Listen up, Rachel. Burns. Equal. My. Fucking. Business. Find another fish to fry.

    [*Sustained beat.* **DYLAN** *restarts his Gameboy and the bleeps are heard.*]

RACHEL: Dylan.

    [*Beat.*]

DYLAN: What.

RACHEL: I don't want you to do that anymore.

DYLAN: Whatever, Rache.

RACHEL: I'm serious, Dylan.

DYLAN: Whatever, Rache. What. Ever. [**LYNN** *enters. She drags a potted wisteria vine through the doors behind her, which is really heavy.* **KACIE** *comes in behind her, wearing a wisteria leaf in her hair.* **KACIE** *wears a backpack and carries a travel mug in her free hand.*] S'up Madre. Ifmomsuglyandgaysaywhat!

LYNN: I'm not saying WHAT and you know it, Dylan. [*Pointing to the outdoor light.*] Did you fix the light yet?

DYLAN: Yes! [**LYNN** *hits the light switch, and nothing comes on.*] D'oh!

LYNN: [*To* **DYLAN:**] That light needs to be fixed or our guests are gonna sit here in darkness tomorrow . . .

RACHEL: Hey Mom.

LYNN: Do you hear me, Dylan? [*To* **RACHEL:**] HEY! You're up! I was just about to make sure you were.

RACHEL: Yes, I got Dylan's really special wake-up call.

LYNN: [*To* **KACIE.**] Oh. We forgot to warn her.

KACIE: [*To* **RACHEL.**] Mom and I are both part deaf. You'll get used to it. [*To* **DYLAN**, *about his attire.*] Nice get-up, Homie Dee. Out of clean AC/DC shirts?

DYLAN: H-hey! Little K-Dog! Good one. Adda girl. [*They exchange an elaborate and well-practiced high-five greeting.*]

KACIE: Why you rocking the paint on your gown, dude.

LYNN: What paint?!

RACHEL: Oh, Dylan got a little paint on the side—

LYNN: What did you do? You got paint on your gown!

DYLAN: No. I protected my clothing.

LYNN: What am I gonna do with you? You're going to be in photos wearing paint. My son, the one wearing paint! [**RACHEL** *goes to the paint can and reads the ingredients.*]

KACIE: At least we'll be able to find him? He won't need a pompom on his head—

LYNN: [*To* **DYLAN:**] This is your commencement gown, dummy. I'm supposed to be proud of you and get teary when you wear it. I'm supposed to sit there and weep, not sit there with a banner that says, "My kid's the jackass soaked in paint!" [**RACHEL** *studies the can of paint.*]

RACHEL: [*Reading.*] Oh, that's a shame. It's acrylic house paint so unless it's watered immediately, it sets. "Immediacy of removal is key."

DYLAN: [*To* **KACIE**, *coughs under his breath.*] Lame!

LYNN: Go on, Dylan. Inside. There's paint thinner in the basement somewhere, try it. Go on, hurry. [*Afterthought:*] And take a look at the washing machine, too. It won't drain again.

DYLAN: Did you overload it?

LYNN: No. It's just swishing around without draining.

DYLAN: Fuck! [**DYLAN** *exits.*]

RACHEL: Since when do you let him talk like that?

LYNN: It's his music. [*Moving the wisteria downstage.*] Help me move this.

RACHEL: I don't think it's his music . . . he's just . . . darker . . . than before. Have you noticed him acting differently, Mom?

LYNN: Yeah, he used to be nicer.

RACHEL: Well, don't you think that deserves a little attention? [**DYLAN** *reenters. He has turned his gown inside out. A big, white tag should protrude from the back.*]

DYLAN: [*About gown:*] See? All better. I fixed it.

LYNN: It works, I guess. Just make sure you cut the tag off the back before tomorrow.

RACHEL: Too bad he can't turn the shed inside out.

[*Beat.*]

LYNN: Oh my GOD. DYLAN! What is this!

DYLAN: What.

LYNN: ORANGE!?

DYLAN: It's a shed.

LYNN: The paint looks like a wave pool! You just slapped the paint on there. You didn't even use tape on the trim!

DYLAN: Yeah. It's a shed.

KACIE: It's not that bad, Mom.

LYNN: It looks like Jackson Pollock painted it! My third graders could paint better than this.

KACIE: I like the color a lot, Mom. It's peppy.

LYNN: And with all those guests tomorrow. Damn. You didn't care at all.

[*Beat.*]

DYLAN: Do you want me to tape it and do it again, Ma?

LYNN: NO. I would like to be pleasantly surprised for once.

DYLAN: Do you want me to go inside and stop helping you for a change?

LYNN: You know, maybe you should.

DYLAN: Was that a yes?

LYNN: You better watch it—

KACIE: GUYS. C'mon, now. Play nice. You don't mean that, Mom.

LYNN: It really would be nice to be pleasantly surprised once in a while, Dylan. It really would.

DYLAN: It really would be nice if you remembered that today I am on vacation. We agreed I was on vacation this weekend. My weekend.

[*Beat. Awkward silence.*]

RACHEL: Okay, so the shed isn't a pleasant surprise, but I have some news that should make you smile, Mom. I did end up qualifying for that scholarship for summer session! The one I told you about? Tuition and fees!

LYNN: Great! So you only need a few hundred for books?

RACHEL: And I can buy them myself. I'll have my job at the library.

LYNN: That's great, Rachel. That helps me a lot.

KACIE: Hold up. I thought college didn't start again until the fall?

RACHEL: I'm doing a summer session, Kace. Six weeks, six hours a day. It's a lot of work, but—

KACIE: So you'll be gone for the tennis tournament? Who will I play with?

RACHEL: Oh. Um, Dylan.

DYLAN: Ix-nay on the ennis-tay.

RACHEL: You stopped playing tennis, too? You were first singles! Why would you quit something you're so good at? [**DYLAN** *gestures rowing a boat.*]

DYLAN: Personally, I trust Summer's Eve.

KACIE: You and I were supposed to play doubles, Rache. I'm finally old enough to do women's league.

LYNN: We don't have time for games this summer, Kace. Besides, your sister is saving me money with her scholarship. Saving Mom money is great news. And we all have to do our part. Like with the kitchen tiles. I wanted Celtic tiles, but I had to order generic glass. I wanted a professional grouter, but I'm settling for . . . Dylan.

DYLAN: WHAT?

RACHEL: I'll help you find a new partner, Kace, I promise.

DYLAN: Tiles! Yeah. Easy. Grout. Hours of labor. Precision. Yep.

LYNN: [*To everyone:*] Enough of this! We need a far more radical change than tiles anyway! [*Abruptly, excitedly:*] SO . . . Who knows why today is a very, very special day? It's BIG . . . It's HUGE . . . It's historic! This is a day that is better than all the others. Do we know why?

RACHEL: I'm home?

DYLAN: I'm on vacation?

KACIE: Dylan's graduating?

LYNN: Yes, I know all that. It's even bigger! Any guesses? [**DYLAN** *raises his hand and shrieks to be called on.* **LYNN** *calls on him.*] Yes. Dylan.

DYLAN: Cuz I get to plant some bush?

LYNN: Exactly! [*About the wisteria:*] LOOK how beautiful this is! HMMM? LOOK. Isn't it just perfect? It's called . . . wisteria.

DYLAN: [*To* **KACIE.**] Her bush is called hysteria! That's killer.

LYNN: No, Wist. WISTeria. See the tag—look at the blooms! They are lavender, Dylan. Lush, beautiful, twinkly lavender cascades . . . all over our yard! Someday! Altogether now . . .

LYNN, KACIE, and **RACHEL:** Wisteria.

LYNN: Dylan? Wisteri . . .

DYLAN: Yea. I fuckin' heard you. It ain't Arbor Day.

LYNN: You party pooper. [*To all, reading from the tag.*] Now, listen. Bask in it: "Wisterias are greatly valued for their large, pendulous flower clusters that occur in the spring and may be white, pink, lilac-blue, or purple in color. The plant climbs by means of twining stems around a supportive structure. Use rope to train it." You train it to twine! You control how it grows! WOW, HUH? Can you picture it?

DYLAN: Hang on . . . [*Considers.*] Nope. But I farted. [**KACIE** *laughs loudly.* **RACHEL** *sneers.* **LYNN** *reaches into the wisteria and searches around.*]

LYNN: And look at this! Look at this. You haven't even seen the best part. Look what I have it all rigged up to do. [*Beat.*] Close your eyes, all of you. Close your eyes. Now . . . [**LYNN** *reaches into the wisteria and flicks a little switch. The tree lights up with white Christmas lights.*] OKAY, OPEN!

[*Beat.*]

DYLAN: It's the Christmas bush.

LYNN: No, it's Southern Italy! The cascades! The lights! We're going to recreate the verandas of Southern Italy back here!

DYLAN: [*In Irish accent.*] Mom, I thought we were liking the Lucky Charms n'all.

KACIE: [*To* **DYLAN.**] I guess a we likea meatball, cabeesh? [**DYLAN** *and*

KACIE *high-five.*]

LYNN: If I train it right, in ten years we will sip wine under a big wisteria tree. We just need a trellis. And we've got all that old wood downstairs . . .

DYLAN: Retardo, we went over warped wood yesterday, remember?

LYNN: No.

DYLAN: Most wood, happy wood, is straight. Some wood, unhappy wood, gets wet, and then it bends. You can't make anything out of a bent two-by-four—

LYNN: What are you saying? You can't make a trellis! They bend!

KACIE: Mom, he can't make it by tomorrow. Not by the party.

RACHEL: And you don't really have a green thumb, Mom.

   [*Beat.*]

LYNN: This is the weekend, guys. My whole address book is coming. All my colleagues. All my friends. All my children's friends. All of my side of the family. All our neighbors. [*About wisteria:*] THIS will make all the difference! A touch of class taking root. [*To everyone:*] Can't you see? Look at it, honestly, and tell me you really, truly, honestly, truly can't see how glorious it will be back here. Can't you see?

RACHEL: I think you should've watered the rosebushes, Mom.

LYNN: [*To everyone.*] I'll water wisteria. [*Beat. Silence. To* **RACHEL.**] Dylan gave you your chore?

RACHEL: Mom, about the compost, I don't feel that I should have to—

LYNN: NOW. [**LYNN** *goes into the shed.* **DYLAN** *and* **KACIE**, *go to the compost, put garbage bags in the cans.* **RACHEL** *just looks at it.*]

DYLAN: [*To* **RACHEL.**] Ha-ha. You got the smack laid down on ya.

RACHEL: She used to have a sense of humor.

DYLAN: Kace. Psst . . . Kace. Huddle Up: Quick huddle. [*Quietly, to* **KACIE.**] I've been thinkin'. This is my party, right? My friends would love this pile of shit. I say we set up Slip N' Slide on top of it and see if she notices. [**KACIE** *laughs.* **LYNN** *comes out of the shed with two pieces of plywood.*]

LYNN: [*Urgently.*] LOOK AT THIS! Dylan, you can definitely make a trellis out of this!

DYLAN: Yeah, Ma. All I need is some scotch tape and fairy dust. And the rope you're looking for is in the toolbox, far right corner.

LYNN: It was for your entertainment that I looked through the basement all morning?

DYLAN: That's right.

LYNN: You're being a real ass today. [**LYNN** *stomps back into the shed.*]

DYLAN: [*To* **KACIE**.] Damn. I was hoping she'd go for "sonofabitch." [*Loudly.*] Get it, Mom? SON of a—

RACHEL: Don't be an idiot. Let's get this over with. So much for a warm welcome home.

> [*Several beats of* **DYLAN** *bagging the compost.* **KACIE** *and* **RACHEL** *drag garbage cans towards the compost. They bag compost.*]

KACIE: Dyl, do it. C'mon, you know.

DYLAN: We gotta shovel, kid. Mom's in a mood.

KACIE: Please? Please, Dylan? Come on, Homie Dee . . . just once?

DYLAN: Okay. [**DYLAN** *begins making low-pitched sounds, almost like yogic breathing. He wields the shovel like a* Star Wars *light saber. Like Darth Vader, to* **KACIE**.] Luke, you must use the force, Luke. Join me and together we shall rule the entire compost galaxy . . . [**DYLAN** *thrashes the shovel at the compost.*]

RACHEL: What's he doing?

KACIE: Vader!

DYLAN: [*As Vader.*] Luke, I am your father.

KACIE: [*Hysterical, as Luke.*] That's not true, that can't be true! [*In despair.*] Nooooooo!!! It's impossible!

DYLAN: [*To* **KACIE**, *as Vader.*] But you are not a Jedi, yet. First you must catch the turd in the garbage can. Ready, Luke? Here it comes . . .

KACIE: [*As Luke.*] My ally is the force, and a powerful ally it is. [**DYLAN** *launches a chunk of compost and* **KACIE** *misses it with the can.*]

RACHEL: Be careful with that—

DYLAN: Not a word outta you, Leia. [**DYLAN** *launches a chunk of compost and* **KACIE** *misses it again.*] You suck, Luke. Focus. Use the force this time. [**LYNN** *comes out of the shed, irritated.*]

LYNN: Dylan, come on! . . .

DYLAN: Don't be distracted by Yoda. Focus, Luke. Be a Jedi. [**DYLAN** *tosses another chunk of compost and* **KACIE** *catches it in the garbage can.*]

KACIE: SCORE!

DYLAN: And Luke scores! Darth . . . is . . . defeated . . . dramatic . . . death . . . sequence . . . [*Suddenly,* **STEPHEN** *appears. He carries an expensive looking camera and a tripod. He clears his throat.*]

STEPHEN: Lynn?

KACIE: Dad. [**RACHEL** *responds with a frozen silence.* **DYLAN** *turns on his game and begins playing.*]

LYNN: Stephen! You're early.

STEPHEN: It's noon. Time for my appointment. [*To* **LYNN.**] That's a rather dangerous game.

LYNN: We were just playing.

STEPHEN: Are you Princess Leia, Kace?

KACIE: She's lame. I'm Luke Skywalker.

STEPHEN: Luke Skywalker should be more careful playing with garbage and shovels. [**STEPHEN** *looks around, unhurried.*] My, what happened to the shed?

LYNN: We're experimenting with the palette. I was thinking maybe beige, but the kids collectively wanted something more . . .

KACIE: Peppy . . .

LYNN: Yes, something more peppy for summer.

STEPHEN: Very bold. There's painting tape in the shed, you know. If you want to fix up the trim.

LYNN: I didn't see it.

STEPHEN: It's in the box below the workbench. I'll get it for you if you like—

> [**DYLAN** *immediately gets up. Goes into the shed. Immediately comes out. Hands* **LYNN** *the tape. Sits back down. Restarts his game. Silence.*]

RACHEL: Um, hi Dad.

STEPHEN: Rachel! I didn't see you back there. What are you doing home?

LYNN: She got in late last night. I was going to tell you today, Stephen.

STEPHEN: I thought you might not have time to get home this summer. Busy making the highest honor roll for the second semester in a row. I saw it in the paper.

LYNN: Rachel's home because she wouldn't miss Dylan's party.

STEPHEN: Well, where's my hug? Or are you too cool for your old Dad? [**RACHEL** *awkwardly crosses to* **STEPHEN.** *Hugs him. Steps away.*] Didn't gain that freshman fifteen, I see.

RACHEL: I run three miles every morning.

STEPHEN: Yes, you look fit. Lovely. And still in pajamas at noon, eh? Someone must be in college.

RACHEL: I slept in today for the first time in months. I got straight A's on my finals and I got a full scholarship for my summer course. I'm taking an Honors language intensive seminar at school. [**STEPHEN** *applauds her.*]

STEPHEN: What does the summer seminar address? Latin and Greek?

RACHEL: Latin.

STEPHEN: Puri sermonis amator?

LYNN: She didn't take the course yet, Stephen. Ask her in September and she'll know.

RACHEL: He said "Am I a lover of pure speech?" I already started studying.

STEPHEN: Of course you did. Well, look at you. That's splendid, Rachel. I've got all my original Latin index cards. I'll lend them to you if you like.

RACHEL: You'll lend them to me if I like?

STEPHEN: Yes? [*Beat. To* **DYLAN**, *about the photo.*] What do you say, Dylan? Shall we begin? [*Beat. Silence.*] Dylan, the regalia suits you. It's a fine accomplishment to finish high school, regardless of where our summer plans take us. We'll all be glad to have documentation down the line. [*No response. Then, to* **LYNN**.] I see this is going to be more of the usual.

LYNN: Dylan, your father is speaking to you.

DYLAN: I hear him.

LYNN: He's congratulating you, sweetheart. Let's be polite.

DYLAN: I heard him. [*Sustained beat while* **DYLAN** *does not acknowledge him.*]

STEPHEN: Lynn, I thought we spoke about these arrangements . . .

LYNN: Dylan. I'm sorry, dear, but I need you to cooperate about what we talked about this morning.

RACHEL: [*To* **KACIE**.] What's he supposed to do? [**KACIE** *shrugs.*]

LYNN: Dylan, honey.

DYLAN: [*To* **STEPHEN.**] I'm wearing the stupid thing. Go ahead.

STEPHEN: I'd prefer if we took them towards the house, if you don't mind. Away from the . . . compost. The light is better. [**DYLAN** *does not move.*] One might argue, son, that this is a small request considering that I didn't force you to attend your last three visitations. [**DYLAN** *goes to the location* **STEPHEN** *wants him to.*] Kacie, Rachel, please join the shot. [*Pause.*] Uh, Lynn if you could . . . make room for the girls. [**DYLAN** *puts his arm around* **LYNN,** *keeping her in the frame.* **STEPHEN** *inspects the shot.*] Kacie, take the leaf out of your hair, sweetheart. [*Looking through the lens.*] Dylan, is your gown on inside out?

DYLAN: No. [**STEPHEN** *sets the camera, pushes the timer, and joins the photo.*]

STEPHEN: It takes just a second here. Look straight ahead and say "graduation!"

LYNN and **STEPHEN:** Graduat . . . [*The moment the flash goes off,* **DYLAN** *removes his cap and gown violently and returns to his game.*]

STEPHEN: [*To* **DYLAN.**] You know, son, it's not too late to include me in your festivities tomorrow. I would still be glad to come, if I were offered an invitation from the graduate. [**DYLAN** *restarts his Gameboy, on highest volume.*]

LYNN: Dylan? [*To* **STEPHEN.**] I'm sorry.

STEPHEN: Me too, it's a shame. [*To* **KACIE.**] Well, what do you say, sweetheart, shall we? I thought we could walk down the street to the park today.

KACIE: Wherever. I'm ready. [**KACIE** *puts her backpack on.* **STEPHEN** *approaches* **RACHEL** *and offers her an envelope.*]

RACHEL: What is it?

STEPHEN: It's a little bonus for making dean's list. Use it for your summer course, if you like. Just a little play money from us. We're really proud of you. [**RACHEL** *does not take it.*] It's impolite to refuse a gift, Rachel.

RACHEL: It's impolite to use the first person plural with me. Dad. [**STEPHEN** *extends the card to* **LYNN.**]

STEPHEN: Lynn? [**LYNN** *takes it.*]

LYNN: Stephen.

STEPHEN: [*To* **LYNN.**] We'll be at the park. [*To* **KACIE.**] After you, my dear. Did you remember your thinking cap?

KACIE: [*Pointing at her head.*] Right here. Bye, Mom.

[**KACIE** *and* **STEPHEN** *exit. Several beats of silence. Then,* **DYLAN** *starts laughing.*]

DYLAN: Rache, that was good. Oh yeah. That check bit? Go hard. Go strong. I have absolutely no idea what you said, but that was the real McCoy right there. POW—

LYNN: No she wasn't. And goddamit it, neither were you, Dylan! Refusing to invite your own father to your party! [*To* **RACHEL.**] And we DO need the money, Rachel. You bet your ass we do. All you two just did was strengthen his fantasy that we're leave-able. And that it's all MY fault that we are.

[*Beat.*]

RACHEL: My palms are sweaty. He's so . . . this is so . . . different. God, he's like—what is he?

DYLAN: Ooooo, can I really answer—

RACHEL: Formal. "That's a dangerous game." "Where's my hug?" "Shall we do this and that?" "I'll lend it to you." He's never asked me for a hug before. [*Pause.*] I mean, that was my Dad right? The one who lived here for twenty years? Has he forgotten?

LYNN: He remembered precisely where his tape was in the shed so that I could fix my peppy shed.

RACHEL: I didn't even get a hello, Mom. Not really. He weighed me and showed off his Latin.

DYLAN: [*To* **RACHEL.**] He was actually pretty talkative today. He usually just tosses us the Dadfare checks like slop in the trough, right Ma?

RACHEL: And Kacie?—"Yes, Dad," "Ready, Dad." Like it's normal or something.

LYNN: It is normal for her! She does this every Saturday! Dylan is only off the hook because frankly, I don't think Stephen could take it anymore.

DYLAN: Autographs available after the show, folks. Thanks. Thank you. No, thank you!

[*Beat.*]

RACHEL: Dad moved from this house straight to Helen Hoebag's. Hasn't Kacie done the math on that one?

LYNN: I don't know what he's telling her. [*Pause.*] Dylan, I mean it. Turn off that game!

[*Beat.* **DYLAN** *pauses his game. In need of a new game, he says:*]

DYLAN: So . . . ahh . . . Is anyone gonna check how much you got?

RACHEL: Don't be tacky, Dylan.

DYLAN: This ain't the Hamptons, babe. [**LYNN** *opens the envelope. There is a note inside, which she reads quickly, and a check.*] Come on big money big money big money no whammy no whammy no whammy no whammy no whammy no whammy—

LYNN: Not bad. Three hundred dollars. [*To* **RACHEL.**] Take it for books.

RACHEL: Is her name on the check?

LYNN: Top left corner.

RACHEL: Then I'm not touching it. [**LYNN** *folds the check and puts it in her pocket.*]

LYNN: [*To* **DYLAN.**] I'll cash it for you then. We can't afford pride.

DYLAN: THREE HONEY! Dude, I can't wait to go to college. [**LYNN** *tosses the envelope in the compost.* **DYLAN** *sees her do this.*] Hey, Ma! Don't destroy the evidence. The checks always come with a note.

RACHEL: They do?

LYNN: Dylan, leave it be.

DYLAN: No, it's good for toilet paper. Two ply, maybe three. Extra absorbency.

LYNN: Dylan, I said LEAVE IT! [**DYLAN** *has the note open and reads it to* **RACHEL.**]

DYLAN: Nooo . . . it's a good one. Check it, Rache. [*Reading.*] "Dear Rachel, we were so pleased to hear that you made dean's list."

LYNN: That's enough. Let's get to work.

DYLAN: [*Reading.*] "Straight A's again! WOW! You've made your father very proud of you. To truly go the distance you have this year is super. Kudos. Although I understand that each of you have responded in their own way to my presence in your life, I am comforted by the knowledge that these things take time. In the meantime, if I remember, dorm food can be awful. Please consider coming over for some home-cooked meals, like chicken marsala over egg noodles, which I've heard is your favorite. I remain lovingly and admiringly yours. Looking forward to meeting you, Rachel. Your friend, Helen." And in parentheses, "and your Dad."

[*Beat.*]

RACHEL: Helen of Troy is grammatically incompetent. She has two split infinitives and a verb that doesn't agree with its antecedent. [**DYLAN** *sniffs the card.*]

DYLAN: I think she has B.O., guys. Oh yeah. [**DYLAN** *brings her the note and sticks it in her face. Beat.* **LYNN** *looks at the note, and then she really looks at it.*]

LYNN: Chicken marsala over egg noodles?

RACHEL: It's only my favorite when you make it. Mom? [*Beat.* **LYNN** *becomes distant. She looks off.* **DYLAN** *comes to her very seriously.* **RACHEL** *should watch this very carefully.*]

DYLAN: Mom? Gimme here. Mom, I said gimme here. [**LYNN** *hands it to* **DYLAN**. *He hacks a loogie into it. Crunches it up, shreds it to pieces, and buries it in the compost pile. Beat. Long silence.*] Where were we? Huh? Mom? [*Beat.* **RACHEL** *and* **DYLAN** *watch her.*]

LYNN: Yes, good. Enough of this. Right? We don't need this, do we!

DYLAN: Mission control, we have take off.

LYNN: We were planting. Wisteria! It was wisteria time. It will have lavender cascades. It will seep into every nook and cranny in a wild, crazy ceiling of exotica. Right, guys? We just need to get it in the ground, give it something to grow over; we have to train it. It will ravish everyone. It will wine and dine our guests. We just have to . . . It WILL be a beautiful new start. Right guys? RIGHT? [**RACHEL** *is silent. To* **DYLAN**.] Right?

[*Beat.*]

DYLAN: Yeah, Mom.

LYNN: Will someone please . . . please . . . say . . . right?

[*Lights fade on* **LYNN**. *Cross fade to Scene 2.*]

Scene 2

Lights up on **KACIE** *and* **STEPHEN**, *sitting on a bench in a park.* **KACIE** *has a math book, a sandwich, and her travel mug.* **STEPHEN** *sits next to her and checks off points on her homework in red pen.*

STEPHEN: This isn't right. Kacie Anne, we went over the placement of x and y on the graph last week. You know better than this. [**KACIE** *is silent.*] What's wrong with your sandwich?

KACIE: There's meat on it. [**KACIE** *drinks her coffee.*]

STEPHEN: You are so full of surprises, Kacie. That comes as a surprise too.

KACIE: What?

STEPHEN: The fact that you're a coffee drinking vegetarian. Your mother doesn't object to you being a thirteen-year-old coffee addict?

KACIE: I buy it on the black market so she doesn't find out.

   [*Beat.*]

STEPHEN: Are you expecting many guests tomorrow?

KACIE: Why?

STEPHEN: I'm just surprised she's gone through with it. I guess she's not embarrassed by the yard.

KACIE: Why are you embarrassed by the yard?

STEPHEN: Well, these things take planning and preparation. Remember Rachel's party last year? [**KACIE** *sips her coffee.*]

KACIE: Nope.

STEPHEN: Your girlfriends from the sixth grade came to a big-girl party? We spent weeks hanging lights? Catering the food? Picking the music? [**KACIE** *shakes her head.*]

STEPHEN: Kiddo, you and I made a banner?

KACIE: I remember you blowing up balloons and laughing. I remember you happy with Mom. My memory's not reliable.

   [*Beat.*]

STEPHEN: It's a beautiful day, Kacie. I am happy to be here, in the park, in the sunshine with my girl. This is nice, isn't it?

   [*Silence.*]

STEPHEN: [*Interested, reading the book.*] Shall we start with the theorems today? Where are your study notes?

KACIE: Right there.

STEPHEN: In purple? [*Firmly.*] Study notes are done in? . . .

KACIE: Pencil?

STEPHEN: Only pencil from now on. Why?

KACIE: So you can erase?

STEPHEN: That's correct. Now, what does this question mark mean?

KACIE: I'm not sure.

STEPHEN: Elaborate.

KACIE: Well, just that I was uncertain of my answer.

STEPHEN: Well, it's simple. Either you double-checked your work and it proved true, or you didn't check it. Did you check it or didn't you?

KACIE: I checked it. I was just tired and momentarily insecure. Don't you ever feel that way about choices you've made? [*Beat.* **KACIE** *swigs her coffee.*]

STEPHEN: You know, Kacie. If you drink coffee at home and at school you're an addict. You're addicted. Are you having trouble sleeping? I can arrange for you to see a specialist. They can prescribe something.

KACIE: Aren't you afraid I might become an addict? [**STEPHEN** *laughs.*]

STEPHEN: Aren't you witty! Student catching the teacher. Touche. [*Laughing.*] Let's hope you don't give me that kind of a whipping on the tennis court today. [*Beat.* **KACIE** *is silent.* **STEPHEN** *reaches into his bag, and pulls out a folded piece of paper with a bow on it. He holds it out to her, but she doesn't take it. He puts it in her lap.*] Here. Take a look. [**KACIE** *unfolds it and starts to read it.*] See? First match: July twenty-eighth at eight a.m. You and I, Kace. Doubles in the county tennis tournament.

KACIE: You want to play with me?

STEPHEN: Of course! Did you know you're old enough to do the adult league this year?

KACIE: But we'll lose. I mean, we'll lose lose.

STEPHEN: [*Warmly.*] You have the most graceful backhand in town! It's a force to be reckoned with.

KACIE: Really?

STEPHEN: Yes! You put real wallop into that swing. Look out! So, what do you say? Can I get us matching headbands? Coordinating outfits? [*Silence.* **KACIE** *searches for words.* **STEPHEN** *warmly responds:*] Listen, that's fine. No pressure. Just think about it. Whatever you want, kiddo. [*Beat.* **STEPHEN** *folds up the paper and puts it back in his bag. He doesn't seem to know what to say. He pulls out some pencils from his bag and puts them in her bag.*] And I brought you some fresh number-two pencils for your test Monday.

KACIE: Thanks.

STEPHEN: You want to bring at least three of them. And certainly, don't forget your calculator. And, you need to have a healthy breakfast, too. And backup batteries for your calculator.

KACIE: Check.

STEPHEN: Do you have gum or mints or some sort of reward for the break?

KACIE: I guess.

STEPHEN: See that you do. Are you ready then? [*More firmly.*] Are you ready to dazzle me, dear?

KACIE: I don't want to do this, Dad.

STEPHEN: Give me some enthusiasm! YES YOU DO! YES YOU'RE READY! NO GAIN IS A PAIN, yes? [*Singing, like a cheerleader.*] Give me an A! Give me a B! Square them and what do you get, KAY-CEE? [**STEPHEN** *laughs.* **KACIE** *is silent.*] Kiddo. You just had twenty-two ounces of Columbian roast! I know you're not too tired. Now, let us hear. You have a professor of mathematics at your disposal. Sing it out. Give me the Pythagorean theorem. [**KACIE** *sighs heavily.*] Kacie.

KACIE: A squared plus B squared equals C squared. Dylan is graduating tomorrow, Dad.

STEPHEN: Speak up. Pronounce it. Have confidence.

KACIE: A squared plus B squared equals C squared.

STEPHEN: Give me the volume of a circle.

KACIE: Pi r squared, Dad.

STEPHEN: The circumference of a circle.

KACIE: Two pi r.

STEPHEN: Give me the area of an isosceles triangle.

KACIE: One half the base times the height.

STEPHEN: Again, the area of an isosceles triangle, please.

KACIE: One half the base times the height.

STEPHEN: One more time: the area of an isosceles triangle is . . .

KACIE: One half the base times the height.

STEPHEN: You're sure?

KACIE: Yes.

STEPHEN: Have conviction. You're certain?

KACIE: Yes.

STEPHEN: Well, you are correct. But, you missed it last time. Give me the volume of a cone.

KACIE: One third pi r squared times height.

STEPHEN: Give me the area of an equilateral triangle.

KACIE: Side squared times the square root of three divided by four.

STEPHEN: Give me the volume of a sphere.

KACIE: Pi squared plus height.

STEPHEN: No.

KACIE: The volume of a sphere is pi squared times height?

STEPHEN: No.

KACIE: Radius times height, isn't it?

STEPHEN: No. Your focus is gone. You've lost your focus. What do we do when we've lost our focus? [**KACIE** *does not react.*] We take a deep breath. We inhale deeply, and we count to thirty. How do we count? One one thousand, two one thousand, three one thousand . . . Kacie. [*Beat.*] This exam could potentially place you in advanced mathematics next year. Carelessness costs points. You must double-check double-check double-check double-check and then double-check your work. You must stay til the last minute. You stay until everyone else has handed their exams in. Do you understand? [*With familiarity.*] Tell me, what do I always say?

KACIE: I don't remember.

STEPHEN: Yes you do. Say it.

KACIE: You can tell who's got a shot at the A by who stays until the end.

STEPHEN: That's right. That's it. The volume of a sphere. Let it echo through the park like a symphony.

KACIE: Dad.

STEPHEN: You know this. Tell me.

KACIE: Stay til the end.

STEPHEN: No. The volume of a sphere.

KACIE: Staying till the end is key.

STEPHEN: The volume of a sphere, please, Kacie.

KACIE: Dylan's graduating tomorrow, Dad.

STEPHEN: The volume of a sphere is . . .

KACIE: Dylan is graduating. It's his graduation.

[*Beat.*]

STEPHEN: When you graduate, I'll be there, Kace. You and I? We check out, right?

KACIE: He's not going to ask you to come.

STEPHEN: If he wanted me there, he would've invited me.

KACIE: Why would he invite you? He hates your ass.

STEPHEN: Who lets you talk like this? Your mother?

KACIE: No . . . it's a direct quote. "I hate Dad's ass."

STEPHEN: Is this because your sister is home, it's gang-up-on-Dad day—

KACIE: No. And, she's not home. Her home is somewhere else now, too.

[*Beat.*]

STEPHEN: I know this might not make sense to you, but I am obeying Dylan's wishes. He says, don't talk to me, so I refrain. He says, don't come, so I'm resisting. What else can I do but honor my children's wishes?

KACIE: I think you ignored a pretty big wish when you moved out.

STEPHEN: Kiddo, sometimes adult things happen in adult relationships. Mommies and Daddies fall out of love. They fall apart from one another. They don't agree anymore on how to handle their children and their dreams. Can you imagine that?

KACIE: Why are you talking to me like I'm three? [*Beat.*] I'm in junior high,

Dad. My gym locker says "Fuckin A" on it.

STEPHEN: Okay, let's . . . please not give me a stroke. [*Beat.*] Let's try this. If all the variables in Column A were proven variables of x and all the variables in Column B were y—

KACIE: I'm gone, Dad.

STEPHEN: Okay. Our proof fell through; the variables didn't align.

KACIE: So you erase the column?

[*Beat.*]

STEPHEN: We're off course. [*Slowly, carefully.*] What do you say we go to my house. I've been dying to show it to you. It's right along the river. There is unparalleled mountain biking and hiking and the view . . . oh, it is so beautiful, kiddo. We'll have lunch: sandwiches, without meat of course, and some fresh decaf? Then, we can take a dip in the pool with Helen, or spend the afternoon in my glorious vegetable garden. I'll show you all around. It's only twenty minutes away.

[*Long beat.*]

KACIE: You have a new garden there?

STEPHEN: Of course, but I miss my chief weed-puller in the worst way, Kace.

[*Beat.*]

KACIE: Come tomorrow, Dad. Don't bring her, but come.

STEPHEN: Life advice from my thirteen year old?

KACIE: Come, Dad. Please.

[*Beat.*]

STEPHEN: Back to business. [*After a pause.*] Now let me hear it. Sing it out. I want to hear the volume of a sphere.

KACIE: I want to hear you say you're not coming. That you're gonna miss his graduation.

[*Beat.*]

STEPHEN: I'm not coming. I'm going to miss his graduation. [*Beat.* **KACIE** *can't make eye contact.*] Kacie Anne, have I told you how much I look forward to our Saturdays? Saturday is my favorite day of the week. I wake up so sad on Sundays because it won't be Saturday again for six whole days. [*Beat.*] I'm going to leave you with this practice exam. You need the practice, especially with spheres. Okay, kiddo?

KACIE: It's pi r cubed. The volume of a sphere?

STEPHEN: Adda girl, Kace! Perfect.

[*Beat.* **KACIE** *rises to go.*]

KACIE: So was Rachel's party, Dad. Perfect. Why don't you give your memory a practice exam.

[**KACIE** *exits.* **STEPHEN** *sits alone. Cross fade to Scene 3.*]

Scene 3

Lights come up on the backyard. **DYLAN** *is playing Gameboy.* **LYNN** *is inside the shed, rattling things about. The wisteria tree is now comically decorated with a tinsel garland and a Christmas star.* **RACHEL** *comes out of the house, dressed for the day. She carries a pretty dress on a hanger and looks irritated.*

RACHEL: Where in the love of God is the iron! [*Without looking up from his game,* **DYLAN** *points to the shed.* **RACHEL** *walks to the shed, then talks to the shed.*] Mom? Where's the iron? It's not in the hall closet, where it's been for two decades.

LYNN: Why?

RACHEL: Why? Because I'd like to iron my wrinkly dress for tomorrow!

LYNN: [*From within.*] Um, I don't know. Look around. Look, um . . . around.

RACHEL: Oh, that's perfect. [*To* **DYLAN.**] I don't suppose you know the mysterious new home for the iron?

DYLAN: Are you high?

[*Beat.*]

RACHEL: [*Seeing wisteria.*] I'll bite. What happened to her bush?

DYLAN: The Christmas elf found some decor in the shed. [**RACHEL** *almost giggles.*]

RACHEL: Is she pissed?

DYLAN: Ho-yeah.

RACHEL: I don't know what's more disturbing. The fact that that's in my yard, or the fact that it took me several seconds to notice. [*At the shed, loudly.*] Mom, I'm going to the mall to buy an iron and spray starch. I need my own anyway. Do you need anything? [**LYNN** *comes out with hands full of weird things from the shed.*]

LYNN: [*To* **DYLAN.**] What time do you have?

DYLAN: T minus thirty minutes til Kace lands back at base, Sarge.

LYNN: Good. [*To* **RACHEL.**] What did you say to me? What do you want?

RACHEL: [*Slowly.*] I'm going to the mall to get a few things.

LYNN: The hell you are! We have less than twenty-four hours to get things in shape back here.

RACHEL: I'll only be an hour. My dress needs to be ironed and you lost our iron. Look—

LYNN: I said no. [**LYNN** *takes* **DYLAN**'s *Gameboy and throws it in the trash.*] And that game is history, Dylan. I'm serious. And for the love of Jesus, do I have to ask you again?

DYLAN: Ask me what, Ma?

LYNN: The same blessit thing I've been asking you to do all morning: that damn compost!

DYLAN: You got it, babe. I was just resting up.

LYNN: How about Mom? Not Ma, not babe, not Madre, not say whats, just plain old respectful MOM.

DYLAN: You got it, Mom. [**LYNN** *goes back into the shed.* **DYLAN** *digs his game out of the garbage.*]

RACHEL: [*To* **DYLAN.**] What's her problem?

DYLAN: It's Saturday.

RACHEL: And we're restricted from the mall on Saturdays?

DYLAN: Until Kacie's back, yep.

RACHEL: That's absurd.

DYLAN: Yep.

RACHEL: [*Noticing the beer.*] So you just sit here and get ploughed?

DYLAN: Hey. Smoke 'em if you got 'em. [**LYNN** *comes out of the shed, furiously.*]

LYNN: I CAN'T FIND ANYTHING I NEED IN THERE!

DYLAN: What are you looking for, Ma? Mom.

LYNN: A sledgehammer! Everything's so bloomin' organized, the most obvious things don't catch your eye. What'd he—alphabetize it?

DYLAN: One sledgehammer. Coming up. [**DYLAN** *goes into the shed. He emerges immediately with a sledgehammer.*]

RACHEL: What do you need that for, Mom?

DYLAN: [*Giving it to her.*] Here.

LYNN: Move. [**LYNN** *goes to the shed and takes a huge bang at it with the sledgehammer.* **DYLAN** *and* **RACHEL** *exchange looks. She does it again, more forcefully.*]

DYLAN: Whatcha doin' there, buddy?

LYNN: The wisteria looks so ordinary and blah over there.

DYLAN: It looks retarded anywhere back here. Why are you beating the shed?

LYNN: The shed is BOLD, and it's in the way of the ideal wisteria placement.

RACHEL: What do you mean, Mom?

LYNN: We just have to get rid of this dumb shed. Problem? Solution! Ugly? Beautiful! Old? New!

DYLAN: No. NO. NO. NO. NO. NO. NO! Mom, listen to me. Listen to the words coming out of my mouth: we are not taking the shed down so you can plant some bush!

LYNN: [*To* **DYLAN.**] Why not? The shed is ugly anyway.

DYLAN: The shed is functional! Functional! Where are you going to put the stuff in the shed?

LYNN: I don't know. We'll build a new shed after the party . . . in the meantime, we can hide the stuff around the side of the house.

DYLAN: Are you fucking kidding me?

RACHEL: Mom, not to point out the obvious, but you just made Dylan paint the shed.

LYNN: Yeah, badly.

RACHEL: But, clearly, you're going to ruin everything in the shed if you dismantle the facade. It will crumble.

LYNN: I can't stand to look at it! [**LYNN** *keeps banging the shed. She is starting to break through a board.*]

DYLAN: [*In dispatch voice.*] Ah, HOUSTON! COME IN HOUSTON! We've got a wild one. [*To* **LYNN.**] She's taking down a shed, alone, with a sledgehammer, so she can plant . . . [*To* **LYNN,** *about wisteria.*] . . . THAT?

LYNN: Precisely.

DYLAN: You leave me no choice, woman. There comes a time when a man has to put his foot down . . .

RACHEL: I think you're going through some sort of an adjustment here, or something, but I think it's dangerous, at best, Mom.

DYLAN: [*Dispatch voice.*] Houston? You're breaking up, Houston. Yeah. I'm gonna have to go in. [**DYLAN** *begins gathering up his Gameboy, stereo, cap, gown, and beer (hidden).*]

RACHEL: [*Gently, to* **LYNN.**] Maybe we should set some realistic goals? Perhaps we should clear it out this weekend, and then take it down some other weekend? You can sit over here and we can discuss it . . .

DYLAN: [*As final words.*] Rachel, tell Kacie she can have my Han Solo second edition figurine. You may have my Metallica box set. [*Loudly, to the gods.*] I will sacrifice myself! I am lamb to the slaughter! I am Obi Wan Kenobi! [**DYLAN** *goes into the shed dramatically, like a martyr.* **LYNN,** *mid-hit, is forced to stop beating the shed.*]

LYNN: Dylan, get out of there. Dylan. Dylan? Goddamnit, come on. DYLAN! GIVE ME A BREAK! [*Softer.*] Dylan. Please? [**LYNN** *knocks on the door reasonably. His game is heard from inside the shed. Exasperated,* **LYNN** *sits down.*]

RACHEL: It's for the best, Mom. Who knows what you were about to smash.

LYNN: People are coming tomorrow. Look at this place.

RACHEL: Yes, but that's all our stuff. We should go through it carefully. You'll just create more work for yourself.

LYNN: What part of "people are coming tomorrow" is unclear? I have twenty-four hours, Rachel, that is all.

RACHEL: Everyone coming tomorrow knows that you're going through a time of . . . [*Carefully.*] Well, no one expects you to be perfect. Now, I think you should take a deep breath, unwind, and come to the mall with me. We can get fro yo and catch up. I haven't even gotten to tell you about school, really.

LYNN: What else.

RACHEL: What else what?

LYNN: What else. I'm not rational. I can't take a shed down. I'm no fun. My yard is a mess. What else.

RACHEL: I was just trying to—

LYNN: You were just trying to what? Go have a sundae. Dylan and I will take care of things. Take care of OUR lawn. [*Loudly.*] Joke's over, Dylan. Come out, now! We've got work to do.

RACHEL: Wait a second!

LYNN: Buy me three irons so I don't lose them all. And staple-gun them to the hall closet so I don't wreck your storage system.

RACHEL: What are you talking about?

LYNN: LET'S GO DYLAN! NOW! [**DYLAN** *comes out of the shed. He is wearing a bicycle helmet in a colorful shade, and he has a gardening spade hidden under his shirt.*]

DYLAN: Ready, Madre? [*Pulling out the spade.*] DRAW!

LYNN: Compost.

RACHEL: [*Slowly, sadly.*] Mom, I didn't mean it like that. I just thought it would be fun to—

LYNN: You know what would be fun? Having some help around here. You want to save some of that stuff? Be my guest.

DYLAN: Then it's demolition derby Madre-style.

LYNN: You. Dig. [**LYNN** *goes to the compost, grabs the shovel, and begins shoveling at the top layer.* **RACHEL** *goes in the shed.* **DYLAN** *sits beside the compost Indian-style, with the spade.*]

RACHEL: [*From within shed.*] So you have no need for the hibachi grill? This is considered garbage?

LYNN: Yep.

RACHEL: You don't want to grill at some point?

LYNN: Toss it!

DYLAN: No BBQ.

RACHEL: Trainer Wheels?

LYNN: Toss.

RACHEL: Croquet set.

LYNN: Toss.

RACHEL: Storm windows.

LYNN: Toss.

DYLAN: Yeah. We don't need those. [**DYLAN** *has begun "shoveling" with the spade, making baby scoops.*]

RACHEL: Birdhouse?

LYNN: Toss.

RACHEL: Easel?

LYNN: Toss.

RACHEL: You don't want your easel, Mom—

LYNN: No.

[*Beat.*]

RACHEL: Birdbath.

LYNN: Toss.

RACHEL: Chalk. Skateboards. Softballs.

LYNN: Toss.

RACHEL: Tennis racquets.

LYNN: Toss.

RACHEL: I learned to play with this one. [**RACHEL** *comes out of the shed with a child's racquet.*] Dad sawed half the handle off so I could hold it, see?

LYNN: Toss.

DYLAN: KEEP! Yo, give it here, Rache.

RACHEL: Yeah, we're keeping it. It's sentimental.

DYLAN: Look, Mom, we've just scored ourselves another shovel.

RACHEL: Hey!

DYLAN: It works good. [*Using the shovel in one hand and the tennis racquet in the other,* **DYLAN** *attacks the compost pile.*]

RACHEL: Dylan! Give it back!

DYLAN: Hey Mom, I think I'm on to something! This is gonna revolutionize the compost industry.

RACHEL: Cute. Give me the racquet.

LYNN: And I'll take the shovel. [**DYLAN** *hands* **LYNN** *the tennis racquet.*] The real shovel. [**RACHEL** *grabs the racquet.* **DYLAN** *bypasses* **LYNN** *and starts shoveling.*] Give me that shovel, Dylan.

DYLAN: No, I'm doing it!

LYNN: Give me the godblessit shovel, Dylan!

DYLAN: No! I'm doing it! [**LYNN** *grabs the shovel and starts shoveling.*]

LYNN: You resent doing anything for me? I'll do it myself.

DYLAN: Give it to me, Ma! It's my job!

LYNN: Well, YOU'RE FIRED.

DYLAN: I'M THE MAN OF THE HOUSE, YOU CAN'T FIRE ME. Now give me the fucking shovel, Mom.

RACHEL: Dylan! Don't talk to her like that! The man of the house? You just stomp around with your dumb Gameboy—

DYLAN: [*To* **RACHEL.**] Butt out, loser! [*To* **LYNN.**] Mom, graduation isn't a big deal for Chrissakes. I don't give a rat's ass about it. No one does. Your dumb shed and your dumb yard and your dumb plant . . . your dumb plant isn't going to grow in this hellhole. You hear me? That gonna make you stop? Huh? Stop shoveling! STOP IT! Would you stop shoveling! [**DYLAN** *and* **LYNN** *have a tug-of-war over the shovel.*]

RACHEL: Jesus! You guys are both certifiable! Who cares? [*To* **LYNN.**] It's garbage. GARBAGE!

LYNN: It's not garbage, it's our yard. We live here.

RACHEL: You're right, I don't. And thank God!

LYNN: What the hell is your problem, Rachel?

RACHEL: My problem? My problem? No, Mom, the question isn't what's my problem! [**RACHEL** *storms over to* **DYLAN** *and yanks his sleeve back aggressively.*] You want to talk about problems? Real problems? Look at this.

DYLAN: Get off me! [**DYLAN** *pushes her arm away violently.*]

RACHEL: You're fighting over garbage while he has a perfectly straight line of burns down his arm. Intentional. Self-mutilation. Look.

[*Beat.* **LYNN** *does not move. Silence.*]

LYNN: Let me see. [*Beat. Silence.*] Let me see your arm, Dylan.

DYLAN: It's not what it looks like, Ma.

LYNN: Now.

DYLAN: She's just in Psych one-o-one—

LYNN: Now. [**DYLAN** *extends his arm.* **LYNN** *pulls back his sleeve. She looks. She is quiet for a minute.*] Oh, that's great, Dylan. That's really cute. You think this is cute? Huh? You think it's cute that I need to worry about this? Is that it? HUH? I need to see this! You're burning yourself?

DYLAN: I dunno.

LYNN: Look at me! You think I need this right now? ANSWER ME! DO YOU THINK I NEED THIS RIGHT NOW?

DYLAN: No.

LYNN: I have to stop what I'm doing and treat you like a baby? You're burning yourself! I need to take you to a loony bin? Is that it?

DYLAN: No.

RACHEL: [*To* **LYNN.**] Some scars are darker than others. This has been going on a long time. It's a cry for help.

DYLAN: Go get your four point zero.

RACHEL: He's got beers over there, he's hiding, Mom. He's been drinking all day, too.

LYNN: Dylan!

DYLAN: I can't listen to this.

LYNN: [*To* **DYLAN.**] No, and you shouldn't. You shouldn't be out here. You don't care about me! [*Increasing pace.*] You don't give a damn about anyone but yourself, do you! You're no help to me, Dylan. You're just dumping more work on me. And don't you worry. I don't need you. I can take it, Dylan. I CAN TAKE IT. You just go on inside and burn away!

RACHEL: Mom . . .

LYNN: GO, DYLAN. GET OUT MY SIGHT.

RACHEL: Mom! Stop it!

LYNN: GET OUT OF HERE!

RACHEL: MOM! STOP!

LYNN: Get out! You're no help to me, Dylan. You're just like your father.

[*Dead silence.* **DYLAN** *freezes in his tracks. He turns around very slowly and looks at her squarely.*]

DYLAN: Make that two men you've driven the fuck outta here, Mom.
[**DYLAN** *exits furiously.* **RACHEL** *runs after him.*]

RACHEL: [*Voice off.*] Dylan! Hey! [**LYNN** *stands alone on stage, stunned and quiet for several beats. Suddenly, with fierceness, she strikes the wisteria as hard as she can, sending it over in a heap. The sound of the car is heard peeling out; she slumps to her knees and weeps.* **RACHEL** *reenters. Frantically:*] Mom! What's the matter with you? He left! He's been drinking and now he's driving! HE LEFT! [*Sustained beat.*] Mom! Mom? Why'd you say that? What's the matter with you? [**LYNN** *doesn't seem to hear* **RACHEL.** Mom? What's the matter, Mom? [*Pause, scared.*] I'm getting Dad. [**RACHEL** *runs off. Lights fade on* **LYNN** *alone on stage.*]

END OF ACT I

ACT II
Scene 1

AT RISE: Later that night, 1:00 a.m. The wisteria tree, still lit up with Christmas lights and lying on its side, is the only source of light on stage. There is a cordless phone on the table. The yard is silent and empty, save the sound of crickets and far off traffic.

After a few beats we see headlights and hear car doors slam. **RACHEL** *enters. She goes straight for the phone and dials numbers.* **STEPHEN** *enters behind her. They both wear jackets and look exhausted.* **STEPHEN** *carries car keys and a map. He trips over a paint can as he enters, which makes a loud commotion.*

STEPHEN: . . . Ow.

RACHEL: Are you okay, Dad?

STEPHEN: I'm not sure this is the wisest place to store her paint cans.

RACHEL: Yeah, no kidding.

STEPHEN: I'll get the light.

RACHEL: Shhh . . . I'm checking messages. [**STEPHEN** *goes to the porch light and turns it on. Darkness. He tries it a couple more times.*]

STEPHEN: The bulb is dead. [**STEPHEN** *goes into the shed despite the darkness. He emerges with a flashlight.*] But old faithful is where it's supposed to be! [**STEPHEN** *turns on the flashlight. Darkness.*] Batteries are dead. Am I on one of these prank TV shows? [**RACHEL** *laughs genuinely.*]

RACHEL: If Dylan has us on candid camera, I'll be pissed.

STEPHEN: Hand me that game thing. Gameboy. I'll use those batteries. [**RACHEL** *hands it to him. He goes to the wisteria tree and crouches near it to see. He puts the batteries from the Gameboy into the flashlight. Meanwhile, **RACHEL** *hangs up the phone.*]

RACHEL: "You have no new messages." You'd think he'd at least call. A courtesy call to say he isn't dead.

STEPHEN: People don't always behave the way we think they will, Rachel.

RACHEL: Except Mom. We thought she'd be late, and sure enough, she is.

STEPHEN: Well, at least half of us are here on time. Let's use our time productively and go over the list while we wait.

RACHEL: We've been over the list, Dad. I think we've thought of every possible place he could be.

STEPHEN: But hearing the list might make us realize new items to add to the list.

RACHEL: Yeah, you're right. Let's hear it.

STEPHEN: You say check. [*Beat.*] Quickee Mart.

RACHEL: Check.

STEPHEN: Park Street Bowl.

RACHEL: Check.

STEPHEN: Pine Street Bowl.

RACHEL: Check.

STEPHEN: Ho Bowl on the Hill.

RACHEL: Check.

STEPHEN: Jefferson Bowl.

RACHEL: Check. Does Dylan bowl?

STEPHEN: He did a couple of times there in elementary school. I know. We're pushing it, but it's one a.m. and we have no leads. [*Beat.*] Waffle Hut.

RACHEL: Check.

STEPHEN: Pee wee Putt Putt.

RACHEL: Check.

STEPHEN: Hot Fudge Franks.

RACHEL: Check.

STEPHEN: Galacticon Cyber . . . ?

RACHEL: Galacticon Cyber Super Station game room. Check.

STEPHEN: Mark's house.

RACHEL: Check.

STEPHEN: Paul's house. Rut and Farley's. That Blake character's.

RACHEL: Check. Checkcheck—

    [*The phone rings.* **STEPHEN** *answers.*]

STEPHEN: Hello? I hear you breathing. May I help you? [**STEPHEN** *hangs up the phone. As if on the list:*] Prankster.

RACHEL: Check. Mom needs to change that number. Pranks are disturbing. [*Pause.*] Actually, a lot of things are disturbing around here. [*Pointing to shed.*] Cut to: visual exhibit A.

STEPHEN: I don't get the feeling she's using Miracle Gro. [*Looking up.*] That's the end of my list.

[*Beat.*]

RACHEL: Do you want . . . I can make us some tea or something?

STEPHEN: That's nice of you. No thank you. I'm fine.

RACHEL: What do we do until Mom gets here? [**STEPHEN** *reaches for the phone.*]

STEPHEN: [*To* **RACHEL.**] Actually, can I borrow the phone? I should touch base at home.

RACHEL: Yeah. [**RACHEL** *hands him the phone; he dials.*]

STEPHEN: [*Into the phone.*] Hi . . . I woke you, yeah, I . . . [**STEPHEN** *goes to the far end of the yard and speaks quietly and quickly into the phone.* **RACHEL** *strains to listen.* **STEPHEN** *hangs up and returns.*] Sorry about that.

RACHEL: Her voice sounded all panicked and loud. She's worried, huh.

STEPHEN: No. I mean, yes, it's late, but she's glad I'm here for you kids.

RACHEL: Yeah?

STEPHEN: Of course. She knows Dylan's my son. And you're my daughter. She understands that you're priorities to me. [*Beat.*] She is eager to meet you, Rachel. I've obviously told her a great deal about you.

RACHEL: Like what.

STEPHEN: Like that you're beautiful, kind, talented, brilliant, and just about the best thing since sliced bread. That I'm intensely proud that you're at my alma mater. Roaming my old stomping grounds.

[*Beat.*]

RACHEL: Dad, I hate school.

STEPHEN: You hate school?

RACHEL: Yeah, I hate it there. It's soul-deadening.

STEPHEN: Well, wow. That's surprising. Your e-mails didn't indicate such a thing.

RACHEL: E-mails generally indicate nothing. That's why they're e-mails.

[*Beat.*]

STEPHEN: Well, what's the problem? Are you in the wrong courses? You said you took Art History? Was that a fluff 'n nutter class?

RACHEL: I took Lit Theory. Modern American Poetry. Adolescent Psych. Philosophy of Antiquity. Geology. And Photography I for my creative outlet class, like you told me.

STEPHEN: No math?

RACHEL: I tested out with a perfect score.

[*Beat.*]

STEPHEN: Are you involved in any extracurricular activities?

RACHEL: All I do is study.

STEPHEN: With a study group?

RACHEL: I study in the library stacks. Behind the bars. Alone. Where the graduate student trolls are.

STEPHEN: Aren't there study groups you can join?

RACHEL: I'm too competitive.

STEPHEN: No. Eager.

RACHEL: [*Fast.*] Poe. Whitman. Longfellow. Frost. Bukowski. Millay. Kerouac. Ginsberg. Ashbery. O'Hara. Carroll. Stevens. Williams. Sandburg. Eliot. [*A challenge.*] The poets on my final exam. Would you like a recitation? I memorized excerpts for the pure fun of being the most prepared.

[*Beat.*]

STEPHEN: Have you made nice friends?

RACHEL: Would you be my friend?!

STEPHEN: Well, is your roommate a nice gal?

RACHEL: Eleven hundred SAT scores; no detectable athletic trophies; extraneous photos of her puppy; eats a lot of mac and cheese. [*Pause.*] Do you know what Kendra thinks about me?

STEPHEN: Who's Kendra?

RACHEL: My roommate, Dad.

STEPHEN: Right. I'm sure neither of us knows how Kendra feels about you.

RACHEL: She told the girl across the hall that she "totally lost" the roommate lottery: a stuck-up uber-dork.

[*Beat.*]

STEPHEN: What's this girl's full name?

RACHEL: Kendra Leary.

STEPHEN: What's Kendra Leary's major?

RACHEL: Undeclared.

STEPHEN: Well, is undeclared Kendra Leary taking an Honors language seminar this summer? Is undeclared Kendra Leary one of the handpicked Dean's Scholars at one of the nation's best schools? Did undeclared Kendra Leary test out of her math requirement? [*Pause.*] She has plenty to envy in you.

RACHEL: Kendra fluctuates between hating me and feeling sorry for me.

[*The phone rings.* **STEPHEN** *answers it. Listens. Hangs up.*]

STEPHEN: How tedious.

RACHEL: Mom is also officially twenty minutes late.

[*Beat.*]

STEPHEN: From one über-dork to another, you are sitting high in my book. You are a focused, articulate, graceful, responsible woman. And I am very proud of you.

RACHEL: Why responsible? Because I ratted out my brother, pissed off my sister, and hurt my mother?

STEPHEN: No, because you did the right thing by coming to get me. Run for help, it's a good instinct. You do the right thing.

RACHEL: That's just my training. I can't do the wrong thing. I can't even pretend to have fun drinking beers with the retarded monkeys at school. [*Beat.*] Dad, can you keep a secret? I mean, Dylan and Kacie will make fun of me if they knew.

STEPHEN: Scout's honor.

RACHEL: At the beginning of the semester when I was trying to make friends, I told everyone on my floor that I had a car. And they were all like, "Oh, the freshman with the car."

STEPHEN: And?

RACHEL: And, so everyone is my best friend when I'm going to do laundry or going to the grocery store off-campus. But come Friday night, when they go to beer pong, or dancing at the Idle Hour, or to the frats, I'm invisible. They'll all do their lip gloss and hairspray in my room and then say good night. Leave me there studying.

STEPHEN: Well, why don't you go? Everyone deserves a little break on a weekend night. Why don't you go, Rachel?

RACHEL: With who, Dad?

[*Beat.*]

STEPHEN: You know, I think I know what's happening here.

RACHEL: What.

STEPHEN: You're forgetting my trick. It always works. When you sit down to work and you have those Kendra Learys and all other demons in your head, you silence them. You say, "Demons, I am Rachel. You will not make me insecure! I am Rachel!"

RACHEL: What do you tell your demons when you're homesick?

STEPHEN: That it's a transition. It'll take time.

RACHEL: When your demons ask you why you e-mailed me the news of your engagement, what do you tell them?

STEPHEN: That I did the best I could? That I'm not good with the phone, Rachel.

RACHEL: When they ask you why I was alone at Parents Day Weekend, what do you tell them?

STEPHEN: Your mother didn't tell me the dates.

RACHEL: I didn't have the heart to tell her the dates, Dad.

[*Beat.*]

STEPHEN: Let's do it this summer. I'll come up, and we can walk the campus. I'll show you my old dorm. Let me make it up to you.

RACHEL: It's a long trip.

STEPHEN: So? Maybe if you had some company in the library stacks you wouldn't feel so alone. We could read together. Do Latin for a weekend.

RACHEL: I can't bring my dad in the stacks.

STEPHEN: Why not? I'm not cool enough to join you and the graduate trolls?

RACHEL: I don't need company, Dad. I need a reason to be working this hard.

STEPHEN: You're doing it for you. You're doing a wonderful job, and you're doing it for you, Rachel!

RACHEL: I was never doing it for me. [*Beat. We see headlights appear in the driveway.*] Ah, finally!

STEPHEN: Let's plan this trip of mine later. I think we should put it in pen on your calendar.

RACHEL: Wow. In pen? [*Two car doors slam.*]

KACIE: [*Offstage.*] HOMIE DEE? HE'S HERE RIGHT? [**KACIE** *runs in, with* **LYNN** *behind her.*]

STEPHEN: Sorry, kiddo. We didn't have any luck.

LYNN: No? Nothing? No one's called? No messages? No word? No sound?

RACHEL: Sorry, Mom. We were two hours up and down Henry Avenue.

LYNN: [*Frustrated, loudly.*] Oh, come on, Dylan! This is ridiculous! He won! I'm a basket case. YES, DYLAN, I AM A BASKET CASE! I did the Indie Five Hundred up and down this town like an idiot! I went through a whole tank of gas! He's made his point . . . [*To* "**DYLAN**":] You've MADE YOUR POINT! I AM SORRY!

KACIE: Mom, let's do your yogic breathing.

LYNN: He's not at any of his friends'. No one's seen him. No one's heard from him. Everything closes at midnight! [*To* **STEPHEN**.] I really thought he'd be gone an hour and then huff home. Who's to say he hasn't hopped a bus to New York or Vegas or who knows where.

STEPHEN: Lynn, we're doing everything we can here. Let's stay calm. We've split up. We've covered ground. But we still have options—

LYNN: WHAT OPTIONS!

STEPHEN: We need to sit down, quietly, and go over our list.

LYNN: We've been over the damn list! I don't wanna hear that damn—

RACHEL: The list really does help, Mom.

KACIE: Hey, did anyone check in the shed? [**KACIE** *goes in the shed. From within:*] Homie?

LYNN: There's got to be SOMEWHERE we haven't considered looking. [**KACIE** *comes out of the shed. She sees the Gameboy on the table.*]

KACIE: GAMEBOY. He'll be back for the Gameboy, Mom! He would never leave it; he's on level three! [**KACIE** *tries to turn the Gameboy on.*]

LYNN: SHIT! WHERE THE HELL IS HE ALREADY?

STEPHEN: Kacie's here. Let's keep it clean. [*Gently.*] Why don't you sit right over here. Pacing doesn't solve anything . . .

KACIE: [*Coldly, to* **RACHEL**.] Hey! Why'd you take the batteries out?

RACHEL: We needed them for the flashlight. [**KACIE** *stomps into the house for more batteries.*]

KACIE: YOU HAD NO RIGHT TO TOUCH HIS GAME, RACHEL!

STEPHEN: Kace! Shhhh!

LYNN: He knows this is sending me over the edge. He wants to make me crazy. This is calculated revenge!

STEPHEN: Now, come on, this isn't personal to you, Lynn. He's just having an adolescent tantrum. [*Beat.* **KACIE** *returns with the Gameboy, which is now beeping wildly.* **KACIE** *walks along the back fence holding the Gameboy up on highest volume.*]

KACIE: [*As Gameboy.*] Here Dylan, Dylan, Dylan. Level three! Come beat me!

STEPHEN: Kacie, quiet now. These poor neighbors have been through enough.

KACIE: [*Whispers, as Gameboy.*] Dylan! Come kick my butt, Dylan!

STEPHEN: [*Tenderly.*] Well, it's past one. As much as I don't want to suggest this, I think it's time we discuss Plan B.

LYNN: What's Plan B?

STEPHEN: Let's sit and converse.

LYNN: What the hell is Plan B?

STEPHEN: [*Firmly.*] Plan B is to call the police to report the car stolen.

RACHEL and **KACIE:** WHAT!?

KACIE: He didn't steal Mom's car!

STEPHEN: I know he didn't steal the car, but it's a means to an end. The police will definitely find the car if we give them the infor—

LYNN: He's my KID. I'm not calling the police on my kid—

STEPHEN: May I finish, please? I don't mean handcuffs. But the fact is, you don't know what he may be drinking or smoking or snorting behind the wheel. This is dangerous—

LYNN: For God's sake Stephen, he's not doing drugs! He's punishing me!

STEPHEN: Do you know that for a fact?

KACIE: His friends aren't druggies, Dad.

LYNN: He's on D.A.R.E. for chrissakes!

STEPHEN: But do you, Lynn, know it to be a fact, with one-hundred-percent certainty, that he isn't—

LYNN: Yes I do.

STEPHEN: Do you search his room?

LYNN: No.

STEPHEN: Do you give him urine tests?

LYNN: No.

STEPHEN: Blood tests?

LYNN: No.

STEPHEN: Breathalyzer tests?

LYNN: No.

STEPHEN: Then you have no means of knowing for sure.

LYNN: Not one that's a test, Stephen.

STEPHEN: Well, intuition isn't going to give us answers. [*Pause.*] Look at the facts: Change in attitude? Loss of focus in school? Dramatic change in appearance? Irritability? Refusal to assume responsibility for—

LYNN: You just described everyone eighteen.

STEPHEN: MAY I PLEASE FINISH A SENTENCE WITHOUT INTERRUPTION! [*Beat. Very softly:*] I beg your pardon, girls. I am very tired.

RACHEL: It's okay. We're all tired, Dad.

KACIE: I'm not tired. [*Beat. The phone rings.* **STEPHEN** *pushes the dial tone button and hangs up without speaking.*] What'd you do that for?

STEPHEN: It's just a prank. You've been getting them all night.

RACHEL: You need to change your number, Mom.

LYNN: We don't get pranks. What kind of prank?

STEPHEN: It's just heavy breathing. The kind Kacie shouldn't hear by accident.

KACIE: Does the breathing sound like this? [**KACIE** *imitates Darth Vader.*]

STEPHEN: Yes?

KACIE: [*Laughing wildly.*] It's Dylan! See? I told you! He's fine!

STEPHEN: Why would Dylan do that?

LYNN: He thinks he's Darth Vader. Where'd it sound like he was? [*The phone rings.*] Give me the phone! Give it to— [*Into the receiver:*] Dylan? I know it's you. It's Mom. It's your Mom and I can hear you breathing, Dylan . . . Don't you hang up, tell me where you . . . [**LYNN** *listens. She hangs it up.*] Loud music and male voices? Like a juke box and muffled conversation.

STEPHEN: Like a bar?

LYNN: Yes, a bar, but not a wine bar. How the hell's he getting into a bar?

STEPHEN: You want to take east of Main or west?

LYNN: West.

RACHEL: I'll go with Dad.

LYNN: No. You stay with Kacie.

KACIE: No way! I'm not missing this! Dylan's in a bar! That's rad!

STEPHEN: Girls, you two stay here. End of story. We'll meet back here at, what? Two?

LYNN: Yeah, two. [**LYNN** *rises and gets her keys as does* **STEPHEN**. *To* **RACHEL**.] Answer the phone if it rings and keep him talking til I can show up there and kill him. [**LYNN** *exits.*]

STEPHEN: And Kace, why don't you let Rachel take you on up to bed once we've gone? [*Confidentially whispers.*] She shouldn't see Dylan when we bring him home . . .

KACIE: [*Whispers.*] Why not?

RACHEL: Because we said so.

STEPHEN: See you at two sharp. [**STEPHEN** *exits quickly.* **RACHEL** *and* **KACIE** *are left alone on stage.* **KACIE** *promptly puts her feet up and begins playing Gameboy.*]

RACHEL: It's time for bed, miss. I'll walk you up.

KACIE: To bed, Kacie. Inside, Kacie. Upstairs, Kacie. You can talk to yourself or I can save you the trouble: I'm waiting up for Dylan. [**KACIE** *plays Gameboy.*]

RACHEL: As the resident authority, I say what. You heard what Dad said.

KACIE: No I didn't.

RACHEL: He said it's time for bed.

KACIE: Go ahead. [*To game.*] C'mon biotch! Bring it!

RACHEL: No, not me go to bed. YOU go to bed. You, the one I'm baby-sitting. I am babysitting you, remember.

KACIE: I'm out of Pampers.

RACHEL: I'll go buy 'em. What's your preference? Huggies or Luvs?

KACIE: I'm sure you know what's best. [*Beat.* **KACIE** *plays.*]

RACHEL: Okay. Enough's enough. I'm gonna count to five, and then you are going to turn off that game and go to bed. One. Two. Three. Four. Four and half. Four and three quarters. Four and nine tenths . . . I'm inching towards the door . . . [*Resigned,* **RACHEL** *returns to the table.*]

KACIE: Five?

RACHEL: Yeah. [**KACIE** *does not move. Cross fade to Scene 2.*]

Scene 2

DYLAN *is at a table in a local bar, holding the phone. Loud music is playing, and there should be a tight light on the area to suggest it is a separate locale. There are several empty beer bottles on the table, and a bowl of peanuts. Under the table is the helmet* **DYLAN** *was wearing at the end of Act I. A freshly poured shot is on the table. He stands to perform his peanut tossing to an imaginary audience in the bar.*

DYLAN: One one thousand. Two one thousand. Three one thousand. And . . . [*Throwing a peanut into his mouth, catching it.*] SCORE! Four one thousand. Five one thousand. Six one thousand. [*Again.*] AND HE SCORES AGAIN! [*To the bar.*] Wally, I scored again! I am the nut MASTA! [**LYNN** *enters.*] Speech? Okay. I'd like to thank the peanuts for their perfect combination of honey and nut . . . and most of all, I would like to thank Heine, for her constant—

LYNN: Dylan! WHAT ARE YOU DOING HERE?

DYLAN: Are you lost, ma'am?

LYNN: Do you have any idea what time it is?

DYLAN: Last call is usually around one-thirty.

LYNN: Get your stuff.

DYLAN: Do I know you? You look kinda familiar . . .

LYNN: You're in a biker bar, Dylan!

DYLAN: Mom, shhh! Don't blow my cover, babe. [*Pointing to the helmet.*] They think I own a Ducati.

LYNN: You called me! I found you! Now, let's go!

DYLAN: I didn't call you.

LYNN: Yes you did. You hung up on me.

DYLAN: Some asswipe is pranking us? I'll kill him. [**LYNN** *picks up the cordless phone on the table.*]

LYNN: Should I press redial?

DYLAN: Go ahead. I ordered you guys a pizza. Pepperoni and mushroom.

LYNN: I know your breathing, Darth.

DYLAN: Okay, you caught me. It was a cry for help. I'm in big trouble, Ma.

LYNN: What kind of trouble?

DYLAN: [*Seriously.*] The most serious kind of all. Sit down. [**DYLAN** *looks like he's going to cry. He hands* **LYNN** *a folded piece of white paper.*]

LYNN: What's this?

DYLAN: [*Painfully.*] Read it.

LYNN: [*Reading.*] Jaegermeister shots—three. Heinekens—eight! Oh Dylan, you're going to be sick! Look at me. Let me see your eyes. Focus right here. How many fingers do I have here?

DYLAN: Hi. Ma.

LYNN: You're going to be puking all day tomorrow! Oh, good God, fool!

DYLAN: That's not even the worst of it. [*Pause.*] Under that. On the bottom. That's where the real ball buster of a problem is.

LYNN: Where?

DYLAN: Down here. What does that say?

LYNN: Forty-five seventy-two.

DYLAN: Yea, see, I only got two fiddy on me. That's where you come in. [**DYLAN** *breaks his serious veneer and laughs wildly.*] Oh come on. You deserved it!

LYNN: I'm sitting here, like an idiot, thinking you're confessing your drinking problems to me.

DYLAN: Nah. This is small potatoes, Ma. I'm far under par.

LYNN: Well that's nothing to be proud of. You know who sits in bars like these and drink that much by themselves? Alcoholics, Dylan.

DYLAN: I'm not an alcoholic, Mom. They go to meetings. [**DYLAN** *laughs.* **LYNN** *does not.*]

LYNN: Dylan, it's one forty a.m. I'm exhausted. I haven't stopped looking for you for the last eight hours. I've been out of my skull and I've been driving around, meeting up with Stephen, looking for your body in gutters. [*Firmly.*] Now I want to see your ass making its way to my car right now.

DYLAN: This ass right here?

LYNN: I'm not joking. [**DYLAN** *sits on the floor.*]

DYLAN: One cheek, two cheek. The floor is cool on this ass, Ma. Try it. My ass is feeling pretty cemented— [**LYNN** *grabs his arm and tries to pull him up.*]

LYNN: Get up.

DYLAN: . . . ooooo . . . ugggghhh . . . feel the burn. . . .

LYNN: Up. Now. [**DYLAN** *puts his arms around her and holds her immobile.*]

DYLAN: Oh! You want hugs! I love hugs.

LYNN: Let go of me! GET UP! Dylan, now!

DYLAN: No hugs?

LYNN: You are going home!

DYLAN: Home, no. Heine—

LYNN and DYLAN: YES!

DYLAN: Yes Heine?

LYNN: NO!

DYLAN: You're confusing me, Ma.

LYNN: [*Furious.*] You listen to me, Dylan. You are the kid! I'm the mother! Mothers know everything and you will do what I say!

DYLAN: You know everything—

LYNN: YES.

DYLAN: I'm glad to hear it. You help me answer a question.

LYNN: Dylan.

DYLAN: What kind of oil does our lawnmower take?

LYNN: What?

DYLAN: I'll make it true or false. [*Pause.*] Is it true that our lawnmower takes two stroke oil?

LYNN: Can't this wait!

DYLAN: I didn't hear an answer there.

LYNN: Yes.

DYLAN: Very good. It is true that our lawnmower takes two-stroke oil. Is it true that a sweating pipe is a leaking pipe?

LYNN: I'm tired, Dyl—

DYLAN: False. Sweating pipe is a verb and it means soldering a pipe together. [*Pause.*] Your car got an oil change twice this year. True or false.

LYNN: I don't know . . .

DYLAN: [*Accelerating in speed and volume.*] True. Tarring a skylight prevents a leak? True. You can make a gutter patch out of a screen and duct tape? True. You can fix a garbage disposal with a vacuum. True. Picket fences are made with pre-made, thirty-six-inch pickets and two-by-three cedar back boards. True. You drive them into the ground twenty-four inches deep. True. Changing the thermostat in a car can take fourteen hours. True. A plumb bob is a weight on a string you use as a level. True. The fuse box is in the basement, right-hand corner. True. The ten foot ladder is in the shed, but the fifth step has a crack. True. The gutters were cleaned in April. Your dryer overheats and blows a gasket weekly. Our Christmas tree lost its needles and we needed a new one. Kacie's bike had a flat tire and the pump didn't work. Rachel's stuff had to be carried up five flights in her dorm. All of the above? TRUE. [*Beat.*] And you know what else?

LYNN: No.

DYLAN: I feel better for the first time in a year. You know why?

LYNN: No.

DYLAN: Because I am a fuck-up who can only do about a third of what you need done. But you know why that's okay?

LYNN: No.

DYLAN: Cuz I am just like my father. Thanks to you, that's TRUE. [**DYLAN** *takes a drink.* **LYNN** *sits, very quietly. Several beats should pass before she speaks.*]

LYNN: I fucked up, Dylan.

DYLAN: Ding. Dong.

LYNN: I didn't mean what I said. People say things they don't mean all the time. You're nothing like your father. [*Pause.*] Fact is, you told me to . . . well you know what you said. Now, that's not something your father would say, is it?

DYLAN: No.

LYNN: I'm sorry, Dylan. Your arm was more than I could take.

DYLAN: I was supposed to be on vacation.

LYNN: You can be on vacation from now on. No compost. No projects. No shed demolition . . .

DYLAN: No party?

LYNN: Yes, party. But you agreed to a party! You want one.

DYLAN: You didn't ask me if I wanted a party. You told me you were throwing me one. I said graduation could suck my balls. You said I had a bad attitude. I said you could suck my balls. You said you needed to have a party because it would be good for you and could I please try not to be an ass.

LYNN: I didn't say that. I wouldn't say that. I wouldn't call my own son an ass.

DYLAN: You called me an ass today, Ma. I didn't want to plant your tree and you said, "You're being a real ass today."

[*Beat.*]

LYNN: Dylan, I'm proud of you and I'd like to throw you a party tomorrow to celebrate. Would you like that?

DYLAN: If you need parties to feel better I'm not going to say no.

LYNN: Do you want a party, Dylan, to toast your graduation?

DYLAN: Yes, if it means you're going to feel better—

LYNN: Dylan, DO YOU WANT A PARTY? I am asking you a question about you! What do you want?

DYLAN: I don't want a party. I don't want to be looked at, and poked at, and cheek-pinched, and asked, "Why aren't you going to college, Dylan?" or "Why'd you quit tennis, Dylan?" or "Where's your Dad, Dylan?"

LYNN: Then we won't have a party.

[*Beat.*]

DYLAN: Good. The shed really does look like shit.

LYNN: It looks like my eighteen-year-old son painted it for me.

DYLAN: It looks like a three-year-old flung his own poo at it. [**LYNN** *laughs. She looks around. She picks up the cigarettes and studies them. She lights one, coughs heavily, then resolves to just resting it in the ashtray.*]

LYNN: God, I haven't been in a bar like this in a long time.

DYLAN: Coulda fooled me. [*Offering her a peanut.*] Want to try a peanut instead?

LYNN: Yea. [*Eating.*] I like it here. There's a rustic, primitive appeal. It could probably benefit from a lady's touch here and there. Murals on the wall. Maybe more wall on the wall. Maybe just some women.

DYLAN: There's a lot of nuts in here, Ma.

LYNN: How did you get in?

DYLAN: Mario Lucheezi.

LYNN: Can I see? [**DYLAN** *shows her his fake ID.*]

DYLAN: I'm Italian, and Italians drive Ducatis. One of these guys is a retired Hell's Angel. [**LYNN** *keeps the ID. She reads.*]

LYNN: These men think you're twenty-seven?

DYLAN: With a baby face. [*Secretly.*] Truth is, they don't care. I have the high score on Space Invaders and Pac-Man. I'm a god to them.

LYNN: Do these men actually socialize with you?

DYLAN: Wally and the guys helped me change the tire on your car last week.

LYNN: Who's Wally?

DYLAN: [*Shouting off, waving.*] YO, WALLY! [*To* **LYNN.**] Wally. [*Beat.*]

LYNN: You know, I used to get good and shitfaced in bars like these, as a matter of fact. I used to drink whiskey, too.

DYLAN: Jaegermeister isn't whiskey.

LYNN: [*Thinking.*] Oh. I must be thinking of something else . . .

DYLAN: [*Listing.*] Jack Daniels? Johnny Walker? Jim Beam? Cutty Sark? Wild Turkey—

LYNN: Dewars.

DYLAN: That's a good choice.

LYNN: [*Uneasy.*] Well, thank you. [*Pause.*] You should've seen me in those days, Dylan. I had a cascade of braids to my perfect twenty-five-inch waist. John Lennon glasses. Knee-high boots. Turquoise jewelry. You father fell madly in love with me the moment he saw me. And with good reason; I looked pretty amazing on the back of a bike, if I don't say so myself. [**DYLAN** *spits his beer out to emphasize his point.*]

DYLAN: BIKE?

LYNN: Yeah, bikes. Harleys, you name it. Where do you think you got your cool from?

DYLAN: Mario, frankly.

LYNN: No, dummy! It's from me. I smoked reefer! I read palms! I went to poetry readings! I toted my easel and painted all day! I was a feisty, arty, beautiful sparkler. [*Sadly.*] I really was.

[*Beat.*]

DYLAN: Mom. You wanna put the helmet on?

LYNN: No!

DYLAN: No one in here knows it matches Kacie's Huffy. They'll just think you're a rockin babe.

LYNN: I can't wear a helmet in public, Dylan.

DYLAN: Yeah. It's an order. Put it on.

LYNN: No.

DYLAN: Put it on! [**LYNN** *puts the helmet on, at first awkwardly, then enjoying herself, looking over her shoulder and smiling.*]

LYNN: I look silly.

DYLAN: You look like a bad ass.

LYNN: It doesn't look ridiculous?

DYLAN: Nah. I'm telling you, you look like a mean motherfucker. All you need is the chaps like Dennis Hopper. [*Singing.*] *Get your motor running . . . head out on the highway . . . looking for adventure . . . pulling over to smoke some weed.* [*Chanting.*] Yea, ma! Hug those curves, smoke that dope, be wild as a bird on a mission for bad assness. Hug those curves, Hug those curves, hug those curves. And, ah . . . BOOM!

LYNN: Boom?

DYLAN: You hit some bush. Drugs kill, Mom. [**LYNN** *stops and takes the helmet off.*]

LYNN: [*Slowly.*] It wasn't a bush I hit. I hit a big, rigid, brilliant, handsome tree. And I got knocked right off my bike. [**LYNN** *hands it back to him. Awkward, long beat.*]

DYLAN: You know he's gone, Mom. [*Beat.*] He isn't coming back. [*Beat.*] He isn't coming tomorrow. He isn't coming back. He chose her. [*Beat.*] He's gone. [*Pause.*] You need to get back on the bike. [**LYNN** *hugs* **DYLAN** *fiercely and cries.* **DYLAN** *hugs her back, just long enough to realize where he is. Feigning suffocation.*] It's cool, Ma. It's cool . . . hey! HEY! Weird woman that definitely isn't my mother, let go now.

LYNN: No.

DYLAN: Ma.

LYNN: No.

DYLAN: Ma!

LYNN: I'm going to do better, Dylan. I am . . . [**LYNN** *pushes* **DYLAN**'s *sleeves up and looks at his arm. She kisses the burns, and hugs him again. About the burns:*] I won't let you do this . . . I'm going to watch you like a hawk . . .

DYLAN: It's not what Rachel says it is.

LYNN: I have to talk to you when you're upset . . .

DYLAN: It's a test of strength . . .

LYNN: I have to pay closer attention . . .

DYLAN: Mom. Listen. [*Pause.*] It's a guy thing that they do in the Army. You and another guy put your arms side by side, like this. [**DYLAN** *takes* **LYNN**'s *arm and holds it against his own, like he describes. He holds the lit cigarette above their arms.*] Once you're in position, you drop the cigarette, and whoever pulls his arm away first has the smaller balls. That's all it is.

LYNN: Who do you play this with?

DYLAN: I play by myself. I have bigger balls than everybody.

LYNN: It's not a game if you play by yourself.

DYLAN: Sure it is. Sometimes I miss.

LYNN: STOP IT! That's bullshit. This is bullshit. I can take you to the hospital, let them pump your stomach, and then wheel you off to the psychiatric ward, you know.

DYLAN: I know.

> [*Beat.* **LYNN** *considers.*]

LYNN: I need to hear you say that this is something we can work on, together.

DYLAN: We can work on it. [**LYNN** *looks around and considers.*]

LYNN: I'm going to have to check your arm every day. Twice a day.

DYLAN: Okay.

LYNN: And I'll take those car keys.

DYLAN: Okay.

LYNN: And you should make sure to have a glass of water so you don't dehydrate.

DYLAN: Mom.

LYNN: And you have to let Wally call you a cab when you're done with your Heine.

DYLAN: Call me a cab? [**LYNN** *hands* **DYLAN** *some money.*]

LYNN: Yeah. I think you've earned a separate exit, don't you?

DYLAN: Right. You drive safe, Mom.

LYNN: I will, Dylan. I will.

> [**LYNN** *exits. Cross fade to Scene 3.*]

Scene 3

Back to the yard. **RACHEL** *plays with citronella candles on the table. She blows it out, relights it. Blows it out, relights it. Meanwhile,* **KACIE**, *who has obviously been ignoring* **RACHEL**, *plays* **DYLAN**'s *Gameboy.*

RACHEL: It's not like the Gameboy is Dylan's homing device, you know. [*Beat.*] Do you even know what a homing device is? [*Beat.*] It's a two-part tracking system. One ends beeps and the other end—

KACIE: I know what home is, Rachel. [*Beat.* **KACIE** *continues to play.*]

RACHEL: It's after two. Way after two. [*Silence.*] Do you want to go watch TV? [*Pause.*] Have a snack? [*Pause.*] Are you thirsty? Bored? Sleepy? [*Pause.*] Are you mute and deaf? [*Beat.*] That's it. [*Exasperated,* **RACHEL** *takes the game out of* **KACIE**'s *hand. It shuts it off.*]

KACIE: Say you're sorry.

RACHEL: No, it's completely tedious and passive-aggressive—

KACIE: [*Fast, overlapping.*] You say you're sorry!

RACHEL: No!

KACIE: Say you're sorry!

RACHEL: I'm not sorry. It stinks that Dylan has problems but I am not sorry that I pointed out the obvious. Mom and Dad needed to know—

KACIE: Dad did not need to know.

RACHEL: Maybe you need to know. Do you want to look his arm up in a mental health encyclopedia?

KACIE: Look up "Rachel." I bet it has a picture of a prissy tattletale away at college where she belongs!

RACHEL: If you came home from college and saw that I had abused myself, what would you do? Would you really say nothing and cross your fingers that your mother—who is acting like a fish out of water—would rise to the occasion?

KACIE: It wasn't you. It wouldn't be you, Miss Perfect. It was Dylan. It was Dylan—

RACHEL: Fine. Put yourself in my shoes. What would you have done?—

KACIE: I'd ask him why he was being a butthead. Did you ask him? Did you say, "Dylan, why are you being a butthead?"

RACHEL: When you love someone, you take action. You go to an authority when they are in trouble.

KACIE: And you think that's Dad?

RACHEL: Dad's the alpha. He's the problem-solver.

KACIE: Earth to Rachel: his problem-solving is a new garden. Herbs, vegetables, and flowers. It's "glorious." [*Beat.*] And they went wallpaper shopping for their kitchen. He showed me the sample in the backseat of the car: Duckie wallpaper. The duckies are wearing bowties. And the bowties are in patriotic colors.

RACHEL: Look, I don't have to explain myself, to what? To you? I don't have to explain myself to a kid! I did the right thing. You're a kid and Dylan's a punk and Mom's a loon and Dad's what we have. He's what I have!

KACIE: Well, Dylan's what I have. [*Beat.*] And you just showed up here and threw him under the bus.

RACHEL: You're thirteen. You don't know anything. You don't even have a learner's permit. You haven't gone to high school. You haven't had a period yet.

KACIE: Yes I have!

RACHEL: Well whatever, you're a kid who should be in bed.

[*Beat.*]

KACIE: Rachel, what happened to you?

RACHEL: I'm a grown-up.

KACIE: You've grown into a suck ass mood.

RACHEL: That's cute, Kace. Is that a noun or an adjective?

KACIE: Both. You are generally suck ass, and you are also in a suck ass mood.

RACHEL: Maybe I just don't fit in around here anymore.

KACIE: Maybe you don't want to.

RACHEL: Maybe the writing's on the wall. I don't even have a bedroom here anymore.

[*Beat.*]

KACIE: Would you like to know how Dylan got your room, Rachel?

RACHEL: Just drop it.

KACIE: Dylan and I were cutthroat competitive over who got it. I mean, we are talking about AC, roof access, and a loft here. We wrestled, we played rock-scissors-hammer, we trash talked, we even threatened wedgies and swirlies.

RACHEL: Swirlies?

KACIE: Someone dunks your head in the toilet and then flushes.

RACHEL: That's sick.

KACIE: So Mom made us draw straws. And I won fair and square.

RACHEL: So how'd he end up getting it? He swirlied you?

KACIE: No. He sat on the stoop and said, all mature-like, "That's cool, kid, you take it. You won it, kid." But I saw his eyes got all shiny and swollen with tears.

RACHEL: He cried over my room?

KACIE: No. I think he cried because he couldn't take losing much more. [*Beat.*] It made his year that I gave it to him, Rachel. He had so much fun moving all his guitars and his posters and his games. It was Dylan's only victory this year. And it's a pink bedroom.

>   [*Beat.*]

RACHEL: I wonder what's worse, actually. Coming home and seeing his study empty for the first time or . . .

KACIE: . . . watching him pack up that study?

RACHEL: Yeah.

KACIE: It's worse for Dylan. He knew they fought over him late at night. He had to help Dad load his car while Mom cried in the basement. And then you left and he lost rides to school, and hellos in the hall, and . . .

RACHEL: Me.

KACIE: You can't do what you did to Dylan, Rachel. He needs us. You might not need me and him, but he needs us. You can't turn on him like that. Do you understand?

RACHEL: Yeah, I do, Kace. [*Beat.*] The truth is, I don't know how to be without Dad. I don't know how to be in this family without him. I'm not sure I know what I'm doing period without him.

KACIE: You know what might help?

RACHEL: No, what?

KACIE: Yoda. Watch *Star Wars* and take notes. When Luke Skywalker has to take the X-Wing into Degaba Swamp he says, "I'll give it a try." Say it.

RACHEL: I'll give it a try.

KACIE: No. As Luke.

RACHEL: "I'll give it a try."

KACIE: And Yoda, he's so smart, he corrects him. He says . . . [*Slowly.*] Try not. Do or do not. There is no try. Rachel.

RACHEL: Okay, Yoda. [*Long beat.*] It's two fourteen. What do you think's taking so long?

KACIE: Who knows. Maybe they went straight to graduation. Secure good seats.

RACHEL: Seriously. [*Beat. They wait.*] Kace, when did you get your period? That's a big deal.

KACIE: Oh, I didn't. I said that for dramatic effect.

RACHEL: [*Laughs.*] That was suckass of you. I just had a guilt trip about not knowing.

KACIE: Well, it could be true. Mom says any day this summer.

RACHEL: Will you tell me when you do?

KACIE: Gross.

RACHEL: So I can . . . buy you a little present or something. Take you to lunch.

KACIE: Oooo, can we make the reservations now?

RACHEL: Shut up. At least you're off the hook for the mortification of dinner with the whole fam like I was. Literally: hell. Dad raised his glass: "To Rachel, who is a woman now and who can conceive" and Dylan stuck a maxipad on the back of my head. [*They laugh a lot.*]

KACIE: Sorry I was with the sitter for that one.

RACHEL: I'm serious though. Do you promise to tell me?

KACIE: Fine.

   [*Beat.*]

RACHEL: Kace? I do need you, you know. Dylan isn't the only one.

KACIE: You do?

RACHEL: I need you to be my tennis partner this summer, for starters.

KACIE: What about school?

RACHEL: I'm too cool for school.

KACIE: Don't say anything like that in front of Dylan. Ever. [*Beat.*] What about your nerd camp?

RACHEL: It's nerd camp. What do you say?

KACIE: Well, yeah. I say we defend our title! We can't let someone else come in last!

RACHEL: That's the spirit. [*We hear a car door slam.*]

KACIE: Oh, finally!

RACHEL: WE'RE BACK HERE! [**KACIE** *runs toward the driveway.*]

KACIE: HOMIE DEE?

STEPHEN: [*Offstage.*] No, it's just me! [**STEPHEN** *enters alone. He goes to the table and puts down his list, map, keys, and jacket. To* **RACHEL**.] Your mother's not here?

RACHEL: No.

STEPHEN: Who's here? There's a car out front.

KACIE and **RACHEL:** There's a car out front?

STEPHEN: Yeah, double-parked in front of the house. I thought maybe it was one of his friends— [*The doorbell rings.*] Are you expecting someone?

KACIE: Weird. I don't know. I'll get it. [*Screams at top volume.*] I'M COMING! [**KACIE** *exits.*]

STEPHEN: Eardrums, Kacie Anne! Wait! It's two o'clock in the morning. Use the peephole! Wait one minute! [**STEPHEN** *exits quickly after her.* **RACHEL** *sits alone in the yard, has a moment to prepare to tell* **STEPHEN** *her news.* **STEPHEN** *returns promptly.*] This house is a funny farm.

KACIE: [*Offstage, very excited.*] PEPPERONI AND MUSHROOM! [**KACIE** *bursts through the door. Does a pizza dance. Chanting like Little Caesars:*] Pizza, pizza, piz-za! Pizza, pizza, piz—

STEPHEN: [*To* **RACHEL**.] Did you order this? At two o'clock in the morning? [**RACHEL** *shakes her head.*]

KACIE: I think it's a gift, Dad.

STEPHEN: From whom?

KACIE: From someone who knows that pepperoni and mushroom is my favorite . . . [*Smelling it.*] And who also knows to dial 338-PIES.

STEPHEN: You have takeout numbers memorized? [*To* **KACIE**.] Doesn't she ever cook?

KACIE: Dylan's building a sign for the front yard that says "This is the house."

[*Beat.* **KACIE** *laughs.* **STEPHEN** *doesn't. He crosses to* **KACIE** *and closes the box.*]

STEPHEN: Kiddo, go put your pizza in the fridge for lunch tomorrow. If you want a snack, you can have a piece of fruit—

KACIE: But Dad it's from Tony's!

STEPHEN: No.

[*Beat.* **KACIE** *exits. But when she gets to the door, she stops and listens to the following.*]

RACHEL: So, I'm not going this summer.

STEPHEN: What's that?

RACHEL: My Latin scholarship? I'm turning it down.

STEPHEN: What?

RACHEL: I'm not going to school this summer. Thought you should know.

STEPHEN: And when did you decide this?

RACHEL: Now. Tonight. Just now.

[*Beat.* **KACIE** *has begun eating pizza while listening.*]

STEPHEN: I'm still not sure I heard you correctly.

RACHEL: Dad. I'm giving Latin a swirlie. I'm flushing my summer class.

STEPHEN: To do what instead?

RACHEL: You're looking at it.

STEPHEN: That's inconsistent with your plans.

RACHEL: Whose plans?

STEPHEN: Your plans! This is what you've worked so hard for.

RACHEL: Well, it's caught up with me. I'm tired.

[*Beat.*]

STEPHEN: If you miss Latin now, you won't be ahead.

RACHEL: I know.

STEPHEN: It's going to set you back. Way back. It's part of the Honors Track sequence.

RACHEL: You make it sound like a death sentence. It's just a title. Honor. What's "honor"?

STEPHEN: It's not a title; it's a choice. What are you going to do here? Work at K-Mart? Read trash? Be a couch potato?

RACHEL: I'm gonna watch *Star Wars* with Kacie and Dylan. All summer.

[*Beat.*]

STEPHEN: Rachel, you're a Dean's Scholar. Don't you understand how rare and fantastic you are, to be a Dean's Scholar? I wasn't a Dean's Scholar.

RACHEL: I just test well, Dad.

STEPHEN: I . . . I don't understand . . . I don't understand your logic at all . . .

RACHEL: It's simple: I forgot to double-check my work. I talked it over with Kacie, and I decided.

[*Beat.* **STEPHEN** *considers this.*]

STEPHEN: Okay, we can work with that. I'll call the university Monday! Perhaps I can arrange an independent study—you and I—to cover the curriculum. We could meet five days a week, say nine to noon, and I could prepare you for the exam so you won't get behind. We can do this, don't you think?

RACHEL: No, Dad.

STEPHEN: But we can do this, you and I!

RACHEL: I'm sorry.

STEPHEN: Oh, Rachel, you're killing me . . . this is painful to hear. I . . . I don't know what to say.

[*Beat.*]

RACHEL: You can say it's okay.

STEPHEN: No . . . this is . . . I can't. [**KACIE** *enters with pizza. She brings* **RACHEL** *a slice and sits with them.*]

KACIE: It's just nerd camp, Dad. Have some pizza with us.

STEPHEN: [*To* **KACIE.**] I said you couldn't eat that! [*Noticing.*] And I thought you were a vegetarian!

KACIE: I quit. Have some. [**RACHEL** *takes a bite of the pizza.*]

STEPHEN: No. No, thank you. [**STEPHEN** *withdraws and sits off.* **RACHEL** *and* **KACIE** *snack on the pizza. The sound of a car is heard pulling into the driveway.*] Ah. Here's your mother, only thirteen minutes late—

KACIE: DYLAN! DYLAN!

STEPHEN: Volume, Kace! [**KACIE** *speeds out to greet* **DYLAN.** *To* **RACHEL.**] We'll see what she has to say about your desire to drop class. [**LYNN** *enters.*]

LYNN: I know I'm late that took longer than I thought it would, hi. [**KACIE** *returns.*]

KACIE: I don't get it. Where's Dylan? He was Vader right?

STEPHEN: You didn't find him? I'm calling the police.

LYNN: No police, that won't be necessary. [*Seeing.*] Oh, Christ. I thought he was kidding about the pizza.

STEPHEN: Who?

LYNN: Dylan.

STEPHEN: You found him! Where was he! Where is he?

LYNN: He's fine. He is not physically hurt or in harm's way. He'll be here shortly.

STEPHEN: If you found our son, why isn't he with you? Why isn't our son being dragged to his room?

LYNN: Because I have left our son in a biker bar, Stephen.

STEPHEN: What! What bar?

LYNN: Foley's Tavern.

STEPHEN: FOLEY'S! What in God's name is he doing there?

LYNN: He's toasting his graduation with a roomful of men who cheer for him while he wins Pac-Man. [*Beat.*] I took his car keys and gave him cab fare and he assured me that when he was done with his Heine, he'd be home.

STEPHEN: What's "his Heine"?

KACIE: His Heineken, Dad.

STEPHEN: [*To* **LYNN.**] I beg your pardon?

KACIE: Heinek—

STEPHEN: [*To* **KACIE.**] No, I heard you! [*To* **LYNN.**] You had better explain yourself right now, Lynn.

LYNN: I think I just did, Stephen.

[*Beat.*]

STEPHEN: [*Laughs.*] Oh. This is a joke! You had me there for a minute. Very rich. Good teamwork, all of you. My son is at Foley's! Very rich. Where is he, in the car? [**LYNN** *shows* **STEPHEN** *the fake ID.*]

LYNN: He uses this to get in. [**STEPHEN** *looks at it. They all do.*]

RACHEL: That's not half bad.

KACIE: [*Laughing.*] Look at the Luchezi grinning! [**STEPHEN** *puts the ID away in his pocket.*]

STEPHEN: [*To* **LYNN.**] Let me get this straight: you left my eighteen-year-old son to drink illegally with bikers?

LYNN: Yes, I did.

STEPHEN: At Foley's!

KACIE: I think that's been established, Dad. [**STEPHEN** *grabs his jacket and keys off the table and storms out of the yard.* **LYNN** *starts after him.*]

LYNN: [*Loudly.*] Oh, gimme a break, Stephen. What are you gonna do? Storm the biker bar? [**STEPHEN** *storms back in the yard.*]

STEPHEN: Your car's blocking mine.

LYNN: And.

STEPHEN: Give me your keys.

LYNN: No.

STEPHEN: Give me your keys, Lynn!

LYNN: I said no, Stephen!

STEPHEN: One of us needs to act like a mature parent! Now give me the keys!

LYNN: When you put it that way, screw you and NO!

STEPHEN: I don't have time for this! Give me your keys, Lynn, or so help me God, I'll drive over your car!

LYNN: You listen to me, I will lie at the foot of the driveway before I let you tornado down there. The answer's no!

[*Beat.*]

KACIE: There's a Huffy in the shed, Dad.

RACHEL: It's got a horn.

[*Beat.* **STEPHEN** *shoots them a look of death.*]

STEPHEN: You two think this is funny? It's ha ha ha funny that your brother's drunk in a bar? That she's left him there with cash flow? This is stand-up comedy to you? [*To* **LYNN.**] It's about as funny as Rachel turning down her full ride this summer!

LYNN: [*Defensive.*] What are you talking about? She's going Monday!

RACHEL: Eh, actually, Mom, I'm not going this summer.

STEPHEN: You missed this, Lynn. She's "tired."

LYNN: Wait, what's going on?

RACHEL: I want to be here this summer.

KACIE: [*To* **LYNN.**] She wants to be here for my period.

[*Beat.*]

LYNN: Don't you need Latin for your special thing?

RACHEL: Yes, but I want to stay home. I miss home.

LYNN: Then that's what you should do. You can take Latin next summer, can't you?

STEPHEN: She'll get behind. It's part of the Honors—

LYNN: She has a 4.0; no one should have a 4.0. [*To* **RACHEL.**] You should be a kid for the summer. Get a job. Or don't, get a tan.

STEPHEN: You see no reason to make her go?

LYNN: No, I don't. [**LYNN** *digs in her pocket and pulls out the check* **STEPHEN** *had presented to* **RACHEL** *in Act I.*] Here's your check back. For her books.

RACHEL: The note that came with it is shredded in the compost.

[*Beat.*]

STEPHEN: Girls, would you excuse us? I have some adult things to say to your mother.

KACIE: We're just gonna listen on the other side of the door—

STEPHEN: Kacie Anne!

LYNN: Go in. All the way in. I'll be in in a minute.

> [*Beat.* **RACHEL** *and* **KACIE** *exit, but they obviously stay on the other side of the door. Long beat.* **STEPHEN** *and* **LYNN** *face each other.*]

STEPHEN: Come, sit down.

LYNN: I live here; you come sit down.

STEPHEN: I'd prefer to stand.

LYNN: Well so would I. [*Beat.*] What can I do for you, Stephen?

STEPHEN: My children are shredding notes from Helen? Putting them in the compost pile?

LYNN: Yeah.

STEPHEN: And this is happening in front of you? Under your supervision?

LYNN: Yeah, it is.

STEPHEN: That's wildly unfair, Lynn.

LYNN: Is that why you sent the girls in? So you can scold me for not framing notes from Helen? You've got some nerve, Stephen!

STEPHEN: I've got nerve? I'm not the one who just wasted our night. When I volunteered my time—the last seven hours to be precise—to look for our derelict son on his inaugural bar crawl, I was operating under the assumption that you were interested in parenting.

LYNN: By parenting, do you mean timing your search?

STEPHEN: [*As if to a jury.*] See? Do you see what I'm talking about? The edge. It's always the edge with you.

LYNN: What do you want me to say? You want me to send you a Hallmark because you looked for your flesh and blood?

STEPHEN: Some gratitude would be nice! Some interest in my opinion! I am half the parental unit after all and I have someone waiting up for me, worried about me—

LYNN: I know exactly what you have waiting for you and I don't care what you think your injuries are. [*With emphasis.*] I ONLY care that our son is THAT LONELY.

STEPHEN: He's not alone! I am here, aren't I? Offering a viable solution to the problem, aren't I?

LYNN: You want to ground him? Send him to juvie? Take away his black clothes? That's not a solution! That's dodging the problem!

STEPHEN: You're the queen of dodging the problem; you've been turning a blind eye. First tennis team, then the math grades, then the friend switch, then the disinterest in college . . . he's been slipping all year. You can't say you're surprised.

LYNN: Your son rolls up his sleeve and puts a burning cigarette to his flesh to see how long he can take the pain, and you're not surprised? How 'bout this: screw you for not being surprised!

STEPHEN: Lynn.

LYNN: The girls aren't back here, I'm saying it! You left him alone! You're the problem, Stephen! Of course he's having trouble; he's learning how to change a tire from Wally, the GODDAMN BARTENDER AT FOLEY'S.

STEPHEN: You LEFT HIM there with Wally. Do you not hear your own lunacy? I'm HERE. It's three a.m. and I'm here, and where is Dylan? With Wally!—

LYNN: You're not here, Stephen.

STEPHEN: No? No! These aren't my arms? These aren't my legs?

LYNN: You haven't been here in two years. One year in actual time, and the year before that in mental time. With the long bike rides and the late nights and the new wardrobe . . .

STEPHEN: You name a single family event I missed. You can't; there isn't one.

LYNN: I don't mean attendance, I mean the man I started this family with. The man who rushed home after school, dying to see me and the kids. The man who lived for his children. The man who beamed—literally, Stephen, you beamed—with pride for them. And the home we created. And the creativity that oozed. We threw the best parties on this block. We turned heads in the mall. We were envied. [*Beat.*] Then boom, teenagers! You couldn't take it. Rachel wasn't valedictorian—

STEPHEN: And you placated her!

LYNN: Dylan threw his racquet on the court—

STEPHEN: And you said the umpire made a bad call!

LYNN: Kacie didn't ace those silly PSATs—

STEPHEN: And you called the test stupid!

LYNN: It is a stupid test! They're all stupid tests! And yes, I had to defend those kids when they had to face your eyes, full of disappointment night after night.

STEPHEN: You didn't defend them, you betrayed me! What did you do with my TV chart, of educational programming? You took it down. You let Rachel drop physics when I said she shouldn't. You let Dylan get his license even though he got a D in Gym—

LYNN: Well, if I knew that letting Rachel drop Physics meant you had the green light to divorce us, I wouldn't have, would I?

STEPHEN: I didn't divorce them; I divorced you, Lynn. What's so impossible to see about that? I divorced you. Look at this place! You. The woman who breaks things with sledgehammers. You. The woman who keeps her home a pigpen. You. Who doesn't know when she paid bills last, or where her car keys are, or where the winter coats went, and who thinks carrot cake is a daily serving of vegetables. You. Who hasn't looked at me with love or lust in her eyes since Kacie was a baby. That's who I divorced. You!

LYNN: Wow. Huh. You've scripted yourself one helluva tale to get laid by. [*As Helen:*] "Poor Stephen, his wife doesn't make salad; poor Stephen, after a long day with three teenagers and a full-time job she doesn't look at him tenderly. Oh, woe is Stephen."

STEPHEN: Outrageous, you—

LYNN: If you were unhappy we could've gone to counseling. We could've worked on this. We could've had a fighting chance. This isn't divorce, you didn't divorce me, Stephen; you screwed Helen. For months you took the clothes off of another woman and then came home and planned your escape. Slept in our bed, across the hall from our children.

[*Beat.*]

RACHEL: [*Offstage.*] No, Kace! Wait! [**KACIE** *enters. She is red-faced and tear-streaked. She looks at both of them.* **RACHEL** *comes in behind her.*]

RACHEL: Kace . . . [**KACIE** *stares at* **STEPHEN.**]

KACIE: You cheated on Mom? With Helen?

STEPHEN: Kiddo.

KACIE: You cheated on Mom with Helen?

STEPHEN: Oh, Kiddo—did you hear that? Oh, no, listen, the truth is not what that just sounded like. [*Beat.*] Let's sit down. I didn't . . . It's not . . . I didn't . . . it's complicated.

KACIE: And you wanted me to help you two garden?

STEPHEN: Sweetheart, it's complicated.

KACIE: You wanted me to swim in her pool?

STEPHEN: Slow down; calm down. Let's talk this through. [**STEPHEN** *tries to embrace* **KACIE. KACIE** *runs out.*]

RACHEL: I'm sorry; I didn't know she was listening. I'll go sit with her—

LYNN: No you won't. I will. [**LYNN** *leads;* **RACHEL** *follows. Beat.* **STEPHEN** *is alone on stage. He paces a little; he strains to listen. Finally, he sits on the back step and waits in the dark. Headlights are visible, then we hear the sound of a car door slamming.* **STEPHEN** *does not move.* **DYLAN** *bursts through the back gate, fully expecting everyone to be outside waiting for him. He doesn't see* **STEPHEN.**]

DYLAN: And the crowd roars! Campers? [*Loudly.*] MA? [*With slight drunkenness,* **DYLAN** *looks around the yard for people. He opens the shed door and peers in.*] Guys? . . . [*He stumbles over the wisteria tree.*] Oh, our wisteria! Sorry, buddy. [*He laughs. Stays on the ground. To the wisteria:*] Rough night? [*Beat. From ground.*] K-DOG! I'M HOME! [**DYLAN** *gets up slowly and starts eating a piece of pizza. He heads for the door.* **STEPHEN** *stirs.*]

STEPHEN: [*Clears his throat.*] Ahe. [**DYLAN** *grabs the flashlight.*]

DYLAN: [*Clears his throat.*] Ahe?

STEPHEN: Ahem. [*Beat.* **DYLAN** *shines it on* **STEPHEN.**] Doing a little night gardening?

[*Pause.*]

DYLAN: I thought you moved out, Big Boy.

STEPHEN: I've been here all night.

DYLAN: Why?

STEPHEN: Why do you think?

DYLAN: I don't know why you do anything.

STEPHEN: I was one step away from calling the police, hospitals. Could you not shine that in my eyes, please.

DYLAN: I'm interrogating you . . .

STEPHEN: I'm not going to ask you again. Stop shining that in my eyes, Dylan.

DYLAN: [*As interrogator.*] "You don't live here, yet you are on the scene of the crime. Why? WHY ARE YOU AN UNHAPPY PAPPY?" [**STEPHEN** *stands up and grabs the flashlight away from* **DYLAN.**]

DYLAN: I am so grounded.

STEPHEN: Yes you are.

DYLAN: Yeah? You gonna come back and enforce all this shit? [*Pause.*] Are you gonna come back?

STEPHEN: No.

DYLAN: Then it's time to sing, Dad.

STEPHEN: To sing?

DYLAN: Nah nah nah nah.

KACIE: [*Offstage.*] DYLAN! [**KACIE** *flies through the door.*] Dylan! [**KACIE** *hugs Dylan fiercely, knocking his balance a little.* **LYNN** *and* **RACHEL** *enter behind* **KACIE.**]

DYLAN: [*To* **KACIE.**] It's the K-Dog. What's up? Wassup, homie? [**KACIE** *doesn't let go yet.*]

DYLAN: Hey! I didn't go to war, Kace. I exited briefly cuz I had a hankerin' for the brew.

KACIE: You're not supposed to bounce without me! That was a deal breaker, Dyl!

DYLAN: I didn't bounce. I bounced right back. Ha ha . . . [*Beat.*] It won't happen again, dawg, I'm sorry. Can I have some skins? [**DYLAN** *goes as if to do their handshake.*] Gimme paw. [*Beat.*] That was pathetic. Try again.

KACIE: No.

DYLAN: Hey, Are you okay? . . . [*Suddenly serious.*] What's wrong? What's wrong with the kid? [*Everyone looks at each other.*] Don't everyone look at each other. What the fuck happened to her?

STEPHEN: That was private talk between your mother and I. Please let me explain. I'm so sorry—

DYLAN: Explain what? What'd you do to her—?

RACHEL: Nothing.

DYLAN: For chrissakes, man! I was gone for one day!

STEPHEN: It's none of your concern.

DYLAN: How'd you have time to fuck more shit up?

STEPHEN: You watch your tone!

DYLAN: WHAT'D YOU DO NOW?

STEPHEN: I'LL TELL YOU WHAT I DID NOW!

LYNN: LET IT GO!

STEPHEN: No, I'd like to respond. To this. To this, "What'd I do now?" What I "did now" was take Kacie to the park to do math today. Didn't I, Kace? I made sandwiches, and went to the park, and I begged her, my own daughter, to come to the house and play tennis, didn't I? Like I do every Saturday, right Kace?

KACIE: Yeah.

STEPHEN: And Rachel, do tell your brother what I did for you today.

RACHEL: You offered to help me in school.

STEPHEN: To privately tutor you in Latin, and you'll have none of it! I am signing up for tournaments, and Latin help, and weekend plans. And in my free time, I am here in the middle of the night looking for this drunkard. Aren't I? [*Beat.*] These are the things I'm doing. I haven't gone away and I haven't missed a thing in any of your lives. So what's the problem here? Why do you all hate me?

LYNN: Don't put that on them!

STEPHEN: I'm doing everything right! I am doing everything by the book, yet look: what a bunch of ingrates I have as children!

> [*Beat.*]

LYNN: Stephen, get out of my yard. [*Beat.*] I said get out. GO. [*Beat.*]

STEPHEN: Kids, don't I deserve to be happy too? Kids! [*Beat.* **LYNN** *opens the fence door.*] Please. Kacie Anne. You don't want me to go, do you? Please Kace? . . . [*As answer:*] No eye contact. Rachel? [*As answer:*] Looks away. Dylan?

DYLAN: Where do I sign. [*Beat. To* **RACHEL.**] Psst! I don't see him moving, do you?

RACHEL: No, I don't.

DYLAN: What do you think, kid?

KACIE: He hasn't budged.

DYLAN: I dunno guys. I guess he's pretending not to hear me, but I can tell he does.

LYNN: Knock it off, Dylan.

DYLAN: Aw. You're kinda cute when you're all pouty, Dad. Isn't he, Mom? Look at his nostrils all flared—Hmmm? Daddy-poo?

LYNN: Dylan. Dammit, you stay over there and be quiet.

DYLAN: No. I don't think so. You asked him nicely. [*Shining the flashlight in* **STEPHEN***'s eyes.*] She said get out. Didn't you hear her? She said GET OUT, DAD.

> [**STEPHEN** *breaks. He grabs* **DYLAN***, slams him into the shed, and pins him there.*]

LYNN: STEPHEN!

KACIE and **RACHEL:** DAD!

> [**STEPHEN** *holds onto* **DYLAN** *forcefully while* **LYNN** *tries everything to get him off* **DYLAN**. **RACHEL** *and* **KACIE** *rush over.*]

KACIE: You're hurting him! He's hurting him—

LYNN: STEPHEN! WHAT THE HELL'S GOTTEN INTO YOU!

DYLAN: You wanna hurt me, you pussy! HUH? YEAH? YOU wanna HURT ME! HERE! DO IT!

> [**STEPHEN** *raises his hand to punch* **DYLAN**. *Realizing what he's about to do,* **STEPHEN** *tosses* **DYLAN** *aside. No one moves.*]

STEPHEN: [*To himself.*] One one thousand...two one thousand...I don't want to hurt him...three one thousand...four one thousand.

LYNN: Jesus, are you okay? Dylan, answer me, are you okay?

DYLAN: I'm fine.

LYNN: Look at me. Let me see your neck—

DYLAN: Mom. I am fine. [**DYLAN** *takes* **KACIE***'s hand.*]

STEPHEN: Five one thousand . . . Six . . . Seven . . . Eight . . . Nine . . . Ten . . .

> [*Beat.* **STEPHEN** *has crouched down and is in a state of shock. He is mumbling.*]

LYNN: [*To kids.*] All three of you over there. Over there!

KACIE: What's he doing?

DYLAN: Is he hurt?

LYNN: No one speaks, no one moves, no one comes near us. Sit there and be quiet. SIT OVER THERE! [*The kids go where she points.*] I know what to do. I'll handle this. [**LYNN** *sits down next to* **STEPHEN** *on the ground.*]

STEPHEN: Eleven . . . Twelve . . . Thirteen . . . Fourteen. [*She sits near him.*]

LYNN: Stephen. Listen to me. Dylan's okay, Stephen. You did not hurt him. We're just going to count it out, okay?

STEPHEN: Fifteen . . . Sixteen . . . Seventeen . . . Eighteen . . . [**LYNN** *takes his hands in hers.*]

LYNN: Good. Give me your hands. Good. Count it out. Take a breath. You didn't do it. You let him go.

STEPHEN: Nineteen . . . twenty . . . twenty-one . . . twenty-two . . . twenty-three . . . twenty-four . . . twenty-five. . . .

LYNN: Good. Let it go. Take a deep breath. Take a deep breath. Look at me. Let it go. You're okay.

STEPHEN: Twenty six . . . . thirty. I'm okay.

LYNN: You're okay.

STEPHEN: I'm okay.

LYNN: You didn't hurt him, Steve.

STEPHEN: No.

LYNN: He's sitting right there. He's fine. [**STEPHEN** *does not look.*]

STEPHEN: I almost . . . God, I almost. I don't hit. I don't hurt my . . .

LYNN: Look at them, sitting right there. [**STEPHEN** *looks at his three children. He looks at* **LYNN.**]

STEPHEN: This isn't me; I'm an A Dad. I get A's. My kids get A's. I was an A, and this was glorious, Lynn . . . we were an A family.

LYNN: Stephen, Look at the way your kids love each other. [*Beat.*] Look at what's growing back here! It's beautiful. Look at [*Pointing.*] THAT. They're beautiful, Steve. You have A's. [*Beat. He sees.*]

STEPHEN: Yes. We do. [*Beat.* **STEPHEN** *rises.*] Dylan . . . I . . .

DYLAN: No.

STEPHEN: Please. [*Beat.*] I am sorry, Dylan. For all of it. [*Beat.*] And I'd like very much to try to . . .

DYLAN: To what?

STEPHEN: To come tomorrow. Would it be all right with you if I were in the bleachers?

DYLAN: It's open to the public.

STEPHEN: Then I will be there. I'll sit on the away side and I'll look for the inside-out gown. [*To* **KACIE.**] And maybe you'll wave hello to me from the other side?

[*Beat.*]

RACHEL: We both will. [*Beat.* **STEPHEN** *turns to go.*] We didn't want you to go. Just so you know, Dad. We've missed you.

STEPHEN: I've missed you, too. [*Beat. No one moves yet.*] Kacie, will I see you next Saturday?

KACIE: I dunno. Maybe.. . .

STEPHEN: Maybe's a good start. [*Silence.* **STEPHEN** *jangles his car keys.*] I guess I'm going to . . . now.

LYNN: Don't be a stranger.

STEPHEN: I won't.

LYNN: Are you okay to drive?

STEPHEN: Automatic pilot. [*Beat.*] I really do hope you have a great party tomorrow, Lynn.

LYNN: Oh. No, I won't. I cancelled it. [**STEPHEN** *exits. He leaves the gate slightly ajar.* **LYNN** *goes to her children and holds them tightly.* **KACIE** *cries a little.*] Are you all okay? Everybody whole? [*Looking at each of them.*] Let's go inside, huh? [*The kids start to file in.*]

RACHEL: Should I get the gate?

LYNN: I'll get it. Pour Dylan a tall glass of water; I'll be right behind you. [**LYNN** *crosses to the table. She gets the pizza, the Gameboy, and the flashlight. She is headed to the gate when* **STEPHEN** *appears.*] God, Stephen, you scared me. What is it?

STEPHEN: I can't go. My car is blocked in. Of course. I'm sorry, I need to move your car. [*Beat.*] Do you know where your keys are?

LYNN: I do. [**LYNN** *pulls the keys out of her pocket.*] I'll let you out.

[**LYNN** *leads the way to the gate, and holds the door for* **STEPHEN.** *She looks around the yard, takes a breath, and closes the door behind her. Lights go down on empty stage.*]

END OF PLAY

Lot's Daughters
REBECCA BASHAM

About the Playwright

Rebecca Basham is a professor of Dramatic Writing and the Director of the Gender Studies Program at Rider University in Lawrenceville, New Jersey as well as a working playwright. She won the 2000 Michael Kanin National Student Playwriting Award for the Kennedy Center American College Theatre Festival for her three-act drama, *Lot's Daughters*, while working on her MFA at the University of New Orleans. That same year, *Lot's Daughters* was awarded the student division Jane Chambers National Playwriting Award. Since its initial production showcased at the Kennedy Center during the KCACTF national festival, *Lot's Daughters* received its professional debut at Diversionary Theater in San Diego, California in 2001 and has gone on to be produced in multiple venues.

After the success of her first play, Basham has had productions and readings throughout the country. *Louisiana LIKK-HR* appeared in the 2003 Homogenius Festival at the Manhattan Theater Source as well as the Cowpoke's Theater in her native New Orleans. *Wrinkles* was produced at the University of New Orleans as a part of the KCACTF in 2004 and then enjoyed a month's run at Diversionary Theater/San Diego in 2005. Basham was commissioned by Sunstar Productions to write the screenplay, *Sons of Italy*, which is slated for filming in Naples and Capri. Most recently, Basham received a funded fellowship from her university to complete her next stage project, tentatively titled, *Echo*.

Basham's work is queer-themed, political, and universal, focusing on the point where tradition must break and be reinvented.

Production History

Lot's Daughters was first produced at the University of New Orleans as a participant in the Kennedy Center American College Theater Festival. It received its world premiere at Diversionary Theater (Executive Director, Chuck Zito) in San Diego, California in October 2001. It was directed by Rosina Reynolds; the set design was by David Weiner; the lighting design was by Shaoann Yo; the dramaturg was Dick Emmet. The cast was as follows:

GERTIE	Katie Reynolds
SUSANNAH	Shannon Diana
WAINCEY	Scott Coker
BROTHER RANKIN	Joe Powers
SISTER RANKIN	DeAnna Driscoll
JUNIOR	Jeremy Shepard
GAYLA FAYE	Karla Kash
HARLAN	Danny Pope

Characters

GERTIE COBB, female, 17.

WAINCEY COBB, male, 25.

SUSANNAH HICKS, female, 18–20.

SISTER RANKIN, female, late forties.

BROTHER RANKIN, male, fifties.

GAYLA FAYE, female, 21.

JUNIOR DOBBS, male, 19.

HARLAN HICKS, male, forties.

CONGREGATION MEMBERS (three to five)

Time

September and December 1944.

Setting

Eastern Kentucky amidst the foothills of Appalachia. A cross-section of an old wooden cabin in a Kentucky holler shadowed by a large, mountainous outcropping of rock. The cabin is partially realistic with half walls and must be equipped with a front entrance and bedroom exit. There is a kitchen table, a coal-burning stove, a washbasin, and a counter with a water pump. Outside the cabin, there is a stump CS with as many trees as possible and a clothesline. A small coal bin should be situated near the cabin. The hilltop graveyard appears at the highest point of the rock outcrop above the cabin and stones must be able to disappear when focus is not on the graveyard. A cross gravestone must be added to the graveyard for Act III, Scene 4. Lighting should reflect the times of day indicated throughout the script. Certain scenes, such as the church service, train depot, and Harlan's place still must utilize free stage areas without placing focus on the cabin. Or, if you choose to do the play less realistically, it is quite acceptable to work with platforms or other conventions.

Act I
Scene 1

AT RISE: Lights come up to the hilltop graveyard strewn with small gravestones. **WAINCEY** *enters and we can hear* **GERTIE** *from offstage.*

GERTIE: [*Offstage.*] Dang, boy! Why you want to drag me way up here? We've been a walkin' since sun-up.

WAINCEY: Hurry up, Gertie! I ain't a meanin' for this to take all day.

GERTIE: [*Entering.*] I'm a comin'. This hill gets bigger ever time I got to climb it. [*Looking around.*] Do you think they can hear you away up there? I come sometimes to talk to Momma when I cain't find nowheres else to turn, but I wonder, does she ever hear me?

WAINCEY: Course she hears you, girl. Don't be a talkin' heathern. Momma always could hear everthing.

GERTIE: I just ain't sure that people can hear once't they's dead. Maybe we're just a talkin' to the dirt.

WAINCEY: Hush. You can hear everthing you want to in Heaven.

GERTIE: Maybe she just wants to sleep peaceful-like without no corn to shuck or plowin' and warshin' to do. Maybe she don't want to listen to the foolishness of a seventeen-year-old girl. Maybe she just wants to rest.

WAINCEY: I don't know where you get some a your notions, Gert. Don't ever feel like Momma ain't a listenin' when you come to talk. You think I'd walk up this mountain and back if'n I didn't think she'd a hear what I come to say?

GERTIE: What about Daddy? You think his ears is as sharp as Momma's? Heaven's purty far away. [*She kneels.*] You think they's a sittin' up there on one a them clouds a hearin' what we got to tell 'em?

WAINCEY: I ain't so sure about Daddy. He could be deaf when it suited him. He always said he could tone out a naggin' woman or a preachy preacher.

GERTIE: He did not! Daddy always said not to say nothin' bad 'bout the Preacher 'cause God can hear everthing. Daddy weren't no sinner like that, Waincey. He surely wasn't a talkin' 'bout Momma bein' no naggin' woman, was he?

WAINCEY: Course not. He's a talkin' 'bout Sister Rankin usually.

GERTIE: Well, that ain't a wonder. She's like a little mule—she'll hee haw and kick till she nigh 'bout wears a body out. I don't see how Brother Rankin fixes up his sermons with that sour, old woman a hangin' on his ever minute.

WAINCEY: Careful, Gert. You're a talkin' bad 'bout the Preacher.

GERTIE: I ain't. I'm a talkin' bad 'bout his wife! [*They laugh, but* **WAINCEY** *sobers quickly.*]

WAINCEY: Well, don't be a talkin' bad 'bout nobody—specially whiles't I'm gone. [*He notices her position on the ground and straightens her skirt.*] And sit up straight and close your skirt. You got to start a actin' like a lady! I ain't a goin' to be around for awhile to keep you outta trouble.

GERTIE: Waincey, I don't want you to go off nowheres. Cain't you just tell 'em you got to stay here and look after your little sister? They surely cain't say "no" to that.

WAINCEY: I guess that'd be a mighty good plan if'n you wasn't but a young'n, but when they found out you's a goin' on eighteen and old enough for marryin', they'd just bust a gut laughin' whiles't they's a throwin' the lock on the jail.

GERTIE: They don't have to know! Peggy Johnson ain't but ten—we could take her over there and say she's me, and then you wouldn't have to go off to Germany.

WAINCEY: You ever seen a time when a lie got you outta somethin'? [**GERTIE** *nods.*] I ain't. 'Sides, we'd be a lyin' to the United States government, and they'd sure as shoot catch us—I know it.

GERTIE: So? What if they did?

WAINCEY: I'd go to jail, that's what. I signed up fair and square, Gert. You want me to be a liar and get locked up?

GERTIE: That'd be better'n a goin' off to fight them Germans. They's mean, Waincey! 'Sides, I wouldn't let you stay locked up long. I'd get Junior Dobbs to ride me over to the jailhouse to visit you. And once't I'd done that a couple a times, and them old jail guards a trusted me, I'd bring you in a basket a biscuits what had a saw hid in it. Then you could break out late one night and come on home.

WAINCEY: Day! You got a life a crime all figured out for the both a us, ain't you?

GERTIE: I been a thinkin' on it. It'd work; I know it.

WAINCEY: I'd rather take my chances with Uncle Sam 'stead a runnin' for the rest a my life with some little heathern, criminal girl. You ought to be ashamed.

GERTIE: I'm just scairt for you, Waincey. What if you get kilt over there?

WAINCEY: I ain't a goin' to get kilt, Gert. I promise.

GERTIE: You cain't do that! You don't know. Didn't Daddy promise me he'd be all right when they pulled him outta the mine? He died that night. You cain't promise me nothin'.

WAINCEY: Oh yes, I can. I ain't a goin' to Germany where all a the fightin' is. I joined the Navy, not the Army, Gert. I'm a goin' to the South Pacific to fight the Yella Perils. Ain't near as much fightin' a goin' on out over that ocean as there is in Europe.

GERTIE: Where's the South Pacific? Who're the Yella Perils? How come I ain't never heard nothin' 'bout any a this?

WAINCEY: It's way out over the ocean. Way past California—past Hawaii even.

GERTIE: Preacher says they's heathern in Hawaii. Sister Johnson told us all 'bout it in Sunday School. She said they eat people there 'cause they ain't heard the word a Jesus. Don't even cook 'em, they just eat 'em raw.

WAINCEY: Look at me, girl. Why, I'm as knotty as a old pine tree. Don't worry 'bout nobody a eatin' on me. 'Sides, I'm a goin' to be tucked in safe on the biggest boat you ever saw.

GERTIE: I ain't so sure.

WAINCEY: I am. I got it all figured out. [*He kisses her forehead.*] I got when I get home figured out, too.

GERTIE: What about it?

WAINCEY: When I come home, Gert, we're a goin' to move to Louahvuhl (*Louisville*). We're a goin' to have us a high old time in the city.

GERTIE: Why in the world would we'ns a want to do that?

WAINCEY: Why not?

GERTIE: We don't belong in the city, Waincey.

WAINCEY: You want to stay in this holler all your life and die early like the rest of 'em? You want to marry Junior and have a bunch a young'ns 'fore you's growed your own self? Or maybe you want to watch me a keel over in the mine 'cause I cain't breathe the coal dust no more. We got to get outta here, Gertie. When we get to Louavuhl, I can get a good job with my Navy trainin'. We can get us a good place to live—we might get a radio or a automobile. Hell! We could get us a Ford, Gertie! And I'm a goin' to buy you all kinds a new dresses and shoes. Seven new dresses if'n you want 'em.

GERTIE: Day! What would I do with seven new dresses?

WAINCEY: Wear 'em! A new dress and a new pair a shoes for ever day of the week.

GERTIE: What do I need with seven pairs a shoes? I got two pair a my own and a pair a Momma's that ain't but a inch too long. Why, I don't even need 'em in the summer time. That's just wasteful.

WAINCEY: It ain't wasteful; it's livin'. No more a bickerin' over the Sears 'n Roebuck. We'll have everthing we's a ever goin' to need: clothes, radios, cars—and a inside toilet!

GERTIE: Your wishin's bigger'n a tent revival the first Sunday a Springtime. We ain't never a goin' to have us a inside toilet.

WAINCEY: Not here we ain't, but we will in Louavuhl, right after the South Pacific. Life's a goin' to be different for us, Gertie. I promise.

GERTIE: You cain't do that! I ain't never asked for nothin' different, have I?

WAINCEY: That's only 'cause you's still a young'n. You don't know enough to ask yet. I's a thinkin' on our future, Gert.

GERTIE: What future's that? The one where you's a goin' to make a load a money off'n somethin' you ain't thought up yet, and then we's a goin' to hightail it to Louavuhl? Preacher says they ain't nothin' but heatherns a livin' in the city, and I ain't a goin'. I don't know what set your mind to it this time, but forget it. We ain't never a goin' to have the money to do it no ways.

WAINCEY: Yes, we are. When I's a signin' up, that Captian started a telling me how I's a goin' off to do my patriotic duty by a fightin' the Yella Perils, then he told me they's a goin' to pay me twenty-one dollars a month whiles't I'm in service. I ain't never had twenty-one dollars at one time in my whole life. I signed that paper right quick.

GERTIE: Ain't nobody a goin' to pay you twenty-one dollars a month to do nothin'. I bet President Roosevelt don't even make twenty-one dollars a month.

WAINCEY: You ever knowed me to lie to you?

GERTIE: Well, no . . .

WAINCEY: I ain't a lyin' now. That officer said they's a goin' to pay it to me, and I'm a goin' to take it.

GERTIE: What're you a goin' to do with so much? It seems sinful to get that much money. How're they a goin' to run the government if'n they's a givin' so much?

WAINCEY: I'm a goin' to send you a little ever month and save the rest. We'll be rich by the time I come on home.

GERTIE: You sure he said twenty-one? Dollars? A month? Don't seem possible.

WAINCEY: Dang, girl! That's more'n I'd get to keep in a lifetime a minin'. Yes, sir! We're a goin' to set up in Louavuhl, and you're a goin' to steal some boy's heart what ain't never even seen the inside of a coal mine.

GERTIE: I done told you a million times that I ain't a gettin' married. Ain't nobody a goin' to tell me what to do. 'Sides, you got to come home first.

WAINCEY: And I done told you I took care a that.

GERTIE: Well, don't think I ain't a goin' to be worried sick till you come home safe. Swear you'll be careful of yourself.

WAINCEY: I swear it, Gert.

GERTIE: Don't try to be some old hero! You ain't a goin' to do nobody a lick a good if'n you're dead.

WAINCEY: Don't worry, Gert. [*He tries to hug* **GERTIE**, *but she resists.*] Come on now. I said I'd take care. I don't want to remember you a standin' there like a misery. Gimme a smile, cain't you?

GERTIE: I cain't. I'm still scairt.

WAINCEY: You? Ain't no need to be scairt. I'm a goin' to be fine.

GERTIE: It ain't that. Well, it ain't just that. I'm scairt a bein' alone. Everbody's been gone so long, I don't worry 'bout bein' alone without 'em, but you and me's been together since I's borned. I'm a goin' to miss you. I'm a goin' to miss a havin' somebody to talk to at supper. What if I forget how to talk 'cause there ain't nobody 'round to talk to? Or worse, what if I turn into some old crazy woman like Miss Watts? She ain't had nobody to talk to in forty years, so she talks to herself. People walk ten feet outta their ways to cut a circle around her. What if I get so lonely, I start a actin' touched or somethin'?

WAINCEY: I never thought on it.

GERTIE: Course you ain't. You're already thousands of miles away out in the ocean. You're alrealy a livin' in Louavuhl and a makin' a fortune for us to spend on shoes we don't need. I don't want to go nowheres. I'm here, and after you leave, I'm a goin' to be here by myself.

WAINCEY: I thought you'd be glad I's a thinkin' on our future. I thought you'd be excited 'bout leavin' the mountain and a havin' new things.

GERTIE: Louavuhl ain't my dream, Waincey. It's yours. I don't want to leave my home. I ain't never thought on leavin' in my whole life.

WAINCEY: I got to go, Gert. I done signed the paper.

GERTIE: So go. I ain't a sayin' you cain't. I'm just a sayin' I'm a goin' to be lonesome. You say you's a thinkin' 'bout me when you signed that paper, but you wasn't. You's a thinkin' 'bout yourself. [*He spins her around to face him.*]

WAINCEY: I was thinkin' 'bout you, Gertie. Just not you right now—you and me in the future.

GERTIE: Well, the future ain't a goin' to keep me company this winter now, is it?

WAINCEY: No, Gert. I guess it ain't. I'm sorry.

GERTIE: I'll talk to "sorry" and eat it for supper later, I reckon.

WAINCEY: Come on, girl. Don't be that a way.

GERTIE: I got to get on home. I've a heap a warshin' if'n I'm a goin' to send you off tomorrow. [*She begins to exit.*]

WAINCEY: Don't go away mad. You ain't even said "hello" to Momma yet. [*She stops and listens.*]

GERTIE: She ain't a listenin' today; I can feel it. Don't stay up here all day. You got to dig me some coal for you leave. And don't be late to supper neither.

WAINCEY: I'll be there on time. I promise. [*She snorts in disbelief. He watches her exit and then turns to Momma's stone.*] I guess you done heard what I come to tell you, Momma. Don't worry—I'm a goin' to take care a Gertie no matter what—I promised that to Daddy, and I meant it. I'll write her ever day—then she won't be so lonely—I cain't believe I didn't even think on her bein' lonesome. I won't be back to talk to you'ns for a while. It don't seem as easy for me to talk to you from nowheres else—I tried it a couple a times—thought I could get over a walkin' this old hill. It don't seem like I can get close enough less'n I'm a standin' right here. Don't you worry none 'bout me, Momma. I'll be back here afore you know it. I promise.

Scene 2

HARLAN *is heard singing "Froggie Went A Courtin'" in black. A still and a stool are placed DR. Lights rise to highlight* **HARLAN**'*s space.* **HARLAN** *sits on the wooden stool beside still. Beside him is a pile of corn which he shucks into a tin bucket in front of him. There is a shotgun on the ground beside him and a jar of corn liquor between his legs. He has obviously been drinking for some time. He shucks while he sings. Song continues as long as necessary.*

HARLAN: FROGGIE WENT A COURTIN' AND HE DID RIDE, UM-HMMM, UM-HMMM. FROGGIE WENT A COURTIN' AND HE DID RIDE, UM-HMMM, UM-HMMM FROGGIE WENT A COURTIN' AND HE DID RIDE [*He picks up a shotgun.*] HAD HIS PISTOL BY HIS SIDE. UM-HMMM. Who's there? Who is it? I got me a gun. [*Pause.*] Show yourself! I'll put a hole clean through you, I will! [**BROTHER RANKIN** *approaches and pauses. He continues in slowly holding a cloth bag with his hands in the air.* **HARLAN** *waves the gun wildly.*] Delmer? Is that you? You almost got your chance't to see the Almighty, Preacher. What're you a doin' up here?

BROTHER RANKIN: I come to talk to you, Brother Hicks.

HARLAN: I ain't your brother, Delmer.

BROTHER RANKIN: I got to say, I'm surprised to hear you a singin', Harlan.

HARLAN: Why's that? I got the right to sing much as any man, I reckon.

BROTHER RANKIN: Course you do. The Lord Almighty 'preciates a song lifted in joy! I'm just surprised to see you joyful is all, what with your wife only been dead a month.

HARLAN: That's all it's been? Seems longer. I cain't rightly get me a good picture of her no more.

BROTHER RANKIN: That's it—a month. Course a body come got a look at your house, they'd think it'd been more'n a year or two. [**HARLAN** *stands and points the shotgun at* **BROTHER RANKIN.**]

HARLAN: What're you a doin' up to the house?

BROTHER RANKIN: I's just a payin' a friendly visit. I come to see 'bout the young'ns and Susannah.

HARLAN: You stay away from my house. I ain't asked for nothin' from nobody. You stay in Happy Top where you belong.

BROTHER RANKIN: Put that shotgun back where you got it. I ain't a meanin' you no harm. Set it on back down now. [**HARLAN** *sets the butt of the gun on the ground and leans it against the stump.*]

HARLAN: What do you want, Delmer? I'm busy.

BROTHER RANKIN: I heard tell that last batch you made's purty sour. I brung you some extry sugar. [**BROTHER RANKIN** *holds out the bag, but retracts it when* **HARLAN** *reaches.*] Not so fast. You got to promise me somethin' first.

HARLAN: I should a knowed. Don't nobody give a man nothin' what they don't ask for a promise first.

BROTHER RANKIN: And people say you ain't a smart man.

HARLAN: What is it, Delmer? You know I ain't got nothin' worth nothin'.

BROTHER RANKIN: I ain't a worried 'bout a gainin' nothin' from you. I just want you to listen for a spell. I've been a thinkin' 'bout them young'ns you got a growin' up like weeds. They got to eat, and you ain't a feedin' 'em.

HARLAN: I feed 'em when I can. They eat when I do.

BROTHER RANKIN: Everbody with a lick a sense knows you drink your supper, Harlan.

HARLAN: What business is it of your'n if'n they eat? You a goin' to feed 'em?

BROTHER RANKIN: No, but I got a plan, Brother Hicks. It'll get those babies fed.

HARLAN: I ain't a goin' to meetin'. I'd ruther starve, and they would, too.

BROTHER RANKIN: I doubt that serious, but I ain't a goin' to fuss with you. 'Sides, they ain't nobody what's got to go to church to get fed. [*He holds out the bag of sugar, and* **HARLAN** *grabs it quickly.*]

HARLAN: What is it, then?

BROTHER RANKIN: Why don't you let me hold on to that jar, Harlan. This might take a minute. [**HARLAN** *hands him the jar, and* **BROTHER RANKIN** *takes a long drink.*]

HARLAN: Now what is it? What do you want?

BROTHER RANKIN: [*Putting his arm around* **HARLAN**'*s shoulders.*] Harlan, the Lord has sent me a vision . . .

Scene 3

Lights rise to mid-afternoon at cabin as **GERTIE** *sits on stump washing on a washboard. A clothesline is strung SL.* **GERTIE** *is muttering/ad-libbing to herself.*

GERTIE: Tellin' me he's a thinkin' on the future. Ha! What future? Ain't nothin' a goin' to happen in the holler nor Louavuhl neither. Thinks he's a big man 'cause he done signed up with a bunch a other fools to go play soldier. I ain't never heard of a Yella Peril! I bet he done made that one up.

GAYLA FAYE: [*Entering and walking slowly toward* **GERTIE.**] Gertie? [*Pause. Louder.*] Gertie? Who're you a talkin' to?

GERTIE: [*Starting guiltily.*] I weren't a talkin' to nobody.

GAYLA FAYE: I just heard you. You's a talkin' to beat the band when I walked up on you.

GERTIE: Well, you shouldn't be a sneakin' up on a body like that no ways.

GAYLA FAYE: I weren't a sneakin' up on you. I's just a walkin' regular. Who was you a talkin' to? Yourself?

GERTIE: Oh, my Lord. It's started already.

GAYLA FAYE: What's started?

GERTIE: Never you mind. What're you a doin' way up here? You's a long way from Happy Top.

GAYLA FAYE: I's just passin' by.

GERTIE: On your way to where? This ain't no place you's just a passin'.

GAYLA FAYE: I just felt like a walk 'fore supper's all. My feet just brung me to the crick, I reckon.

GERTIE: Well, your feet's done made a long trip for nothin'. He ain't here.

GAYLA FAYE: Who ain't here?

GERTIE: Waincey. He's gone to town. I'm surprised you didn't see him there and save yourself the trip.

GAYLA FAYE: I ain't a lookin' for Waincey. I just wanted me a walk's all.

GERTIE: You ain't come to see me. We ain't never had no love lost 'tween us.

GAYLA FAYE: You ain't over that, Gertie? Seems like a million years ago to me.

GERTIE: I don't know what you're a talkin' 'bout.

GAYLA FAYE: Yes, you do. Let me see if'n I can help you to remember. Jack Beel's a helpin' you outta your Pa's wagon at Redenair's store, and I walked by, and he chased after me so fast he left you a standin' with your foot a danglin' off the buckboard. I didn't do nothin' but walk by, Gertie. You cain't hold it agin me for that.

GERTIE: It's the way you walked by, Gayla Faye Dobbs.

GAYLA FAYE: I didn't do nothin' but put one foot in front the other.

GERTIE: It ain't the feet's got 'em a runnin' after you.

GAYLA FAYE: What do you think it is, then? [**GERTIE** *walks swinging her hips wildly.*]

GERTIE: It's your bee-hind a swayin' like a tornado's done got stuck in your dress.

GAYLA FAYE: [*Laughing.*] I don't walk that a way, Gertie.

GERTIE: Well, not quite that hard, but almost, Gayla Faye, almost!

GAYLA FAYE: I've missed you, Gertie.

GERTIE: You ain't.

GAYLA FAYE: I know you ain't never liked me much, but that's only 'cause you's jealous 'bout Jack. I never liked him. I want you to know that straight.

GERTIE: I wish you hadn't a walked by him quite so's regular then. I might a had a chance't with him 'fore the Beels up and moved to Dee-troit.

GAYLA FAYE: I'm sorry. I guess I's just bein' greedy is all. I'm a payin' for it now, though, if'n that makes you feel some better 'bout it.

GERTIE: Married life ain't what you thought it'd be?

GAYLA FAYE: No, but then I never figured on bein' married to Old Senior, neither.

GERTIE: What's it like?

GAYLA FAYE: I don't know.

GERTIE: You been married almost six months! How you a goin' to say you don't know?

GAYLA FAYE: I try not to think 'bout it much.

GERTIE: Can I ask you somethin'?

GAYLA FAYE: Uh-huh.

GERTIE: What's it like, you know, at nighttime? Do you like it?

GAYLA FAYE: Why, ain't you a sinner, Gertie Cobb.

GERTIE: Never mind. I didn't mean nothin' by it.

GAYLA FAYE: I'm just a funnin' with you. I don't mind you a askin'. I'd a asked too, if'n I'd knowed somebody to ask.

GERTIE: Well?

GAYLA FAYE: It weren't nothin' like I thought it'd be. I 'member when I'd kiss on some boy 'fore I's married, and it seemed like the kissin' would last forever and ever. You could feel the fire a heatin' up in your toes and right quick it'd be a lickin' at your neck. Heat travels like that when you's a kissin', but you know that. [**GERTIE** *looks at the ground.*] Don't tell me you ain't never even kissed a boy. What about Jack Beel?

GERTIE: We never made it to the kissin' 'fore you walked past Redenair's store. I's too mad to let him try after that.

GAYLA FAYE: Goodness, Gertie. We got to find you a boy to kiss on 'fore they marry you off, and you don't know the difference.

GERTIE: What're you a talkin' 'bout?

GAYLA FAYE: Well, when Waincey and me's a kissin', it was powerful different than when Senior kisses me.

GERTIE: Lord, Gayla Faye. Don't be a talkin' 'bout kissin' on Waincey. I won't be able to look at him over the supper table without a laughin'.

GAYLA FAYE: I know it's hard for you to believe since he's your brother and all, but Waincey's one a the best kissers I ever knowed.

GERTIE: How many boys have you kissed, Gayla Faye?

GAYLA FAYE: Just one or two. Don't get all ruffled-up and righteous on me. You's the one done brung it up.

GERTIE: I'm sorry. Why you think it's so different with Senior?

GAYLA FAYE: Could be 'cause I don't love him, I reckon. Or, it could be that he just ain't no good at it. Could just be that he's old enough to be my Pa. I don't rightly know.

GERTIE: Why'd you marry him then, and break poor old Waincey's heart if'n you didn't love him?

GAYLA FAYE: You're such a young'n, Gertie. You think I wanted to marry

Old Senior? I didn't have much to say about it. Sister Rankin saw me and Ted Coffee a holdin' hands one service—the next thing I knowed, Preacher's at the house a tellin' Daddy how I ain't a good girl no more. Daddy beat me somethin' fierce. Next day, I's engaged. Week later, they married me off to Senior.

GERTIE: You know it almost kilt Waincey when he got back from a huntin' and found out you's a goin' to marry Senior.

GAYLA FAYE: Why didn't he come after me then? I waited ever night that week. I fell asleep a tellin' myself he's a goin' to come get me, and we's a goin' to run off to Louavuhl like he talks 'bout all the time, and everthing's a goin' to be all right, but he never come got me.

GERTIE: I reckon he figured you done made up your mind.

GAYLA FAYE: But I didn't; they made it up for me.

GERTIE: You coulda said, "No."

GAYLA FAYE: You ever seen anybody say "No" to Preacher or my Daddy?

GERTIE: Well, no . . .

GAYLA FAYE: That's 'cause there ain't nobody what's ever done it. I didn't have no choice.

GERTIE: Why Senior do you think?

GAYLA FAYE: That's simple. He's the only man in town what's got a little money. His wife's been dead a couple a years now, and his young'ns is almost growed. Daddy says he's to a age where he can 'preciate a young wife like me. He's always got food, too, 'cause a the slaughterhouse. Momma and Daddy's eat regular since I got married. My daddy traded me for supper's all.

GERTIE: [*Embarrassed.*] I, uh, I got to get cookin'. Waincey'll be home soon. I'd ask you to stay for supper, but I know he'd feel funny 'bout it, so I cain't do that.

GAYLA FAYE: That's all right. I weren't expectin' nothin' to eat. I got to get on home and cook some up myself 'fore Junior and the young'ns tear the house apart.

GERTIE: Bye, then. [**GAYLA FAYE** *waves tentatively and begins to leave.* **GERTIE** *runs after her.*] Gayla Faye?

GAYLA FAYE: Uh-huh?

GERTIE: It was good to talk to you. You know, without everbody a millin' round like at meetin'. It was good to talk with you.

GAYLA FAYE: Thanks, Gertie. [*Pause.*] Gertie?

GERTIE: Uh-huh?

GAYLA FAYE: Will you do me a favor? Tell Waincey I come to say goodbye. I heard he's a goin' off tomorrow. Tell him I, well—just tell him I said to take care a hisself. Okay?

GERTIE: I'll tell him. [**GAYLA FAYE** *exits.* **GERTIE** *enters cabin.*]

Scene 4

Laundry and tub are removed. Lights rise to mid-evening inside cabin. **GERTIE** *is sitting at the table with the supper plate. She is agitated and sits fidgeting with the plate. She stands and heads toward the slop bucket by the front door as* **WAINCEY** *enters the cabin.*

GERTIE: Where have you been? It's a goin' on nine o'clock. I's just about to dump your plate in the slop bucket.

WAINCEY: Hold up on that plate, now. I'm right hungry, and I'll 'preciate it much more than Old Tommy. [*She hands him the plate, and he calmly crosses to the table and sits.*] You a goin' to hand me a fork? Or should I just use my fingers? [*She hands him a fork.*] That's better. This fried chicken looks better'n a swimmin' hole on the Fourth a July. You must a been a cookin' all day.

GERTIE: They's some biscuits, too. You want one? [*He nods, and she grudgingly gives him one.*] How 'bout some taters? [*He nods, and she plops some on his plate.*] They's some blackberry cobbler, too, for after. I thought I'd make us somethin' real special. [*Pause.*] So, we know where I been all day—behind the warshboard and the stove. Where have you been?

WAINCEY: I went to see the preacher.

GERTIE: On a Saturday afternoon? What for?

WAINCEY: I got to thinkin' on what you said up at the graveyard—'bout bein' lonesome and such whilest I'm gone.

GERTIE: What's that got to do with Brother Rankin?

WAINCEY: Where do people usually go when they got problems that they cain't figure out? To the preacher.

GERTIE: My bein' by myself ain't no trouble to drag the preacher into—

Dang burn it! You're a goin' to have Sister Rankin a breathin' down my neck for the whole next year. Waincey Cobb! You've done gone and made it worse than ever.

WAINCEY: Calm down, Gertie. Me and Preacher done figured out the whole thing. Sister Rankin ain't a goin' to bother you—no more'n usual anyways.

GERTIE: Lord, I hate to think of what you two pea-brains has done figured out for me, but you might as well tell me quick and get it over like castor oil.

WAINCEY: Well, I went on up there a thinkin' maybe you could go and live with the Rankins whiles't I'm gone. Josephine is our fifth cousin, remember.

GERTIE: [*Exploding.*] You what? I ain't a goin' to live with that sour old woman that ain't got nothin' to do but gossip and snitch and spy on people so's she can be the first one to catch 'em a doin' somethin' she's done gone and made a sin. I ain't a goin' to do it. I'll walk myself right outta this cabin and go and live in the mines. I swear it! I cain't believe you's ever thought to punish me so hard so's you can go gallavantin' around. You've done gone touched. If'n you want to go so bad that you's a willin' to see me into misery so's that you can do it, just go! But you call off Josephine Rankin 'fore you do, or I'm a goin' to join the Navy myself! [*He continues talking as if he never stopped.*]

WAINCEY: But, I figured out halfway there that that wouldn't be a fair deal for nobody. Josephine'd just make you sourer than buttermilk, and you'd likeaways run her into a early grave.

GERTIE: Uh-huh.

WAINCEY: I done decided that you a livin' with the Rankins wouldn't work, but I still didn't know what to do, so I went on over and had me a talkin'.

GERTIE: [*Nervous.*] Well, it must a been purty serious to keep you so late.

WAINCEY: It was serious, Gert.

GERTIE: [*Very nervous.*] Um, you said you'ns had done figured it out? What exactly did you figure on?

WAINCEY: I'm a goin' to get married. Then, when I leave, you won't have to stay alone.

GERTIE: Oh, is that all? I reckon Brother Rankin had you a ready-made wife in his coal shed, and you's a goin' to get married in the mornin'. I cain't believe you had me so upset over a little funnin'. Imagine a tellin' me I's a goin' to have to live with Josephine Rankin.

WAINCEY: I ain't a funnin', Gert. I'm a fixin' to get married, but not tomorrow morning—in about a hour.

GERTIE: What are you a talkin' 'bout? You ain't even courted nobody since Senior Dobbs went and married Gayla Faye. [**WAINCEY** *empties food into slop bucket.*]

WAINCEY: You leave Gayla Faye outta this. I told you I didn't never want to talk 'bout her again. [*He exits cabin to sit on steps.*]

GERTIE: [*Joining him.*] She's just up here a couple a hours ago. She come to tell you goodbye. Don't seem like she's too happy a bein' hitched up with Senior.

WAINCEY: Well, that ain't none a my business, now is it. [*Pause.*] When I's at Brother Rankin's house, he told me 'bout a girl named Susannah Hicks. Seems she's a been havin' a real hard time gettin' along with her daddy since her momma died, and she's been a comin' up to the church to talk to Preacher 'bout it. He said I ought to go to her daddy's house and see 'bout her comin' to work for me since I'm a goin' to be makin' all that money in the service. I figured she could help you out 'round here.

GERTIE: Hicks? Day! Her family ain't nothin' but trash.

WAINCEY: Why'd you say they's trash, Gertie?

GERTIE: 'Cause they's dirty. That old man don't even try to take care a nothin'. He ain't never worked—you seen that old shack they's a livin' in? It's filthy. Always has been, and it's a gotten worse since Eva died. Don't none of them young'ns never go to school—not since Pinky Hicks gave Darell Lee Redenair the lice five year ago.

WAINCEY: Are you a Christian, Gert?

GERTIE: Course I am, so's I know cleanliness is next to godliness. Have I ever missed a day a Sunday School? Don't I read from the Bible ever night the way Momma taught me to?

WAINCEY: Readin' the Bible and a goin' to service don't make you a Christian, Gert. Learnin' 'bout the Lord's teachins and a makin' 'em a part a your life is what it means to be a Christian. I *have seen* where Susannah lives. I saw it tonight when Brother Rankin took me over there. And you're right, it's a piss poor little shack in the middle of a rotten tabacca field, but that ain't none of them young'ns fault, now is it? And, yes, they's dirty. They's so dirty, you could plant pole beans in the top soil on their feet, and watch them beans grow and climb right up to the top a their heads, but they don't want to be that a way. That daddy of their'n ain't no good, but those young'ns cain't be expected to know any better than what they growed up with. When we's a ridin' up that overgrown, muddy little rut they call a drive to the shack, I said to Delmer, "Lord, Preacher, what have you done got me into? I think we ought to turn 'round and just forget 'bout a hirin' this girl." But then, I saw Susannah a draggin' in from the chicken coop where they's only one scrawny, old rooster, and I took a mind to go on ahead. Susannah ain't nothin' to look at, Gertie, but she looked up toward us in our wagon from the dust a that front yard, and I saw Momma, just like I seen her a hundred times when you's a baby. Momma never was dirty like Susannah, but they got the same eyes.

GERTIE: What in the world are you a talkin' 'bout?

WAINCEY: They both got the same tired, old eyes. Susannah cain't be more'n a year or two older'n you, but she's a startin' to look like a old woman. She'll be ancient at forty and dead by fifty. I made up my mind, right then and there, that I's a goin' to offer to let her come to work for me, no matter what Harlan Hicks wanted to ask for her.

GERTIE: And he wanted you to marry her?

WAINCEY: That's right, and I'm a goin' to do it.

GERTIE: But, why? You don't even know that girl. How're you a goin' to be married to somebody you don't even know? I know I said I's a goin' to be lonely here by myself, but don't you think you've gone a little far? I surely don't think nobody 'spects you to marry somebody you never even met 'fore tonight so's I'll have company to talk to at supper.

WAINCEY: It started out for you, Gertie, but it changed somewheres along the way. Somewheres between the wagon and the chicken coop, I got a feelin' for this girl.

GERTIE: But you don't even know her.

WAINCEY: I know her. Just like I knew Momma. I know her like I know ever woman in this holler I ever met. I cain't help 'em all, but I wasn't a goin' to sit there a knowin' I left one to the mountain.

GERTIE: I just don't understand how you can marry a stranger, Waincey.

WAINCEY: She ain't a stranger to me, Gert. Even though I ain't even spoke to her yet, I've known her all a my life. 'Sides, would you rather I didn't marry her, and then you'd have to move in with Josephine Rankin?

GERTIE: What a choice! Oh, all right. I choose Susannah.

WAINCEY: Good. [*Pause. He re-enters cabin.*] They's one other thing I got to tell you, Gertie.

GERTIE: [*Re-entering.*] Day! I don't know if'n I can stand much more!

What in tarnation is it?

WAINCEY: Harlan wouldn't let me take Susannah, less'n I said I'd marry her.

GERTIE: You done told me that.

WAINCEY: And to marry her, I had to trade somethin'.

GERTIE: What?

WAINCEY: Well, you know he don't work much.

GERTIE: Not at all from what all a Happy Top can tell.

WAINCEY: Those young'ns is real hungry, Gert.

GERTIE: Yeah?

WAINCEY: Well, I said I'd, well, I had to promise to . . .

GERTIE: Waincey, you better not a told that drunk I'd cook regular for 'em or somethin'.

WAINCEY: It's worse than that, Gert.

GERTIE: It cain't be no worse than that.

WAINCEY: I'm glad you feel that a way. They's real hungry. I had to promise to trade Old Tommy for Susannah.

GERTIE: NO! You cain't trade Old Tommy. Daddy give me that pig. He's mine! You ain't got no right.

WAINCEY: They's *hungry*, Gert. And I couldn't get Susannah outta there less'n I promised the pig.

GERTIE: Oh, you're one for the promisin', ain't you! Well, you just go outside and promise you're a liar 'cause you ain't a givin' my pig away to no trashy layabout what's too lazy to feed his family.

WAINCEY: I done said I would, Gert. And I ain't a takin' it back. Them hungry faces was more'n I could stand. Be a Christian, Gert. What's a pig compared to hungry young'ns?

GERTIE: But Daddy give me Old Tommy.

WAINCEY: And Daddy'd want you to give him away. I don't want to hurt you none. Most a the time, I let you have your way. Some'd say you're spoilt. This time, you're a goin' to have to do what I say. The pig's a goin' home with Harlan, and I don't want to hear you say a word 'bout it. You're a goin' to do the right thing here, ev'n if'n I got to force you to do it.

GERTIE: Why's this mean so much to you? I ain't never seen you like this.

WAINCEY: Them eyes. They just broke my heart.

GERTIE: You ain't never asked me to do nothin' you wouldn't do yourself have you?

WAINCEY: Not once't, Gert, and I won't ever.

GERTIE: Okay, then. You can have Old Tommy.

WAINCEY: Thank you, Gertie. I knew you's a good girl.

GERTIE: But I don't have to like it.

WAINCEY: No, you don't, but the Lord 'preciates your sacrifice all the same. [**HARLAN, BROTHER RANKIN,** *and* **SUSANNAH** *enter.* **WAINCEY** *and* **GERTIE** *exit cabin and stand inside at front door.* **SUSANNAH** *stands off to the side as* **BROTHER RANKIN** *and* **HARLAN** *meet* **WAINCEY.** **WAINCEY** *grabs the slop bucket.* **SUSANNAH** *is very dirty and is wearing rags; she carries a bundle wrapped in a quilt.*]

HARLAN: Waincey Cobb, you in there?

WAINCEY: Mind your manners there, girl. Remember, you's a Christian. Howdy there, Harlan.

BROTHER RANKIN: You a ready to get this marriage a goin'?

WAINCEY: Yes, sir. I am.

HARLAN: Hold up there! We got business to take care of first. I know you's probably a itchin' to get to the weddin' night, but I got to see this hog first. Maybe it ain't good enough to trade for a full-growed girl what's trained up right.

BROTHER RANKIN: Harlan, I done told you, Old Tommy's one a the finest hogs in Kentucky, and you ain't a gettin' no bad deal. 'Sides, all you been a talkin' 'bout all the way up here is how glad you's a goin' to be to have one less mouth to feed. Let's get this marriage a goin'.

HARLAN: I don't trust neither a you no further than I can spit my chaw. I want to see his pig first, or they ain't a goin' to be any marryin' a goin' on tonight.

WAINCEY: [*Carrying the bucket.*] I don't see nothin' wrong in a lookin' at Old Tommy first, Preacher. We got to get him fed anyways. He's a goin' to eat good tonight. We wouldn't a want to keep him from his last good supper.

HARLAN: What's that supposed to mean? You a tryin' to say I cain't take care a no pig good as you? Let me tell you, boy . . .

WAINCEY: No, sir. I meant no disrespect. I just figured you's a take him from here straight to Dobbs' butcher shed's all.

HARLAN: Damn right!

GERTIE: No! You cain't take Tommy; you just cain't do it.

WAINCEY: Hush, Gert. Take Susannah into the house and give her some a that cobbler you's so proud of. Me'n the men's a goin' to go look at Old Tommy, and make sure he's fit enough to trade for this fine girl. [*Men exit.*]

GERTIE: [*Staring harshly.*] Well, come on. [**GERTIE** *enters cabin and crosses to sink.* **SUSANNAH** *stands in place.* **GERTIE** *goes back to door.*] Don't just stand there like a bump on a log. [**GERTIE** *re-enters and crosses to sink.* **SUSANNAH** *crosses to bottom of steps.* **GERTIE** *goes back to door.*] Get in here, girl. [**SUSANNAH** *enters the cabin tentatively.*] Sit down a the table. I'll fix you a plate. [**SUSANNAH** *sits.* **GERTIE** *fixes her a plate, but then trips when bringing it to her.* **SUSANNAH** *reacts violently and falls out of her chair and cringes.*] I'm so sorry! Lord, I could tear up a brass jackass. Did I just scare you? [**SUSANNAH** *sits.*] You ain't got to be afeared of me. [*Pause.*] Don't you like chicken? [**SUSANNAH** *nods "Yes."*] Then what's wrong? Go on and eat you some then. [**SUSANNAH** *begins to eat slowly, but quickly begins to devour the food hurriedly without chewing.* **GERTIE** *looks at her with compassion.*] Well, I'll be. I guess we'll have to work on your table manners some, I reckon. [*Crossing to pump and back with plate of chicken.*] Here, honey—have all you want. [**SUSANNAH** *takes another piece as* **HARLAN** *enters and calls.*]

HARLAN: Susannah! Get on out here and get married! That pig's enough to feed the family for a month or two. [**HARLAN** *exits.* **SUSANNAH** *takes a piece of chicken and sticks it in her pocket on the way to the door.* **GERTIE** *follows.*]

GERTIE: You ain't got to do that. There'll be more when you's finished a joinin' the family. I promise.

SUSANNAH: [*Gruffly as if she hasn't talked for a long time.*] You promise?

GERTIE: I do. [**SUSANNAH** *puts the chicken back on plate and exits cabin as all men enter.*]

BROTHER RANKIN: Susannah, you stand here, girl. Waincey you stand to the side of her. Gertie, you come over here by Waincey. Harlan, you stand on Susannah's other side. [*Picking up Bible.*] Sacred bretheren, we are gathered her tonight in the sight of God . . .

Scene 5

The next day. Lights rise to cabin in early afternoon. **JUNIOR** *enters and stops CS.*

JUNIOR: Gertie? [*Yelling.*] Gertie? Where are you girl? [*At cabin.*] Gertie? Gertie, you here? [*He shrugs and crosses to the stump where he begins whittling. He hums for a beat, then begins to sing "Blue Moon of Kentucky" in a voice that he thinks is wonderful. He is interrupted by the noisy entrance of* **GERTIE** *and* **SUSANNAH** *who enter laughing from the creek. They are wet, and look as if they've put on their clothes without drying off.*] Day! What have you two been a doin'? Wadin' with your clothes on?

GERTIE: Oh, hi, Junior. Nah, we fell into the crick.

JUNIOR: How in tarnation did you'ns a do that?

GERTIE: We's a fishin'.

JUNIOR: Was you a tryin' to catch catfish with your hands? [*Seriously.*] If'n you use a pole, it's easier.

GERTIE: [*Exaggerating—it's a "fish story."*] Um, nah . . . Well, Susannah here hooked her a big 'un, and I had to help her bring it in. We's set on fish for supper, but the dang thing's so big, it pulled up both into the crick.

JUNIOR: That ain't a crick, Gertie. It's a full-blowed river. You got to be careful. What happened to your poles?

GERTIE: We only took the one 'cause I didn't want to take a chance't on ruinin' Waincey's—you know Daddy give it to him, and he's mighty particular 'bout it—and that dang catfish a dragged mine into the crick.

JUNIOR: Well, I'll be. I'm a goin' to have to try my fishin' round here. I ain't never heard of a catfish big enough to drag two full-growed girls into the crick. I surely ain't.

GERTIE: He's a granddaddy all right! Susannah, why don't you run on into the house and get dried off? You don't want to catch your death a standin' around in wet clothes. [**SUSANNAH** *exits into cabin and then into bedroom.*] What're you a doin' way up here in the middle of the day, Junior? Don't your daddy need you at the slaughterhouse?

JUNIOR: It was kind of slow today. I just decided to pay you a little visit.

You know, Waincey asked me to look in on you ever now and then—make sure you got enough coal and such, make sure everthing's a goin' all right.

GERTIE: [*Laughing.*] Who're you a tryin' to fool? You know Waincey ain't never asked you to stop by here, more like he told you to stay away whiles't he's gone.

JUNIOR: Now why would you be a thinkin' that?

GERTIE: 'Cause he thinks you're goofy!

JUNIOR: That ain't true. Lyin's a sin, Gert.

GERTIE: That's why I don't do it.

JUNIOR: Waincey used to like me 'fore Daddy went and hound-dogged his sweetheart.

GERTIE: How is Gayla Faye?

JUNIOR: Snotty. She ain't but a year older'n me, but you'd think she's my real momma a tellin' me what to do all the time—how to eat and dress and talk. I'm purty tired of her, to tell the truth. I didn't know we's a goin' to get a foreman in the house when Daddy went a courtin'.

GERTIE: [*Laughing.*] It cain't be all that bad.

JUNIOR: It is, but that's all right. It's just set me to thinkin' it might be time to get on out a Daddy's house and start a family of my own.

GERTIE: Don't tell me you done found you a wife in Brother Rankin's coal shed, too.

JUNIOR: Huh?

GERTIE: Never mind. Who're you a goin' to marry and when's the lucky day?

JUNIOR: Well, that kinda depends on on you, I reckon.

GERTIE: Me? I don't see where I got a good nothin' to do with it.

JUNIOR: [*Standing.*] I want you to marry me, Gertie. I want it real bad. [*Kneeling.*] Will you?

GERTIE: What are you a talkin' 'bout? What's got into you, Junior? We's like brother and sister—why we ain't never even kissed each other, or walked to meetin' or nothin'. I've been a funnin' with you since we's in the first grade with Sister Smith. What is it with you men a wantin' to get married overnight?

JUNIOR: [*Earnest.*] It ain't overnight, Gertie. I been a wantin' to marry you since we's young'ns and Sister Rankin had you throwed outta church for a month of Sundays.

GERTIE: Lord, Junior, don't be a bringin' that old story up. You know it nigh 'bout embarrasses me to death. That old woman thinks a smile's a sin.

JUNIOR: Well, we's all a smilin' that day. Least most a us was. I reckon Sister Rankin didn't think it's funny, but I always thought it was kinda cute, myself.

GERTIE: I told you I didn't want to talk 'bout it, so hush.

JUNIOR: I'm just a usin' it so's you'll know how long I been set on a marryin' you. It surely has been a mighty long time. That Sunday when we's a leavin' meetin' in Daddy's buggy, I told him square, "I'm a goin' to marry that girl, Pa. I am." Course, he laughed at me then 'cause I weren't but five, but I told him last night when Gayla Faye's a wallerin' 'bout me trackin' mud crost her floor, "I think it's time for me to go get Gertie, Pa." He just looked at me for a minute, then he said, "Well, Son, I guess you been a thinkin' on it long enough. Go ask her." He told me he didn't 'spect me back for work till I's promised. So, here I am, Gertie. You a goin' to marry me or what?

GERTIE: No.

JUNIOR: [*Crushed.*] How come?

GERTIE: I'm sorry, Junior. I weren't a tryin' to be so short. You just took me by surprise is all.

JUNIOR: I can understand that. Why don't you take some time and think on it a little while—you probably really want to do it—I just knocked the wind outta you a askin' so sudden. You got to know though, Gertie, it ain't sudden for me. I been a thinkin' on it for fourteen years now.

GERTIE: That long? But why ain't you never said nothing 'bout it before this? You ain't even tried to kiss me. How do you know you's in love with me?

JUNIOR: Now, I ain't never said I love you, Gertie.

GERTIE: No, you ain't.

JUNIOR: I do a course, but I ain't never said it 'fore now.

GERTIE: A course.

JUNIOR: We could, you know, well, try that kissin' on for size and see if'n it don't help you to bend your mind toward it.

GERTIE: You ever kissed a girl?

JUNIOR: Course I have. Kissed a bunch.

GERTIE: Like who?

JUNIOR: Marlene Temple.

GERTIE: She don't count. I heard she kisses everbody.

JUNIOR: Seems to me she should count double then. Why don't Marlene count?

GERTIE: She just don't, that's all.

JUNIOR: All right. I kissed a girl over to Happy Top at the last tent revival.

GERTIE: I's there. When did you break away for kissin'?

JUNIOR: After the snakes and right before the strychnine. While'st the old folks was a talkin' in tongues—nobody ever even noticed I's a missin'.

GERTIE: Well, I reckon that counts, and I'll be generous and let you have Marlene, but two still don't make a bunch. You need at least three for that.

JUNIOR: There is one more, but I ain't a goin' to tell you that story. You'll just have to take my word for it.

GERTIE: Who is it?

JUNIOR: I ain't a goin' to tell. It wouldn't be right.

GERTIE: Didn't you just ask me to marry you?

JUNIOR: Well, yeah . . .

GERTIE: If'n you expect me to be your wife, you got to tell me everthing they is to know, don't you?

JUNIOR: I'll tell you when you say, "Yes."

GERTIE: Tell me now or the answer is a flat-out, big, ole "No."

JUNIOR: Gayla Faye.

GERTIE: [*Horrified.*] Day, Junior! You done went and kissed your daddy's new wife?

JUNIOR: They wasn't married yet! We's awalkin' home after Sunday school, just a talkin' friendly, you know? And then, outta nowheres, she stopped in the middle of the path. I thought she done got a sticker in her foot or some-thin', so I asked if'n I could help her out, and she grabbed me by the arms and kissed the bee-jesus outta me. I didn't want to hurt her feelin's none, so I kissed her back. She's purty good at it, too.

GERTIE: Does your daddy know?

JUNIOR: I'm a walkin' and a breathin', ain't I? Course he don't know. He come home with 'er her less'n a week later and said, "Junior, this here's your new momma." Said her daddy said she's ripe for the pickin' and Daddy ought to take her off'n his hands 'fore she got into trouble.

GERTIE: What'd you say?

JUNIOR: What could I a said? I said, "Welcome to the family, Momma."

GERTIE: Was you hurt?

JUNIOR: Not hurt, just surprised like.

GERTIE: I cain't even imagine.

JUNIOR: It's a queer day, that's for sure.

GERTIE: [*Pause.*] I guess you've done you some kissin' then.

JUNIOR: Guess I have. You a goin' to let me kiss on you a little bit?

GERTIE: I ain't decided yet. [*Pause.*] You ever touched a woman?

JUNIOR: What a you mean?

GERTIE: You know. [*She motions to her breasts.*] Here. You ever touched a woman here?

JUNIOR: Why, sure. I am nineteen year old.

GERTIE: What'd feel like?

JUNIOR: Well, it was soft and kind a pillowy.

GERTIE: No, I mean, what'd it make you feel like?

JUNIOR: Huh?

GERTIE: Did it make your tingle in your belly and kinda sour-apple sick all at the same time?

JUNIOR: I reckon I got to tinglin', but it weren't really in my belly.

GERTIE: Where? Your chest?

JUNIOR: No, well, you know . . .

GERTIE: [*Embarrassed.*] I ain't a talkin' 'bout that. A dog can tingle down there. I mean did it make you so's you wanted to jump outta your skin and hop inside a hers? Or did it just make you scairt?

JUNIOR: [*Insulted.*] Well it didn't make me scairt, Gertie. I ain't afeared a no woman nor no part of her. You come up with some a the craziest notions I ever heard. Why you think it would a made me scairt?

GERTIE: Not just scairt, but afeared and excited all at the same time—didn't it make you feel that a way?

JUNIOR: No, ma'am. Don't nothin' make me scairt. Scairt didn't have a thing to do with it.

GERTIE: How did it make you feel then?

JUNIOR: Kinda squirmy the first time, but excited, too. Real excited now that you mention it. You want me to try it? Then I can tell you fresh.

GERTIE: Don't be sinful. I was just a askin'. I's just a wonderin' is all.

JUNIOR: Well, you got to kiss me now—you done got me started.

GERTIE: Started on what?

JUNIOR: Never you mind. Just kiss me back, Gertie. I'll show you what it feels like. [*He kisses her clumsily.*] See? Don't that make you excited?

GERTIE: I'm not sure I'd say, "excited," Junior. More like odd.

JUNIOR: Huh?

GERTIE: You's just too much like a kissin' on Waincey.

JUNIOR: Don't tell me Waincey's been a kissin' you on the mouth!

GERTIE: Course not! I mean it's the same feelin' I get when I kiss Waincey on the cheek, or the way I used to feel when Daddy'd tickle me and kiss me when I's a young'n. It's real nice, but it don't make me feel wifely.

JUNIOR: That's all right, Gertie. I's just gettin' warmed up. I didn't want to scare you none. [*He grabs her and kisses her.* **GERTIE** *responds politely, but it's clear she is not moved. While they are still in a clutch,* **SISTER RANKIN** *enters.*]

SISTER RANKIN: Gertie Cobb! What in the Lord's name do you think you's a doin'? [*They break apart guiltily.*]

GERTIE: We wasn't doin' nothin', Sister Rankin.

SISTER RANKIN: Well it sure looks like the Devil's nothin' to me. And your brother only gone a day! I knew you's a sinner. I knew it that day you flipped your dress up over your head and showed the whole Congregation your drawers. I had to have you throwed out of meetin' for a month.

GERTIE: I was only three years old!

SISTER RANKIN: That don't matter. The Devil done put his mark on you early, girl. You's probably born a loose woman. No angel child of three's a goin' to show the world their drawers.

GERTIE: You hush! My daddy told me it weren't nothin' to be 'shamed of. He said all young'ns is naturally innocent, and the sin is a makin' 'em feel shamed.

SISTER RANKIN: If'n your daddy had been a better Christian, he might not be dead now.

GERTIE: [*Flying at her.*] You take that back, you bitter, old . . .

JUNIOR: [*Catching* **GERTIE.**] Both a you'ns stop it now. GERTIE! Calm down. [*She fights him.*] Settle down, Gertie. NOW! [*She stands still.*] Sister Rankin, you owe us a apology. Gertie and me's just decidin' to get married, and we's a stealin' a kiss to seal the promise. Everybody does that.

SISTER RANKIN: Everbody don't kiss like that less'n it's their weddin' night, and folks with the proper respect for the Lord don't even do it then.

JUNIOR: We weren't a sinnin', Sister Rankin. We's just a sealin' our promise. Right, Gertie?

GERTIE: Maybe.

SISTER RANKIN: When's the weddin' then? Don't look like you two ought to wait too long.

JUNIOR: We ain't set a date yet, but we don't plan on a waitin' much. Why, I've already talked to Brother Rankin—I been saved. He's a goin' to baptize me tomorrow at meetin' so I'll be sinless as a young'n a goin' into my marriage with Gertie.

GERTIE: [*Panicking and backing away.*] We got to wait till Waincey comes home. He wouldn't like it none if'n we did it whiles't he's gone off to war.

SISTER RANKIN: You're sure enough right, sister. Waincey wouldn't hold no truck with you'ns a foolin' 'round whiles't he's out to service. I still ain't satisfied that there ain't been no sin committed here. Junior, you go on home now. You need to so some heavy prayin' afore you's a goin' to be worthy of God's cleansin' waters.

JUNIOR: But me and Gertie's still got us some talkin' to do.

SISTER RANKIN: Seems to me, the talkin' was over with. You get, now. Get on home or I'll take a hickory switch to you; you ain't too big yet. [*Chasing* **JUNIOR** *offstage.*] I won't stand to come acrost sin and not stop it. Go on home, Junior. [*He begins to exit.*]

JUNIOR: Oh, all right. Ain't no sense to fight you.

SISTER RANKIN: [*Following.*] Because God and righteousness is on my side, and don't you'ns forget it.

JUNIOR: I'll come get you tomorrow for meetin', Gert. I'll walk you and Susannah to the Church. [**SISTER RANKIN** *moves toward him threateningly. He exits.*]

SISTER RANKIN: I should a knowed you'd be up to no good. I knew I'd better get on up here 'fore too long and see what's a goin' on. Now I see, the wages of sin have already trapped you in their fiery claws. Repent, girl! [*Kneeling.*] Kneel with me, Gertie. Pray for the Lord's forgiveness.

GERTIE: I ain't a goin' to do it. I ain't done nothin' wrong. You see sin in the air, Josephine Rankin.

SISTER RANKIN: It is in the air. Sin is all around us, and we's a goin' to breathe it in if'n we's not careful. Sin's like the coal dust; it swirls so thick we cain't help but breathe it in, and if'n we don't figure that out and walk outta that deep, dark mine of eternal damnation, we're a goin' to get so's we cain't breathe nothin' good. Kneel with me and pray, Sister Cobb. Kneel and pray for your eternal soul. [**GERTIE** *kneels.*] Lord, this girl is a vessel of sin. Just a empty vessel, Lord, a waitin' for somebody to fill her up. Let it be you, Lord. Fill this girl full a your light and protect her from Satan who's always ready with a pitcher a sin a waitin' to pour. [*Pause.*] Our Father, who art in Heaven . . .

SISTER RANKIN and **GERTIE:** . . . hallowed be thy name. Thy kingdom come, thy will be done, on Earth as it is in Heaven. Give us this day our daily bread, and forgive us our trespasses, as we forgive those who trespass against us. Lead us not into temptation, but deliver us from evil. Amen. [**GERTIE** *quickly stands.*]

SISTER RANKIN: There, Gertie. We've started you on the narra path. [*She stands.*] The Lord's road is a steep and rocky climb. I feel sure this dose'll cure you for the minute, but I 'spect you at meetin' tomorrow, you hear me?

GERTIE: [*Cowed.*] Yes, ma'am. We'll be there—me and Susannah.

SISTER RANKIN: That's right. Bring her too. She don't come from no Christian family, and I'm more'n sure she needs a savin', too. I begged and begged Waincey to listen to reason and set you girls up in my house where I could keep a eye on the both a you—if'n I find any more foolishness a goin' on 'round here, I'm a goin' to have to pack you'ns up and bring you to the house with me'n Delmer.

GERTIE: There won't be nothin' a goin' on here, Sister, that you cain't take a part in. I swear it.

SISTER RANKIN: You think I don't know what it's like to be a young'n in the summertime, Gertie?

GERTIE: No, ma'am.

SISTER RANKIN: I know what it's like to be young and foolish; I seen enough of it in my time. When I's a little girl, my momma keeled over of a coughin' fit and died whiles't she's a makin' Daddy's breakfast. Did you know my daddy's a preacher, too?

GERTIE: Yes, ma'am. I heard my daddy tell it.

SISTER RANKIN: Best preacher this side of Zula Mountain he was. Some might say he's stern, but I loved him, Gertie. I surely did. He raised me on his own from the time I's four. Used to tell everbody what a good little girl I was—how I minded good and proper.

GERTIE: I'm sure you's a sight.

SISTER RANKIN: I was a sight in them days. It's a long time ago now, though. [*Pause.*] I did everthing my daddy told me to, Gertie. Ever little thing—'cause he knew God made women weak. When he told me to pray for the weakness of all women, I prayed hard. I know how it feels to want mirth and joy and only know hardship. My daddy's the only one that taught me a doin' what I's told was the Lord's work for me. [*Pause.*] But you ain't got no daddy, nor nobody else what's here to look after you. So, you're a goin' to have to listen to me . . .

GERTIE: Yes, ma'am.

SISTER RANKIN: Them boys looks like fun, don't they?

GERTIE: No, ma'am.

SISTER RANKIN: You ain't got to lie. Ever girl thinks a handsome boy's all they's ever a goin' to want. But you'll see, Gertie. They's dirty and low-down at heart. You don't need you a boy, girl. You need a man what's a goin' to give you the holy light a God's protection. Boys just fade away when the sin's done been committed. [*Pause.* **SISTER RANKIN** *kisses* **GERTIE** *on the forehead.*] Now, I got to get on home and get the supper cooked for Delmer. I'll see you tomorrow mornin', Gertie. No excuses. The Lord won't accept excuses and neither will I. [*She exits.* **GERTIE** *enters cabin where* **SUSANNAH** *enters from bedroom with a brush.*]

SUSANNAH: What're we a goin' to have for supper since that catfish done got away?

GERTIE: [*On edge.*] Don't be a throwin' my lies back up in my face, Susannah. It ain't funny, and I ain't in no funnin' mood anyways.

SUSANNAH: I'm sorry, Gertie. I'm sorry 'bout the whole thing.

GERTIE: Well, you look better. Leastaways you's clean. Sit on down, and I'll comb out your hair. [*She does so. Pause.*] Susannah?

SUSANNAH: [*Lulled by combing.*] Uh-huh?

GERTIE: Why didn't you tell me you couldn't swim a lick?

SUSANNAH: [*Quietly.*] You wanted me to be clean, Gertie.

GERTIE: I didn't want you to drown yourself.

SUSANNAH: I weren't a tryin' to. You wanted me to be clean, and I's so dirty. I just thought if'n I could wade out deep, but still touch bottom, that I could finally get all a the dirt off'n me. I know the crick's got holes in it, but I didn't 'spect the bottom to give out so sudden like that. I swear, I didn't think we's a goin' out that far. I just felt all that cool water and the soap, and all of a sudden I wanted to be clean, too. I'm sorry I scairt you.

GERTIE: Well, I's only scairt 'cause I didn't want nobody to think I done went and drowned you. You only been here a couple a days.

SUSANNAH: Nobody'd think that 'bout you, Gertie. You're too good.

GERTIE: That's a laugh. Sister Rankin's just outside a tellin' me what a plumb sinful, loose woman I am.

SUSANNAH: You shouldn't pay no mind to her. She's just a lonely, old woman.

GERTIE: Lonely? She ain't lonely; she's got the preacher.

SUSANNAH: That don't make no never mind. You can be lonely in a field full a people same as when you's by yourself.

GERTIE: Are you lonesome, Susannah?

SUSANNAH: I always has been, but maybe not so much anymore.

GERTIE: [*Pause.*] You have beautiful hair, you know that?

SUSANNAH: Ain't nothin' purty 'bout me. You can clean me up if'n you want to, I'm still a goin' to be dirty.

GERTIE: [*Pause.*] Susannah? I didn't mean to touch you like that when we's a flailin' in the crick. I's just a tryin' to get a hold of you is all, and you's soaped up and slippery as a snake . . .

SUSANNAH: Touch me like what, Gertie?

GERTIE: You well, you ummmm. You know . . . on the . . .

SUSANNAH: I knowed you's a doin' your best to save me, Gertie. That's all I know.

GERTIE: Good. I just didn't want you to be scairt or nothin'.

SUSANNAH: I weren't scairt of the touchin', Gertie. I weren't scairt a you a'tall. Once you grabbed a hold a me and held on like you wasn't never a goin' to let go, well I weren't afeared of nothin' then.

GERTIE: Was you scairt before that?

SUSANNAH: I was afeared of the water, I reckon. At first it was peaceful—like and warm, but then when I went under, it got cold and rough. That water was almost alive and a swirlin' around me like it weren't never a goin' to spit me out. I felt like I's a bein' held down 'gainst the ground, 'ceptin' the ground kept a rollin', and there weren't nothin' a stoppin' it. [*Pause.*] Then I felt you, Gertie—'gainst my back, a gropin in that murky water to find me. Your hands was desperate and good a holdin' on, and I felt safe—like nothin' bad could ever happen to me again—like I'd come home.

GERTIE: You are home, Susannah. Here with me. This is your home.

END OF ACT I

ACT II
Scene 1

Lights rise to early morning of the next day. **GERTIE** *is standing CS outside the cabin pacing. She is wearing a yellow dress and is ready for church.*

GERTIE: [*Yelling.*] Susannah? Come on! Girl, you're a goin' to make us late for the service, and Sister Rankin's a goin' to write us up in her book! SUSANNAH! [**SUSANNAH** *emerges from bedroom and crosses to top step. Her appearance is totally changed. She is wearing a powder-blue dress and her hair is "fixed." She glows with a beauty hereto unseen by* **GERTIE** *or the audience.*]

SUSANNAH: Here I am, Gertie. I'm sorry I took so long. These hairpins took me some gettin' used to. [*Pause.*] Do I look all right? I tried really hard. Do I look all right?

GERTIE: [*In wonder.*] You's a sight.

SUSANNAH: I'm sorry. I thought I did okay. Is it the dress? I knowed you said it was your momma's, but I thought it was a purty good fit.

GERTIE: The dress is fine, Susannah.

SUSANNAH: Then it's these dang burned shoes, ain't it? Your momma took real good care of 'em, Gertie, but they's kinda high for me. I feel like a new calf what's just got her legs a walkin' round in 'em. I'll just go on in and change.

GERTIE: NO! Don't you go nowheres.

SUSANNAH: I tried really hard to look so's you wouldn't be 'shamed to sit with me, Gertie. I'll just go on in and change.

GERTIE: No, Susannah. You cain't do that.

SUSANNAH: I reckon you think I'm a lost cause. But you got to know, I ain't never a goin' to be purty like you. I tried though; I surely did.

GERTIE: Susannah, you're 'bout the purtiest thing I ever seen.

SUSANNAH: Don't make fun a me, Gertie. I know I ain't purty. Please don't make fun a me.

GERTIE: I ain't a makin' fun, Susannah.

SUSANNAH: I'm just a tryin' to look respectable. Do I look all right?

GERTIE: [*Unable to hide her awe.*] You look . . . you look . . . Why, Susannah, you're beautiful.

SUSANNAH: [*Shyly.*] Thank you, Gertie. You're beautiful, too. [*Pause.*] Are you ready to go?

GERTIE: I's a waitin' on Junior. He said he's a goin' to come to walk us to meetin'.

SUSANNAH: I don't mind a waitin'. I ain't big on meetin'. I ain't even been to Church since Momma died. She only made us go when Harlan's out on a drunk anyways. It don't matter if'n we's late to me.

GERTIE: I don't know. I hate bein' late. 'Sides, I ain't in the mood for Sister Rankin's snotty remarks on tardiness. We don't need no boy to walk us anyways, now do we?

SUSANNAH: I don't 'spect so. I ain't never had me a boy a walkin' me nowheres before.

GERTIE: Well, Waincey always walks me to meetin', but he ain't here.

SUSANNAH: No, he ain't here.

GERTIE: We'll just set to a walkin' ourselves, I reckon.

SUSANNAH: All right.

GERTIE: [*Hesitating briefly.*] You wanna hold my hand?

SUSANNAH: Thank you, Gertie. [*They join hands and exit.*]

Scene 2

In black the congregation (all players except for **WAINCEY***) can be heard singing "I'll Fly Away." As lights rise, we see* **BROTHER RANKIN** *standing and* **JUNIOR** *kneeling before a makeshift church of benches where* **CONGREGATION** *sits R and L of* **BROTHER RANKIN**—*leaving the feeling of an open church.*

BROTHER RANKIN: In the name of the Father, and of the Son, and of the Holy Spirit! Rise from these holy waters, boy. Rise and call yourself a man a God.

CONGREGATION: Praise the Lord! [**JUNIOR** *wipes the water from his forehead.*]

BROTHER RANKIN: Don't be so quick to wipe away the Lord's blessin', Junior. You've a long time in this life to stand dry and parched a wishin' for the Lord's glorious and forgiving waters. Don't be so quick, boy, to dry out and stand amongst us sinners. [*He lays hands on* **JUNIOR.**] You are blessed in the waters of our Lord. Amen, Lord!

CONGREGATION: Amen!

SISTER RANKIN: Praise the Lord!

BROTHER RANKIN: Now, go on down and sit with your intended. Share with her the wisdom of being born again and saved in this lifetime. [JUNIOR *takes a seat between* **GERTIE** *and* **GAYLA FAYE**.] Good mornin', brothers and sisters! How 'bout a HALLELUJAH for this purty day on God's green Earth!

CONGREGATION: Hallelujah!

SISTER RANKIN: Praise the Lord!

BROTHER RANKIN: Come on, brothers and sisters! You can do better'n that sickly little hallelujah for the glory of the Lord. We've done gone and saved one a our own. We've taken a sinner amongst us and brought to the Lord a saved soul! I said HALLELUJAH!

CONGREGATION: [*Louder.*] Hallelujah!

SISTER RANKIN: [*Louder still.*] Praise the Lord!

BROTHER RANKIN: Each and ever one a us ought to be down on our knees a thankin' the Lord that they's baptism to save us. WHY? Because all a us is sinners! We cain't help it. Ever since Eve gave into the Devil and took the first bite of sin, we ain't a been able to help it. Yes sir, Eve was weak—just like ever one a us here tonight is weak. Lord, we ask you to forgive us for a bein' weak. We's sinners, brothers and sisters, 'cause we cain't say "no" to temptation. We's a bein' tempted all the time—whether it's by money or glory or somethin' else. Ever minute of ever day we's weak. And the Devil's promise of a easier life is one we'd a like to believe in. We're like Eve, a hopin' the Devil knows how to cure our troubles, that takin' a bite from temptation's mouth'll make us better, educate us up, help us to find a easier world to live in. Just like Eve, we want to take a bite a that apple 'cause the promise is sweet. We can taste the good, sweet taste a cider ever time he thrusts that apple into our'n faces, now cain't we? Yes, sir! The promise of temptation is sweet. It leads us to a thinkin' we'ns can chew and fill our bellies with new learnin', but the fruit of temptation is a bitter seed to bear, brothers and sisters. A eatin' a that apple leads right back to this here. This minute a knowin' we has shunned God's eternal light for the shriveled stink a hell! God knows what we need to do, not Satan. God knows that even in the hard times when he leads us through the rocks and briers thrown acrost our path that we just need to believe. The Lord our God takes care a us when we turn away from temptation. Turn away from the Devil, brothers and sisters. Allow the light a God to cover you in his wonder and glory. Hallelujah!

CONGREGATION: Praise the Lord!

SISTER RANKIN: Hallelujah!

BROTHER RANKIN: Course now, everbody cain't wait out temptation, and I'm a goin' to tell you some scripture what shows us the dangers of a givin' in. They's once't a man named Lot in God's ancient world, and he had him a wife and two growed daughters still at home. They's evil men a livin' in the town where Lot and his family was a dwellin', and God sat himself down with Abraham and talked on the evil of this town. Even though Abraham was against it, God decided he's a goin' to have to destroy Sodom and Gomorra 'cause the men there had done set themselves up with other men. So God sent him his finest angels to tell Lot to take his family and leave their home 'cause Lot was a righteous man. When them angels got inside Lot's house, them Sodomites came to the door and banged on it till it nigh' bout fell off the hinges. "Where are the men which came in to thee this night?" they said, and they set to bangin' some more. "Bring them out unto us, that we may know them." Like any good Christian, Lot bolted that door even tighter agin' those evil men, and then he offered his daughters as sport so's them angels could remain pure. Those angels weren't afeared a course cause the Lord was a protectin' 'em. They told Lot to get his family ready, and they's a goin' to lead them out a that den of iniquity that very night. Lot got 'em all together and ready to head for the mountain outside a Sodom— oh, 'bout ten miles away I reckon. Right 'fore they left, them angels told everbody, "Don't look back, now. The mighty fire a the Lord will burn your eyes." Then they headed out to the holy mountain away from sin. Halfway outta the city, Lot's wife heard a rumblin', and the Devil whispered, "Look back, woman." Lot's wife give into the Devil's temptation, and brothers and sisters, she went agin' God's word and looked back. The fire of the Lord was just too much for a woman to bear, and she was turned into a pillar a salt. The rest of the family made it up onto the side of the mountain, and the angels left them there safe in a cave they done found. A couple a days went by, and Lot's daughters a got to thinkin'. Now we all know there ain't nothin' more sinful than a woman that ain't got nothin' to do but sit and think. I said, "Hallelujah!"

CONGREGATION: Hallelujah!

SISTER RANKIN: Praise the Lord!

BROTHER RANKIN: The Devil started a whisperin' in those girls' ears. "You're the only ones left in the whole, wide world," he said. "God's done went and kilt everthing and everbody." When the Devil starts a whisperin' in your ears, brothers and sisters, he can trance you into almost anything. Them daughters sat down in the cave whiles't Lot was out a huntin' up some food, and they came up with a plan. When Lot come home that night, they made him some supper, and then they give him some wine. Now you know Lot was a good, Christian man, or God wouldn't a saved him from the destruction of Sodom. He weren't used to drinkin', and them girls counted on that. They got him drunk, they surely did, and then them daughters lay with their own daddy so's that they could bear babies and the world wouldn't end. Lot was so lost in that haze of drunkenness—he didn't even know them daughters come into the bed with him. Satan had made them believe that's the only way. The Devil handed them a apple and said, "Eat," and they bit into the Devil's sin right quick. Them daughters was smarter than a tick. They tricked their daddy into a givin' them babies—Moab and Ben. If'n they could a just waited out temptation, they'd a seen men a walkin' in the valley what could a given 'em sons. If'n they could a just waited it out, God would a taken care a them, but they couldn't do it 'cause they smelled the sweetness of the Devil's apple, and they laid in sin with their own daddy to have their bite. We ain't got to be like Lot's daughers, brothers and sisters. We know that God is a comin'. We's all sinners now 'cause a Eve, but if'n we can learn to wait out the temptation, brothers and sisters, we can defeat the Devil at his own dinner. Hallelujah! Praise the Lord.

SISTER RANKIN: Praise our merciful Jesus!

CONGREGATION: Amen!

BROTHER RANKIN: Now, let's all sing in jubilation to the Lord! [*Begins singing.*] I'LL FLY AWAY, OH GLORY [**CONGREGATION** *joins in.*] Who's a goin' to testify?

CONGREGATION MEMBER: I will, Brother! [**CONGREGATION MEMBER/MAN** *kneels before* **BROTHER RANKIN** *and prays. His words are swallowed by the singing of the* **CONGREGATION**. *He doubles over on his knees sobbing.* **BROTHER RANKIN** *prays over the man and he gets up and goes back to his seat.* **SISTER RANKIN** *stands and begins praying out loud and waving her arms. Her words quickly become nonsensical as she begins rocking and speaking in tongues.*]

BROTHER RANKIN: Who else is a goin' to testify? Who else wants the light of the Lord within their heart? [**CONGREGATION MEMBER/ WOMAN** *kneels before* **BROTHER RANKIN**. *Singing becomes louder and intensifies.* **SISTER RANKIN** *becomes louder as well.* **BROTHER RANKIN** *prays over the* **WOMAN**, *and she is helped back to her seat.*] We got more'n two sinners here tonight. I know it. Who else is a goin' to cleanse hisself a the Devil's sin? [*Pause.*] Susannah Cobb! Come forward and testify, girl.

[**SUSANNAH** *doesn't move.*] Come forth! [**SUSANNAH** *sits and shakes her head violently.* **JUNIOR** *and* **MAN** *push her toward the front.* **SISTER RANKIN** *is still talking in tongues—faster and louder.*] Confess your sins, Susannah! Confess before your brethren and your God. [*She doesn't move or speak.*] Confess! Confess the sin that stains your soul! [**BROTHER RANKIN** *pushes* **SUSANNAH** *to her knees as she screams in anguish and then faints.*]

SISTER RANKIN: Graph. Rana out ay tangasarsh cana tad senon and. Ga de lat so. Dootre ingt, rahn toe sisi tay weng laot nay. [*She opens her eyes and lapses into English.*] I knowed this girl was a sinner. I knowed it the first time I laid eyes on her. [*She closes her eyes again.*] Happa kan tag day losss no ikmon nooooooo rand pay nokka nokka nokka gunt weeeeek asongi mak a kayda loooooowt. [**SISTER RANKIN** *collapses and joins* **SUSANNAH** *on the floor.*]

Scene 3

Lights rise to moonlight outside cabin. **GERTIE** *enters supporting* **SUSANNAH.**

GERTIE: We's almost there. Hang on just a minute. I'm a goin' to get you there. [**SUSANNAH** *falls.* **GERTIE** *picks her up, and they enter cabin.* **GERTIE** *seats* **SUSANNAH** *at table and exits into bedroom. She re-enters with a quilt and places it around* **SUSANNAH**'s *shoulders.*] There. How's that? I think I'll put us on a pot a coffee. Could you drink some coffee, Susannah, or should I fix you some milk? [**SUSANNAH** *doesn't acknowledge question.* **GERTIE** *busies herself with coffee things.*]

SUSANNAH: [*Staring straight forward.*] You think they had names, Gertie?

GERTIE: Who, honey?

SUSANNAH: You think they had names?

GERTIE: Who're you a talkin' 'bout?

SUSANNAH: Lot's daughters.

GERTIE: I don't rightly know. I'll have to look it up in the Bible.

SUSANNAH: I done looked it up. I looked it up the last time Brother Rankin spoke on 'em. I looked it up in Genesis. The Bible don't give 'em no names.

GERTIE: You can read, Susannah? You never come to school.

SUSANNAH: Sister Smith taught me a little after Sunday school sometimes.

GERTIE: Maybe you just skipped over the part with those girls' names in it; you think that might be it?

SUSANNAH: No. I went to Redenair's. Old Harold can read purty good. He read it to me, and I made him read it over and over so's we could be sure he didn't just miss them names.

GERTIE: Well, I'm sure they got 'em. Don't nobody go around forever without nothin' to be called. How'd anybody get 'em to come home for supper?

SUSANNAH: But they ain't writ down nowheres.

GERTIE: Ain't that funny.

SUSANNAH: You know how you can picture somebody, even if'n you ain't met 'em yet 'cause a their name? Like I know what a Josephine looks like afore I ever meet her. She's mean and pinched up—and I know what a Sarah's like—she's kind and knows everthing good. You know how that goes, Gertie.

GERTIE: I guess so.

SUSANNAH: Well, I cain't get me a good picture of them daughters, Gertie. I see two girls, young—almost women—and they both got dark hair, long hair. They's kinda slender, you know, from the back, but when they turn around, they ain't got no faces. I dream 'bout 'em all the time. These two daughers a plowin' in their daddy's field, a workin' together and a livin' together, they seem almost peaceful when I dream 'bout 'em like that, but then they go and turn around, and they ain't got no faces—there's just white skin—they're blank. Those girls need names. They got to have names.

GERTIE: Susannah? You a goin' to be all right?

SUSANNAH: I thought 'bout namin' 'em myself. I thought I'd call one Rachel and the other Sarah. But that means I'm a given faces, and I cain't do that. They got faces of their own—I cain't give 'em new ones. I just cain't do it. I cain't give 'em their names.

GERTIE: Course you cain't, Susannah. Don't you worry 'bout them girls' names. I'll ask Brother Rankin for 'em the next time I get a chance't to talk with him.

SUSANNAH: NO! You cain't ask him, Gertie. You cain't.

GERTIE: But he'll know if'n they got names. He's the preacher.

SUSANNAH: He'll give 'em the names he wants 'em to have, Gertie. He'll give 'em the names of sinners 'cause he can. Don't let him name 'em. They's not sinners.

GERTIE: But they tricked Lot into layin' with 'em, Susannah. That's a sin. That's a powerful, big sin.

SUSANNAH: [*Pleading.*] Don't let him name 'em, Gertie. He'll name 'em sinners. [*Becoming progressively more hysterical.*] They didn't want to do it! Maybe it was Satan like Brother Rankin said, but more like it was Lot a tellin' 'em. Satan spoke through Lot. Lot said, "Drink the liquor, girl. You got a duty, and your momma cain't do it no more. Drink, girl. Drink. Do your duty for the Lord." Satan spoke through Lot, Gertie—you cain't let Preacher name 'em—they ain't sinners.

GERTIE: [*Kneeling with her.*] Susannah! What's wrong with you? Calm down, honey. Hush. Don't cry. Calm down.

SUSANNAH: Gertie—I have known sin. Momma weren't dead three days 'fore Daddy come into the bed with me. "You got a duty, girl. Your Momma's gone. You got to take on her duty." I weren't a goin' to do it, Gertie. I weren't a goin' to lay there and let him sin on top a me. I scratched and scratched. I bit him on the lip, and then I bit his hand when he tried to cover my mouth. I kicked and yelled and cried and prayed in his face a hopin' the word a God would stop him. He's drunk, though, and the more I yelled the more he laughed. He straddled me, and I kicked hard. While'st he's a lyin' there sick, I run out the house and swore I weren't a goin' back to that house a sin. I ran all the way to Happy Top and banged on Brother and Sister Rankin's door. They made me tell 'em what was wrong. I's 'shamed, so I told 'em Harlan had tried to beat me 'cause he's drunk. They put me to bed. Next mornin', Sister Rankin goes off to town, and Preacher come into my room while I's still a sleepin'. "I am the Lord," he said, "I am your Lord and Savior. What sins have you done committed, girl?" I told him I ain't committed no sin. "I ain't a sinner," I said. He accused me a lyin'. I told him Daddy didn't just beat me, he come after me. Brother Rankin said I's a temptation many a man couldn't resist since purty women come from the Devil. He said I must a done something to tempt Daddy into it. Then he slid into the bed with me. He said, "Pray with me, girl. You are woman and temptation in the flesh. Open your mouth, daughter. You are the child of Eve, a sinful woman let loose in Paradise. Open wider, child. I would rather dwell with a hungry lion than to live with the wickedness that is woman. Suck, girl." He kept a sayin' I's evil, Gertie, and I wanted to pray, but I couldn't say nothin'. I couldn't talk 'cause I was a chokin'. I was "Daughter." I was "hungry, evil woman." I was "Eve's child." He took away my name, Gertie, and now I don't have no face.

GERTIE: [*Crying and stroking* **SUSANNAH***'s hair softly.*] Oh my Lord. Oh my Lord. You poor baby. Oh my Lord.

SUSANNAH: Preacher sent me home. The next time Daddy's drunk, I didn't even try to fight him. I just laid there a waitin' for him to finish. [*Pause.*] I've knowed sin, Gertie. I am sin. Don't look at me—I ain't fit for you to look at.

GERTIE: I cain't do nothin' but look at you Susannah—I ain't been able to take my eyes off'n you all day—you ain't a sinner, Susannah; I couldn't love a sinner. [**SUSANNAH** *begins weeping.* **GERTIE** *embraces her and begins to rock her back and forth.*] You ain't a sinner; I couldn't love a sinner. You ain't a sinner; I couldn't love a sinner. You ain't a sinner; I couldn't love a sinner. [*She pulls back and wipes* **SUSANNAH** *'s tears.*] Hush, now, Susannah. [**GERTIE** *slowly kisses* **SUSANNAH** *'s cheek.* **SUSANNAH** *brings her hand up to touch where* **GERTIE** *kissed her.*]

SUSANNAH: You cain't love me, Gertie. You don't even know me.

GERTIE: I know you, Susannah. I love you. [**GERTIE** *bends in and kisses* **SUSANNAH** *'s face, eyes, cheeks, and finally mouth.* **SUSANNAH** *and* **GERTIE** *kiss tentatively at first, and then with all of the passion that was missing from the* **JUNIOR/GERTIE** *kiss.*]

SUSANNAH: Your lips is so soft and warm—you make me feel soft and warm.

GERTIE: That's what love feels like, Susannah. [*They kiss as lights fade.*]

Scene 4

Three months later. Landscape needs to be changed to reflect winter. Lighting should appear gray throughout. **GERTIE** *is sitting at the kitchen table, sorting through homemade Christmas ornaments and decorations. She is in a wonderful mood and sings.*

GERTIE: JINGLE BELLS, JINGLE BELLS, JINGLE ALL THE WAY . . .

GAYLA FAYE: [*Entering with a basket.*] Gertie? Gertie you home?

GERTIE: Season's greetin's, Gayla Faye. Come on in.

GAYLA FAYE: I done brought you some popped corn that we'ns had left over. I thought you'n Susannah could make you some garland.

GERTIE: Thank you. That was mighty nice a you to think 'bout us.

GAYLA FAYE: Where's Susannah? Ain't she home yet?

GERTIE: Said she wanted to take her a walk up to the crick'n look for pine cones for the decoratin'.

GAYLA FAYE: She did? Well, I seen her in town less'n a hour ago.

GERTIE: Oh, well, she must a went to Redenair's. We's a runnin' low on flour. What're you a doin' up in the holler?

GAYLA FAYE: I just got a hankerin' to talk with you I reckon. Lord, I ain't seen you in a month a Sundays—I's worried you done took sick or somethin'.

GERTIE: Nah. I'm feelin' purty good. That's a heck of a long way to walk when you could a just asked somebody in town if I was a ailin'.

GAYLA FAYE: Well, I told you I a wanted you to have the corn, now didn't I?

GERTIE: Don't get your feathers ruffled, girl. I said "thank you"—I surely do appreciate it.

GAYLA FAYE: I'm sorry, Gertie. Seems I swing back and forth 'tween sweet and sour here lately. It ain't you.

GERTIE: What is it then?

GAYLA FAYE: T'ain't nothin' much, I reckon, 'ceptin' I'm 'bout to have a young'n.

GERTIE: Well, I'll be! I didn't think old Senior had it in him! You'ns been married almost a year—we thought he's past it.

GAYLA FAYE: I thought on it like that, too. Oh, Gertie, what am I a goin' to do?

GERTIE: Ain't you happy?

GAYLA FAYE: I am happy. I'm so happy I just want to burst.

GERTIE: Then what's a botherin' you so?

GAYLA FAYE: I got a secret. A powerful, big one.

GERTIE: What is it?

GAYLA FAYE: I shouldn't tell you. But, it's 'cause a this secret that I'm scairt for my baby.

GERTIE: Gayla Faye, bein' scairt is natural—but we been a havin' young'ns round here forever—babies is more regular than the tabacca crop—you ain't got nothin' to worry 'bout.

GAYLA FAYE: Maybe I do. Oh, I got to tell somebody! Somebody what ain't a goin' to tell soon's they get the chance't.

GERTIE: What're you a goin' on 'bout?

GAYLA FAYE: Gertie, I done somethin' awful bad.

GERTIE: There ain't nothin' that bad to get into 'round here.

GAYLA FAYE: There's plenty enough, I reckon. Can you keep a secret, Gertie? I'm serious. You cain't be a tellin' a soul. [*Pause.*] It ain't Senior's baby, and I don't care a bit! WHEW! Goodness to gracious that felt good. I been a itchin' to say it out loud almost a month.

GERTIE: Day!

GAYLA FAYE: It ain't Senior's and I'm happy it ain't. Tickled pink—plumb, outright proud that that old man ain't got it in him after a year, but somebody else's got in me after only once't.

GERTIE: Oh my Lord, Gayla Faye. What're you a goin' to do?

GAYLA FAYE: I don't know. I just don't know. [*Pause.*] I guess I'm damned now, ain't I, Gertie?

GERTIE: I don't know. I just don't know. [*Pause.*] Whose is it? Did he force you?

GAYLA FAYE: [*Laughing.*] Likeaways it was the other way around. I purty near had to hold him down and cut his britches off. I'm darn near sure it's his first time at that.

GERTIE: Shush.

GAYLA FAYE: You worried I'm a goin' to make it any worse by sayin' the truth? I'm already damned, Gertie. Might as well make it whole hog to goodness.

GERTIE: Does Senior know?

GAYLA FAYE: I'm a walkin' and a breathin' ain't I? Course he don't know. He's all swelled up like a banty rooster with a hen house full a chicks—thinks he's somethin' else.

GERTIE: You a goin' to tell him?

GAYLA FAYE: Now what do you think? You think I'd get outta that house alive once't I told him how I spread my legs for some young, wonderful, handsome boy what ain't got a ounce a fat nor a wrinkle on him? I might as well drown me'n this young'n out in the crick.

GERTIE: Can you live with it?

GAYLA FAYE: With what?

GERTIE: Livin' a lie—wakin' up ever day a your life and a knowin' you's done damned yourself and that little young'n? Can you live with it?

GAYLA FAYE: You ain't never been in love, has you Gertie?

GERTIE: Now why would you want to start on some foolishness like that?

GAYLA FAYE: 'Cause nobody what's been in love could a look me in the face and ask me if it's worth a damnin' myself for.

GERTIE: I have been in love.

GAYLA FAYE: Oh, Gertie. Jack Beel don't count. You wasn't but a young'n when he's in town.

GERTIE: I ain't a talkin' 'bout Jack Beel.

GAYLA FAYE: Who, then?

GERTIE: Well, now. That ain't really no never mind to you.

GAYLA FAYE: It's Junior, then, ain't it? He ain't right for you, Gertie—he's always a runnin' 'round with anything in a skirt. Why I heard tell he's a messin' with Marlene just last week over to the Happy Top meetin'. Is it Junior, Gertie? Is it? 'Cause I don't think you's strong enough to tie yourself up with Junior. That's a goin' to take somebody with a little more gumption, I reckon.

GERTIE: Like who?

GAYLA FAYE: [*Evasively.*] Oh, I don't know. Somebody what's got a little more notion of what a man wants.

GERTIE: I know enough.

GAYLA FAYE: Oh, do you? Where you done gone and learned it then?

GERTIE: Hush up, girl. I ain't a learned nothin' you need to worry yourself 'bout. 'Sides, it weren't Junior I's a talkin' 'bout noways.

GAYLA FAYE: Oh. Well, who is it then? I know! It's Walter Reedy from Zula. I seen the way he's always a lookin' at you in church.

GERTIE: Lord, no! I ain't never been that hard up.

GAYLA FAYE: Tell me, Gertie.

GERTIE: I cain't. It ain't none a your business any old ways.

GAYLA FAYE: [*Laughing.*] Gertie's got a fella. Gertie's got a fella.

GERTIE: Hush up. You ain't got a lick a sense in you sometimes. I'm glad my brother didn't get hitched up with you. You ain't nothin' but a trollop. Hush that laughin'!

GAYLA FAYE: [*Pressing* **GERTIE**'s *hand against her abdomen.*] You feel that, Gertie? Just that little bump that's a swimmin' in there? That's life, Gert.

Right inside a me. They's a tryin' to take it away from me. Makin' me marry a old man what cain't even get hard half a the time 'cause he's too old to remember what livin's like. I got life inside a me, a swimmin' 'round and a waitin' to come out. I'm full of it, and there ain't nobody what's a goin' to take it away from me. Nobody. I can feel ever little change a happenin' to me. My stomach a swellin' and my paps a gettin' fuller—ever inch a me is changin' this very minute—ever inch a me's a livin' and nobody but me cain't even see it. Now, if that damns me, so be it—I'm a sinner and a trollop and a no-good whore, but you know what? I'm sure a goin' to have me a good time on the way to Hell. Now come on, Gertie. You can tell me. I told you enough. You done you some kissin' now, ain't you? I can see it in your face. Tell me, what's it feel like? It's just like fire, like I told you last summer. You can feel that heat all over your body when he kisses you, cain't you? Fire a lickin' at your legs and then a travellin' up inside a you. You can feel it, too, cain't you.

GERTIE: Shut up.

GAYLA FAYE: You ain't never been in love, Gertie. You's too scared a the Devil for lovin'.

GERTIE: I made it all up. I's tellin' you a tall tale so's you wouldn't think I's backwards.

GAYLA FAYE: [*Sympathetic.*] Don't you worry, Gert. It'll happen to you one a these days. You'll find yourself a sittin' at this old table a stringin' popcorn and a singin' Christmas carols while life's a kickin' at your belly. You's young yet; it'll happen.

GERTIE: [*Halfheartedly.*] Maybe.

GAYLA FAYE: It will, Gert, and it'll be your secret—all a that life swelled up inside a you a waitin' to break loose. It'll be your secret—all a that life.

Scene 5

Lights rise to later that night. Somewhere on the mountain. **JUNIOR** *enters walking quickly followed by* **GAYLA FAYE** *carrying a small suitcase.*

GAYLA FAYE: Why are you a runnin'? Cain't we take our time'n enjoy the night?

JUNIOR: They's a million other nights ahead a us, Gayla Faye. I'm a hurryin' 'cause I want to get outta here'n start our new life. I want to get there quick and forget everthing else that's come before you'n me.

GAYLA FAYE: You know your daddy ain't never a goin' to forgive us for this, Junior. You know that, don't you?

JUNIOR: I reckon I do.

GAYLA FAYE: Can you live with me a knowin' we done went and broke your daddy's heart?

JUNIOR: That baby's mine, ain't it?

GAYLA FAYE: Yes.

JUNIOR: Then I guess you can stop a askin' me questions.

GAYLA FAYE: I just don't want you to do nothin' you cain't live with.

JUNIOR: I can live with just about anything nowadays, Gayla Faye. Stop a worryin' and come on.

GAYLA FAYE: [*Not moving.*] Junior?

JUNIOR: Come on!

GAYLA FAYE: Why me? I thought you's in love with Gertie. Why'd you pick me?

JUNIOR: 'Cause God told me you's the one.

GAYLA FAYE: Be serious, Junior.

JUNIOR: [*Seriously.*] I had a dream that night you come into my room— I was at the crick a fishin', and a catchin' catfish one right after the other, and I's a slappin' them fish on the ground just as quick as I could get the first one off the hook. I's a havin' me a high old time 'til I pulled me out a big one that had the longest whiskers you ever saw. Then that darn fish started a talkin'. Said he's ready to make me a deal. He told me to throw my line one more time, and I did. This time though, I didn't pull up no fish. I pulled up a woman what had gills and could breathe underwater. I threw her on the pile and she started a writhin' and a twistin' and all a them fish turned into women. They's a layin' on the bank like that, all pushed up together and naked. I got me a hoe—I don't know where it come from— and I started trying to cut 'em up, you know like a snake? But ever time I cut one in half, two'd grow back. I's scared to death and a screamin'. Then I woke up and you's a standin' over me with the moon behind you from the window. You looked just like a angel with a halo a standin' there like that. That's when God told me you's the one. [*He grabs her and kisses her hard.*] Now come on, girl. Let's get a movin' 'fore Daddy and Sister Rankin figure it out. [*He pulls her offstage.*]

Scene 6

Lights rise to morning of the next day. **GERTIE** *enters dragging a small Christmas tree.*

GERTIE: Come on, Susannah! Keep a movin'—we's almost there.

SUSANNAH: [*Entering with axe.*] I'm a tryin', Gertie. I just don't feel too good today.

GERTIE: What's wrong with you? You been peaked all week.

SUSANNAH: I don't know, Gertie. I just had a awful sour stomach lately.

GERTIE: Maybe we ought to take you to town to see Dr. Mason. He fixed my arm good when I broke it a totin' wood.

SUSANNAH: I don't think we need to do that. I must a just ate somethin' didn't agree with me, that's all. It'll go away. I'm sure on it. 'Sides, what if we run into Sister Rankin again? What're you a goin' to tell her about us not a goin' to meetin' no more? We's a runnin' out a excuses, Gertie.

GERTIE: If'n she don't quit comin' 'round and botherin' me, I'm a goin' to tell her the truth and see what she thinks a that.

SUSANNAH: [*Shocked.*] You cain't do that. Why, she'd die of a fit or some-thin'. 'Sides, you promised me you'd never tell nobody.

GERTIE: I won't tell her nothin'; I don't break promises, but she nigh about dares a body to tell her what she sure don't want to hear. 'Sides, she wouldn't believe it noways. She'd just tell everbody we done went and got the Devil inside a us. It wouldn't be worth it. [**GERTIE** *picks up end of tree.*]

SUSANNAH: We could go to the Pentecost church 'stead a the Holiness if'n you want to go.

GERTIE: I ain't set on church right now, Susannah. Don't seem right to go somehow.

SUSANNAH: [*Softly.*] Why not, Gertie?

GERTIE: What do you mean, "Why not?"

SUSANNAH: Is it because a what happened to me? 'Cause that was done by a preacher, Gertie, not God. I don't want to have soured you on God. You's too much of a Christian for that.

GERTIE: Help me get this tree into the house.

SUSANNAH: Or is it somethin' else?

GERTIE: What else could it be? I ain't a goin' to church right now 'cause I don't want to is all.

SUSANNAH: But you told me you ain't never missed a day a church in your life till Waincey left. All churches ain't the same, Gertie. Just 'cause one man done wrong, don't mean church is bad.

GERTIE: Well, our'n is, and it's the only one I ever knowed. I ain't a goin' back. Now, I want to get this dang burned Christmas tree in the house. [*They enter cabin and put tree in stand.*] Brrr. It's cold in here. It's colder in here than it is outside. I never could understand how the house could be colder than the darn air. [**SUSANNAH** *moves to* **GERTIE** *and wraps her in her arms.*]

SUSANNAH: Don't that feel better? I got some heat in these old arms to keep you warm. See? That's better, ain't it? [**GERTIE** *leaves her embrace and sorts through decorations in box.*]

GERTIE: I got to get this started. Why don't you get some coal from the bin, and put it in the stove?

SUSANNAH: [*Pause.*] All right, Gertie. [*She exits cabin and fills coal bucket. She re-enters cabin and shovels coal into stove.*] That'll make us warmer.

GERTIE: [*Absently.*] Should do the trick. [**SUSANNAH** *crosses to* **GERTIE** *and tries to embrace her again.*]

SUSANNAH: I like the other way, though, don't you?

GERTIE: [*Breaking away.*] Susannah! It's daytime. Don't be a doin' stuff like that in the daylight. I done told you a hundred times.

SUSANNAH: Why not, Gertie? It ain't like we got nosy next-door neighbors now is it? The closest people's three or four miles away. Who's a goin' to see us?

GERTIE: You never know who's a goin' to sneak up on you. Wasn't Junior a waitin' on us that day we come back from the crick a drippin' wet, and didn't Sister Rankin come out a nowheres and catch him and me a kissin'? You never know.

SUSANNAH: You never told me you and Junior's a kissin' when she come.

GERTIE: I told you he come to ask me to marry him, didn't I?

SUSANNAH: Yes, but you never told me you's a kissin' on him.

GERTIE: Well, it didn't mean nothin', Susannah. It's so no account, I forgot all 'bout it. 'Sides, I's real confused 'bout my life that day.

SUSANNAH: You kissed him since?

GERTIE: I ain't even seen him since he got baptized. How'm I a goin' to be a kissin' on somebody I ain't even seen? Don't be foolish, Susannah.

SUSANNAH: Well, it was daylight when you's a kissin' on Junior, now wasn't it?

GERTIE: It surely was, and I got caught! I almost had to marry that boy 'cause Sister Rankin caught us a kissin'.

SUSANNAH: [*Laughing.*] Is that it? Are you afeared you's a goin' to have to marry me?

GERTIE: [*Seriously.*] No, Susannah. I'm afeared they's a goin' to try and take you away from me.

SUSANNAH: Oh, Gertie. We ain't a doin' nothin' wrong.

GERTIE: Then how come we don't want to tell nobody 'bout it? When other girls is in love that's all they seem to do—walk around a tellin' everbody what'll listen how much they's in love. [*Pause.*] I want to believe they ain't nothin' wrong with us, Susannah. I surely do. But I ain't never heard tell 'bout no together women like us, have you? Have you heard tell of any other women that lives together like us? I'd surely like to know if'n you did.

SUSANNAH: I ain't, Gertie. But I never heard on it a bein' no sin neither. Did you?

GERTIE: Not that I can remember. But what if it's a sin nobody ain't never thought on before? What if it is? My life feels so different, so good, Susannah. I don't want to know.

SUSANNAH: I feel different, too. I ain't never felt nothin' like this before now—where I cain't get enough of somebody, where I work with 'em all day and sleep with 'em all night, and I cain't stand the five or six minutes we got to be apart. It ain't a sin to feel this good. We ain't a sinnin' far as I can see.

GERTIE: But those men got me scairt, Susannah.

SUSANNAH: What men?

GERTIE: The men in the story a Lot.

SUSANNAH: What men you a talkin' 'bout?

GERTIE: Those men in the town what banged on the door and wanted to "know" the angels. Did they just want to make friends like? Don't seem like the Lord would a destroyed a whole town if'n they only wanted to get to know 'em better. What if "know" meant they wanted to . . . wanted to . . . well, you know.

SUSANNAH: I don't believe that story no more, Gertie. I don't believe nothin' 'bout it. I think Preacher made it up.

GERTIE: Why would you think on it that way?

SUSANNAH: So's he could tell us how sinful women is.

GERTIE: But didn't you say you looked it up in the Bible? Didn't old Harold read it to you out loud?

SUSANNAH: Well, yeah . . .

GERTIE: Then Brother Rankin couldn't a made it up, now could he.

SUSANNAH: I reckon not. But maybe it weren't no true story to begin with. Maybe the man that went and wrote that story's just like Delmer Rankin. Maybe he's a evil man, too, and he wanted to keep the women in their'n place by a tellin' 'em how evil that women's always been. Maybe that man had his own reasons like Preacher does. I don't think that story's true at all.

GERTIE: But God wrote the Bible, Susannah. You know that.

SUSANNAH: I know that's what we've always been told, Gertie. But are you sure? Seems to me God's been too busy a creatin' the world and a plannin' disasters and miracles and such to set himself down and write a big book like the Bible. I'd bet on it. The Lord must a sent some a them men a vision or somethin' and said, "It's time to write the word a God." I don't think they could a come up with it on their own—why, they didn't even have them schoolhouses back then. Maybe somewheres, sometime, this man that wrote the story a Lot snuck his old tale in for his own reasons. He's just like Preacher—he wanted us to think that we's a goin' to always be evil. I don't think God thought up that story, Gertie. Sounds like somethin' old Satan sat around with all the other fallen angels and thought up. Maybe the Devil came to those men and said he's the Lord and for them to write down that story. You cain't change your whole life on it. God couldn't think a somethin' that evil. Evil takes the Devil and people who's a goin' to listen to him.

GERTIE: Maybe you're right, Susannah. But you forgot the one sin we's sure of.

SUSANNAH: [*Getting angry.*] Which one's that? The one where we ain't a goin' to church no more, or the one where we's in love?

GERTIE: The one where I'm a layin' with my brother's wife. You forgot that one, Susannah.

SUSANNAH: You are bound and determined to make us a sin some way, ain't you?

GERTIE: Adultery is a sin. I'm sure a that one.

SUSANNAH: Me and Waincey ain't really married, Gertie. We ain't never been together. Lord, he left the mornin' after the marryin', and you know I stayed in bed with you on my weddin' night. We ain't had no chance't to even get to know nothin' 'bout each other.

GERTIE: But, you got the ceremony outta the way, didn't you? You said, "I do." You's married in the sight a God whether you know each other or not.

SUSANNAH: No we ain't, Gertie.

GERTIE: Susannah, I stood there and witnessed it myself. I saw you'ns do it. You cain't tell me I dreamed it up.

SUSANNAH: You saw us get married all right, but who married us?

GERTIE: Brother Rankin.

SUSANNAH: That's why we ain't really married. That man ain't a man a God, and it don't count. I ain't married 'cause the Devil whispered the service, and that ain't no true marriage.

GERTIE: Waincey thinks you's married. Don't he write stuff to you in his letters from the service and call you his wife?

SUSANNAH: He does, but he's a good man. I can tell from his face—the way he looks all tender when he's a talkin' to you 'bout somethin' you don't want to hear—and soon as he gets home from service, I'm a goin' to tell him why I ain't his proper wife. He'll understand, Gertie. Waincey is a good man.

GERTIE: He is a good man, Susannah, but you got to figure, he ain't a *perfect* man. What if he thinks what we been a doin' is a sin? What if it is a sin? He surely won't let sinnin' go on.

SUSANNAH: Then we'll leave here, Gertie. You can tell him that you love him, and that you'll surely miss him, but what we done gone and found ain't a goin' to be nothin' nobody's a goin' to make us do without. We'll go somewheres else is all.

GERTIE: Why is the answer that we got to leave our home? I just don't figure on it. Why do we always got to leave here to get what we want? Waincey said it first, and now you're a sayin' it too.

SUSANNAH: I ain't said no such thing. I just said if'n Waincey don't hold no truck with us, then we'll just have to go somewheres else. If, Gertie, only if.

GERTIE: I just don't see where leavin's a goin' to solve all the problems we done made for ourselves.

SUSANNAH: You think on me as a problem, Gertie? I sure don't want to be a problem to nobody.

GERTIE: Course I don't think on you like that. You know what I mean.

SUSANNAH: I don't. You don't want nothin' to do with me 'cept when it's dark and nobody cain't see—even me—or God. You think God cain't a see what we's a doin', Gertie? Is that what you think?

GERTIE: Don't be heathern, Susannah. You know God can see and hear everthing he wants to. You know that same as me.

SUSANNAH: Well then, if'n what we's a doin' is a sin—why ain't God struck us down yet?

GERTIE: I don't know.

SUSANNAH: You're afeared a joy is all. You're scairt a feelin' this good. Sister Rankin's done convinced you feelin' good's a sin.

GERTIE: That ain't true. That crazy, old woman ain't convinced me a nothin'.

SUSANNAH: Well that's who you're a actin' like. [*Parodying* **SISTER RANKIN.**] Everthing's a sin, Gertie Cobb. Everthing. Why sin is in the air we breathe to stay alive.

GERTIE: How'd you know she told me that?

SUSANNAH: She does that "Sin is like coal dust in the air, and we cain't help but breath it in" speech for everbody—and she's done convinced you it's the truth. I don't care if it is. I'm a takin' deep breaths now. Deep! I want to breathe it all in 'cause it feels so wonderful. Stand with me, Gertie. Take a deep breath! [**SUSANNAH** *stands breathing deeply, audibly and defiantly.*]

GERTIE: Stop it, Susannah! You're a goin' to make yourself faint if'n you don't stop a breathin' that a way.

SUSANNAH: Only if you're a feared a livin', Gertie. Only then. I'll walk off a this mountain a holdin' your hand anytime you want me to. We can start us a new life somewhere so far out in the woods, or so closed in in the city that nobody will ever pay us no nevermind. But you got to want to hold my hand. You're a goin' to have to want to come with me. You have to want to take deep breaths. You want that? Or are you too worried we's a goin' to offend the Lord or one of the tranced-out holy rollers that have done claimed Him for their own? God ain't offended by love, Gertie, but maybe you are . . . [*Pause.*] Or maybe you ain't really in love. Is that it?

GERTIE: You know that ain't it, Susannah. I love you so much it makes my heart ache to look on you. I'm afeared a losin' you if anybody's to find out how much I love you. I want to hold your hand, Susannah. You know I love you.

SUSANNAH: Then show me, Gertie. Right here. Right now, with the sun a shinin' on our faces. Show me in front a God that you love me. Show me. [**SUSANNAH** *takes* **GERTIE** *into an embrace, and they kiss.*]

SISTER RANKIN: [*Offstage.*] Gertie? Gertie! Come on outta there! I got news! [**GERTIE** *breaks from* **SUSANNAH** *guiltily and stands in fear.* **SUSANNAH** *starts to exit into bedroom, but is stopped when she sees* **GERTIE** *wiping her mouth.*]

SUSANNAH: [*Hurt.*] It don't show, Gertie. She cain't tell by lookin' at you.

GERTIE: [*Impatiently.*] Go in there and get straightened up. [**SUSANNAH** *waits at door until* **SISTER RANKIN** *is at doorway. She gives* **SISTER RANKIN** *a cold look and then exits into bedroom.* **GERTIE** *stealthily streaks flour on her face, and exits doorway to join* **SISTER RANKIN**.]

SISTER RANKIN: I got some news for youn's.

GERTIE: Hi, there, Josephine.

SISTER RANKIN: Where you been? I been a callin' since the bluff.

GERTIE: I's bakin' some biscuits. I had to get the flour off a me. What news you brung?

SISTER RANKIN: Waincey's a comin' home tonight.

GERTIE: What? Is he all right? What happened?

SISTER RANKIN: I don't know, Gert. They come a telegram for you to Redenair's store. Old Harold brung it to me 'cause he thought somethin' might be wrong. I did, too, so's I opened it. Here. [*She thrusts a piece of yellow paper at* **GERTIE.**]

GERTIE: [*Reading.*] Gertie. Stop. Brother on train. Stop. Arrive Zula, 9:42 p.m. Tuesday. Stop. That's it?

SISTER RANKIN: That's it.

GERTIE: You sure they wasn't no other piece but this?

SISTER RANKIN: I'm sure. You want to walk in with me?

GERTIE: No. I reckon me'n Susannah'll walk it in a while. Can we get a ride from town to the station when we'ns get there?

SISTER RANKIN: Surely. I'll get Delmer to hitch up the team.

GERTIE: All right. I guess we'll be there in a hour or so.

SISTER RANKIN: [*Softly.*] Gertie?

GERTIE: Yes, ma'am?

SISTER RANKIN: Don't worry. I ain't a goin' to tell on you.

GERTIE: [*Shaken.*] Tell what?

SISTER RANKIN: That you ain't a been comin' to church. I know you's a good girl even if you done strayed with Junior. The Lord'll take you back in and take care a you.

GERTIE: Junior? I ain't seen hide nor hair a Junior since that day he got baptized. I swear it, Sister Rankin.

SISTER RANKIN: You sure? Ain't nobody seen him since last night. We's a thinkin' he's done run off to build your weddin' house. You sure you ain't seen him?

GERTIE: I swear. I ain't seen him since that day.

SISTER RANKIN: Well, I'll be. I'm a goin to have to run by Senior's and see if Gayla Faye's outta the bed yet. I stopped by this mornin', but Senior said she's feelin' poorly and a sleepin' in. You girls hurry up now.

GERTIE: Yes, ma'am. [**SISTER RANKIN** *exits quickly.* **GERTIE** *collapses on the stump.* **SUSANNAH** *exits bedroom, peaks through window, and then joins* **GERTIE** *outside.*]

SUSANNAH: Well, did she talk you into goin' to meetin' tomorrow night?

GERTIE: No. To the train station in Zula in about a hour.

SUSANNAH: The train station? Why on Earth would she want you to go to the station in Zula?

GERTIE: Both a us got to go, Susannah. Not just me. Both a us.

SUSANNAH: Why?

GERTIE: To pick up Waincey.

SUSANNAH: [*Startled.*] What?

GERTIE: Waincey's a comin' home, Susannah. Tonight.

SUSANNAH: You sure?

GERTIE: Go get dressed. You'll want to look purty for your husband.

SUSANNAH: Gertie?

GERTIE: Go get dressed, Susannah. We ain't got no time left. [**SUSANNAH**

exits. **GERTIE** *resumes chant from Act I.*] I ain't a sinner. You couldn't love a sinner. You ain't a sinner. I couldn't love a sinner. We ain't sinners 'cause God cain't love sinners. [*Pause.*] Oh Lord, watch over us tonight. I know you's busy. I do. But we's a goin' to need you, Lord. Me and Susannah and Waincey. Be merciful.

END OF ACT II

ACT III
Scene 1

Set must be converted to train station platform. Lights rise to weak moonlight. **GERTIE, SUSANNAH,** *and* **SISTER RANKIN** *are standing on platform waiting for the train. We hear the roar of the train and its whistle. A spotlight shines in from off stage as if the train has stopped further down the line. It is cold. The wind howls as the three stand shivering on the platform in worn coats. A* **MAN** *enters carrying crates and crosses in front of the platform.*

GERTIE: 'Scuse me, Sir? Why're they a stopping way down there?

MAN: They's a loadin' the coal, I reckon. [*He exits.*]

GERTIE: Oh.

SUSANNAH: Maybe we done got the wrong train, or the wrong day or somethin'. Ain't nobody else out here anyways.

GERTIE: Telegram said 9:42 on Tuesday. That's it.

SISTER RANKIN: There he is! There's Waincey! He's a walkin' this a way now.

GERTIE: Why's he got them sticks?

SUSANNAH: Looks like he's hurt. Go get him, Gertie. [**GERTIE** *runs off toward the light.*]

SISTER RANKIN: [*Pause.*] Susannah?

SUSANNAH: Yes'm?

SISTER RANKIN: Is there anything you'd like to tell me 'fore Gertie gets back with your husband?

SUSANNAH: [*Softly.*] No, ma'am.

SISTER RANKIN: [*Turning* **SUSANNAH** *to face her.*] Why ain't you and Gertie been a comin' to meetin'?

SUSANNAH: 'Cause Gertie didn't want to go.

SISTER RANKIN: And why's that? Come on honey, you can tell me.

SUSANNAH: [*Softly.*] I cain't tell you nothin' that you don't already know.

SISTER RANKIN: Well, if'n I knowed already, I wouldn't be a askin', now would I?

SUSANNAH: [*Firmer.*] Leave it be, Josephine. Leave it be.

SISTER RANKIN: [*Changing tactics.*] The Lord come to me yesterday evenin' and told me there's been somethin' evil a goin' on up at the Cobb house.

SUSANNAH: [*Hard.*] You been a lightin' bushes on fire again, Josephine?

SISTER RANKIN: Don't be heathern. Why are you a stoppin' Gertie from a comin to meetin'?

SUSANNAH: I ain't a keepin' Gertie from nothin'. Now leave it be!

SISTER RANKIN: [*Getting excited.*] Why are you a denyin' that sweet girl the love and light of God?

SUSANNAH: [*Angry.*] What light? What God? Your God's a liar. [*Whispering.*] Now, hush up, you silly, old woman. [**SUSANNAH** *turns away from her and looks toward train* **SISTER RANKIN** *grabs her by the arm and spins her around.*]

SISTER RANKIN: I don't know what you done to Gertie, but I knowed you's evil from the first time I laid eyes on you. Showin' up at my house a bangin' on the door in the middle of the night!

SUSANNAH: Daddy had done beat me, Sister Rankin. I told you that.

SISTER RANKIN: [*In righteous full voice.*] I knowed your dress was teared a little, and your hair was a mess, but there weren't a bruise nor scrape on you nowheres, girl. [*Mean and threatening, but softer.*] He didn't beat you, or if'n he did you probably deserved it. Purty girl like you's just a askin' for trouble a stayin' in a house with a full growed man and no wife around.

SUSANNAH: He is my daddy. I weren't askin' for nothin' but a safe place to sleep when I come to your door. I didn't get nothin' I *asked for*, and you and me both know it.

SISTER RANKIN: [*Angry.*] What's that supposed to mean, girl?

SUSANNAH: Search your *Christian* heart, woman. You know what I'm a talkin' 'bout. You can fool any of the others you want, but we both know what happened in your house. We know why you had to go to town that mornin'.

SISTER RANKIN: You're touched. I don't know what you're a talkin' 'bout.

SUSANNAH: You cain't stand to hear 'em a cryin' and a callin' out the Lord's name, can you Sister? So's you get yourself outta that house while Delmer's a sacrificin' angels and a callin' 'em "Children a Eve." You cain't stand for Lot to already count you as a pillar a salt while he's a layin' with his daughters.

SISTER RANKIN: [*Livid and shaking* **SUSANNAH.**] Shut up, you harlot! You're a talkin' with the Devil's tongue.

SUSANNAH: [*Struggling to free herself.*] Don't you touch me. [*She pushes* **SISTER RANKIN** *to the ground.*] You know what he's been a doin', and you'd rather run to Redenair's store than hear them a cryin'.

SISTER RANKIN: [*Clutching her chest.*] You've done lost it, girl. You don't know what you're a sayin'. You've done gone and tainted Gertie with your Devil's lies, ain't you? You're a witch! Is that why she ain't been a comin' to church? You've done witched her! I knew you's evil from the first minute I laid eyes on you. Kneel and pray with me, girl. It's the only way. Kneel and pray! [*She clutches chest with one hand and extends the other to* **SUSANNAH**.] Kneel! Testify your sins unto the Lord.

SUSANNAH: [*Keeping her distance.*] I don't have to kneel to testify, Josephine. [*Looking straight at* **SISTER RANKIN** *throughout the monologue.*] I've always walked a narra path, Lord. I've kept to myself, dirty and lonely since I's thirteen so's Harlan wouldn't notice me. I took to sleepin' in the chicken coop after Momma died so's I'd smell so bad he couldn't want me. I only run off that one night, Lord, 'cause Harlan tried to force me, dirt and stink and all. And where did I run, Lord? To your servant's house to be safe. They took me in, Lord, and gave me a bed for the night. Next mornin' early, your servant come into my room, "I've come to help you repent," he said. Then he slid into the bed. He put his hand upon me. He forced me to touch him. He made me pray twixt his legs. He held my head down and made me say his prayer. [*Angry parody of the experience.*] Lord, I take you into my mouth to sanctify. Lord, you are my master and my maker. Lord, I am a child of Eve. I am daughter bound to honor my Father. I am a wicked woman who must be cleansed. [*Accusing.*] You run off to town, Josephine. You knew what was a goin' to happen. You knew.

SISTER RANKIN: [*Agitated and bordering on hysteria—whispering.*] Hush up, girl! You're outta your head. You don't know what you're a sayin'.

SUSANNAH: I know what I'm a doin' just like you knowed what you's doin' when you got dressed and went to town. [*Pointing her finger at* **SISTER RANKIN** *and spitting.*] I curse you, old woman. I curse you for bein' quiet. I wait for God's vengeance to visit you in the middle of the night. Your silence is the sin. You knew what he was a doin', and you didn't do nothin' 'bout it. [*Kneeling.*] I curse you as God curses a liar and a thief to eternal damnation. You lie to everbody—you ain't no Christian—and you help him by bein' quiet. You help him to sin. I damn you to the hell you've done made for yourself. I curse you.

SISTER RANKIN: [*Desperate.*] You cain't do that. You ain't the Lord. You cain't curse anybody.

SUSANNAH: I curse you.

SISTER RANKIN: [*Wailing.*] Take it back! TAKE IT BACK! [*Pause.*] I couldn't look back. I couldn't say nothin'. The fire of the Lord would a burned my eyes. I couldn't look back. I didn't leave, Susannah. I heard him a goin' into your room whiles't I's still in the bed. "Confess. Confess, Susannah," I heard him say, then I heard the springs on that old mattress give way. "Confess." I snuck up to the door. I listened, but I couldn't look. I would a been burned to nothin'. What could I a done? I stood there long as I could bear it. I had to get dressed; then I snuck out back and came in when I heard him on the stairs. What could I a done? The Lord gave the handmaiden Hagar to Abraham, and his wife, Sarah, didn't say nothin'. Sarah didn't say nothin'. What could I do, Susannah? I couldn't look. I would a been turned to salt. [*She is sobbing hysterically and begins rocking and talking in tongues.*] Appa nay any. CRASHMAYTA! Rroooootsa, somba kay lie me day sot!

SUSANNAH: [*Hard and cold.*] It ain't a goin' to work with me, Josephine. Ain't no baby talk a goin' to fix your sin. You are a SINNER.

SISTER RANKIN: [*Clutching chest.*] GREEEE! Dea, reeeek a swayt lay! [*Weakly.*] Deag me tay! [*Weaker still.*] Say no, say no more. [*She dies quietly.*]

GERTIE: [*Offstage.*] Susannah, I need some help with . . . [*Entering.*] Oh my Lord! [*She kneels and tries to revive* **SISTER RANKIN.**] What's wrong with her? What happened? Oh my God. Get somebody! SUSANNAH! Go and get somebody!

SUSANNAH: She's dead, Gertie.

GERTIE: What happened?

SUSANNAH: I don't know, Gertie. I don't know. I think she . . . I don't know.

GERTIE: Oh my God. [**GERTIE** *cradles* **SISTER RANKIN**'*s head in her lap and begins to rock. Lights begin to fade.*] Our Father, who art in Heaven . . .

Scene 2

The next morning. **SUSANNAH** *is seated at table drinking coffee. She is dressed in a long flannel nightgown and heavy socks. Her hair is a mess. She is crying softly.* **GERTIE** *enters from bedroom dressed in black.* **GERTIE** *walks to stove and pours herself a cup of coffee.*

GERTIE: Susannah? Why ain't you dressed yet? It's almost time for the viewin'.

SUSANNAH: I cain't go, Gertie. I just cain't. I been a sittin' here since early this mornin' a tryin' to tell mysef I got to go, but I just cain't do it.

GERTIE: Susannah, this ain't like skippin' church. We got to go, or people's a goin' to start talkin' for sure.

SUSANNAH: Talkin' 'bout what, Gertie? 'Bout you and me? They ain't a goin' to know 'bout you and me just 'cause Josephine Rankin keeled over dead at the train station.

GERTIE: No, not us. Not that at all. I ain't worried 'bout that.

SUSANNAH: What then?

GERTIE: Well, we's the last ones with her. It's a goin' to look a might queer if'n we don't go into town for the viewin'.

SUSANNAH: I cain't go, Gertie. Tell 'em I'm too worked up 'bout seein' her die in a fit like that.

GERTIE: Is that what's a botherin' you?

SUSANNAH: That's a part of it.

GERTIE: What's the rest of it then?

SUSANNAH: Oh, Gertie, you's such a young'n sometimes.

GERTIE: I ain't.

SUSANNAH: I've done ruint you, Gertie. Go on to town.

GERTIE: I don't want to go without you.

SUSANNAH: [*Hard.*] Well, when you grow up you'll figure out sometimes wantin' don't make a bit a difference. Now, go on.

GERTIE: [*Taking* **SUSANNAH**'*s face in her hands.*] Wantin' makes all the difference. It changes your life.

SUSANNAH: [*Quietly.*] Not always for the better, it don't. [**GERTIE** *looks into her face for a long beat. She bends forward and kisses her on the corner of the mouth—almost on the cheek. Although this is not a sexual kiss, it should be filled with longing.*]

GERTIE: Always for the better, Susannah, 'cause not a wantin' means you's dead and gone, and I want to be a livin'.

WAINCEY: [*Entering noisily on crutches from bedroom.*] Mornin'. What's for breakfast? I am truly hungry this a mornin'.

SUSANNAH: They's some biscuits on the stove I cooked early this a mornin'. They's some sweet butter, too. I ain't made no more'n that. I'm sorry, Waincey. I ain't used to a man bein' in the house and a needin' to get fed. I'll make you some eggs, if'n you want 'em.

WAINCEY: Biscuits is fine, Susannah. These look like a feast after what I been a eatin' on in the Navy. [*There is an uneasy silence while he eats at the stove.*]

GERTIE: Susannah ain't a feelin' good this mornin', Waincey. She's a goin' to stay here 'stead a goin' to the viewin'. You and me can walk it though.

WAINCEY: You all right, Susannah? What's ailin' you?

SUSANNAH: It ain't nothin', Waincey. I just ain't a feelin' up to it.

WAINCEY: Well, I don't reckon Sister Rankin'll mind.

SUSANNAH: I don't reckon she will. [**SUSANNAH** *begins crying and gets up and exits into bedroom.* **WAINCEY** *and* **GERTIE** *stand looking at each other for a beat.*]

WAINCEY: That poor, old critter. She's a takin' it purty hard, ain't she?

GERTIE: I s'pose so. [*Pause.*] You ready to go?

WAINCEY: Nah. My leg's a hurtin' a might this mornin'. You go on. I'll keep Susannah company and come to the service tomorrow.

GERTIE: But don't you want to come to the viewin'?

WAINCEY: I reckon I done seen me enough dead people to last me a whiles't. You go on ahead.

GERTIE: But people's a goin' to think you and Susannah stayed home 'cause you . . .

WAINCEY: 'Cause a what, Gertie?

GERTIE: 'Cause you want to . . . you know . . .

WAINCEY: She's my wife, Gertie. It's only natural for me to want to take care of her. [*Pause. Harder.*] You go on now. And quit a worryin' 'bout people so much. You ain't a been too worried 'bout 'em whiles't I's gone, or you'd a been to meetin' more.

GERTIE: Who's been a talkin'?

WAINCEY: Quit a worryin'; it won't do nothin' but make you a worrywart. Go on, now. [**GERTIE** *looks at him and then exits.* **WAINCEY** *butters another biscuit and crosses to table to sit.* **SUSANNAH** *enters and walks to stove to pour a cup of coffee.*] How much coffee you drunk since last night, Susannah?

SUSANNAH: Oh, Waincey! You scairt me. I heard the door a closin', and I thought you and Gertie had done gone.

WAINCEY: I didn't mean to startle you none. I'm sorry.

SUSANNAH: You ain't got nothin' to be sorry for. I've drunk a pot or two, I reckon.

WAINCEY: It won't help you. You ought to try and get some sleep.

SUSANNAH: I cain't sleep. I keep a seein' Josephine a fallin' on that platform. I dream I'm a stuck to the ground, and I cain't move a lick to help her. I just see her face a twistin' up and a turnin' blue.

WAINCEY: You got to sleep. Susannah. It'll pass.

SUSANNAH: I ain't so sure.

WAINCEY: I see 'em, too.

SUSANNAH: See who?

WAINCEY: Men a dyin' right in front a me. I couldn't do nothin' but step over 'em and keep a goin'.

SUSANNAH: They's been so much a goin' on, we ain't even asked you how you got hurt over there.

WAINCEY: It ain't much of a story.

SUSANNAH: Well, it's gotta be somethin'.

WAINCEY: I's just a sittin' on deck and everthing was peaceful-like. I was thinkin' on home and a wishin' I's a walkin' in the hills or a scrappin' with Gertie. I's thinkin' on sittin' at the breakfast table a gettin' to know my new wife a might better. I's purty homesick, I reckon. Wasn't a day went by I didn't dream on comin' home. I got to say, Susannah, livin' here sure seems to agree with you. You're a lookin' as purty as a field full a March lilies.

SUSANNAH: [*Laughing.*] And my eyes must look like black-eyed Susans.

WAINCEY: You look just fine to me. [*Pause.*] Well, there I was a sittin' and all of a sudden, I heard a roarin', like a airplane, and I looked around, but they wasn't any fighters up there, so I's confused for a minute. The next thing I knowed, a airplane out a nowheres had done crashed on the long end a the ship.

SUSANNAH: A airplane? Where'd it come from? Did it hit you?

WAINCEY: Nah, that ain't what did it. See, we all jumped up and a started runnin' 'cause we didn't have no kind a warnin' at all. We all run on over to it and was a tryin' to put out the fire it'd done made on the deck.

SUSANNAH: It just fell outta the air from nowheres?

WAINCEY: Not exactly. It was one a them Jap planes.

SUSANNAH: And one a our'n had shot it down?

WAINCEY: No. [*Pause.*] That Jap soldier had crashed his plane into us on purpose.

SUSANNAH: You mean he was a meanin' to crash it like that?

WAINCEY: That's right. And when I's a runnin' up on it, I's one a the first ones to get there, a part a the engine exploded and hit me in the leg purty hard. Doc says I still got a part a that Jap plane inside a my leg.

SUSANNAH: Does it hurt awful bad?

WAINCEY: No so much anymore. The doc said the pain'll go away, but I'm always a goin' to hobble a little. A souvenir from the South Pacific.

SUSANNAH: Why do you think he did it?

WAINCEY: 'Cause they's a noble people.

SUSANNAH: What a you mean?

WAINCEY: See, the Japs'd ruther die than to be dishonored—and they got a whole bunch of 'em thinks they's a goin' to be dishonored if'n the Americans win the war—so they go up in them airplanes and crash 'em on purpose so's they can kill any a us they can, and escape a livin' a life a shame all at the same time.

SUSANNAH: Day!

WAINCEY: They'd ruther die than live the way somebody else wants 'em to. I thought they's crazy at first, but I reckon they's somthin' to be said for a livin' and a dyin' the way you see yourself a doin' it.

SUSANNAH: You know, we's married, and I don't even know your real name.

WAINCEY: [*Embarrassed.*] It's Solomon. Ain't nobody called me that, though, since Momma died.

SUSANNAH: Why do they call you Waincey?

WAINCEY: When I's born, my brother, Jimmy Lee, weren't but about four year old. He told my Daddy that "Solomon" was too big a name for a scrawny runt like me 'cause I weren't no bigger than a "waincey" little pig. The name just stuck, I reckon.

SUSANNAH: That's a funny story.

WAINCEY: Well, most people'd say it's a funny name, but it don't bother me most a the time. I met pigs what's better'n some people.

SUSANNAH: Waincey?

WAINCEY: Yes, ma'am?

SUSANNAH: Them Jap soldiers—you reckon they's happier dead?

WAINCEY: I don't rightly know, Susannah, but one thing's sure—they don't feel no dishonor.

SUSANNAH: You a goin' to the viewin'?

WAINCEY: I will if'n you'll go with me—I need some help a gettin' there.

SUSANNAH: All right. Gimme a couple a minutes to get dressed. [*Pause. She exits into bedroom.*]

WAINCEY: You take all the time you need. I ain't a goin' nowheres. [*Softly.*] I got all the time in the world to sit here and wait for you. [*Full voice.*] Just tell me when you's ready.

Scene 3

The next day. Late afternoon. Lights rise on **GERTIE** *and* **SUSANNAH** *entering front yard. They are dressed for* **SISTER RANKIN**'s *funeral.*

GERTIE: It was a purty service for the winter time, weren't it?

SUSANNAH: I reckon it was purty all right.

GERTIE: What's wrong with you? You ain't half here. You been a actin' odd since that night at the train station.

SUSANNAH: My belly's a botherin' me's all. I just don't feel very good, Gertie. Seems like I been a wantin' to retch for 'bout the last week or so. 'Specially since that night at the train station.

GERTIE: I guess it's hard on you a watchin' her die like that. Don't take it to heart, though. She's nigh 'bout fifty. Don't seem like nobody lives much past that. 'Sides, I think she's still in shock over Junior and Gayla Faye a runnin' off like that.

SUSANNAH: Senior's too old for Gayla Faye. He should a 'spected somethin' like that to happen. Old men shouldn't be a courtin' young'ns.

GERTIE: I 'spect you's right, but it seems double sinful to run off with your husband's son, don't you think?

SUSANNAH: Not if you got the son's baby a swellin' up inside a you. It was wrong for 'em to run off like that, but who're we to be a judgin' somebody else's sinnin'?

GERTIE: What are you a talkin' 'bout?

SUSANNAH: Our sins. You's the one that told me we got 'em.

GERTIE: I only did that 'cause Josephine's a hollerin' in the yard, and I's scairt.

SUSANNAH: You wiped me off'n you, Gertie. You should a never let me come into your life. I ain't nothin' but sin a wallkin' on two legs. You's right to wipe me off'n you like that.

GERTIE: No, I weren't. I weren't right. What's got into you? Two days ago you's a tellin' me that feelin' good weren't no sin—that love couldn't offend the Lord. Just two days ago you's a tellin' me to breathe deep! Now we're sinners a walkin' on two legs? What's different, Susannah? Not a thing. I love you. I'm a goin' to love you no matter what. [*She attempts to embrace* **SUSANNAH**, *but she resists.*]

SUSANNAH: It's daytime, Gertie. Somebody'll see.

GERTIE: So? Who's a goin' to see? They ain't nobody here.

SUSANNAH: What if somebody was to come?

GERTIE: Waincey's off with the men; ain't nobody a goin' to come and you know it.

SUSANNAH: Then, God, Gertie. God's a goin' to see us out here in the daytime.

GERTIE: Just like he's seen us before. He's seen us already, Susannah, and he don't care 'cause we's in love. Didn't you tell me the Lord ain't offended by the sight a love?

SUSANNAH: But that was different.

GERTIE: How? How was it different two days ago?

SUSANNAH: 'Cause I hadn't seen retribution yet, Gertie. I hadn't seen Waincey all twisted up. I hadn't seen Josephine a layin' at my feet dead 'cause I done kilt her. I hadn't seen the sin. I didn't know Satan's a talkin' through me. I know now, Gertie. I know.

GERTIE: I think you's a talkin' in tongues 'cause I can't believe nary a word you's a sayin'.

SUSANNAH: It's all 'cause a me, Gertie. I kilt her. And my sins is what got Waincey wounded.

GERTIE: How?

SUSANNAH: I said Waincey weren't my proper husband 'cause I didn't want it to be that a way. The Lord heard me, Gertie. He heard me, and he sent that Jap plane to crash into Waincey's ship. He sent him home to us crippled 'cause I'm a sinner.

GERTIE: Susannah, you's a actin' the fool. Your words ain't got that much power. Delmer Rankin ain't no man a God—you's right—it weren't no proper marriage. You a sayin' all a that didn't cause Waincey to get hurt.

SUSANNAH: No? Then how'd I kill Sister Rankin with nothin' but my words?

GERTIE: Doctor Mason said she had her a heart attack.

SUSANNAH: I cursed her, Gertie. I accused her a knowin' everthing, I surely did. I cursed her, then she started a talkin' in tongues, and she keeled over dead. I kilt her.

GERTIE: You told her 'bout Delmer?

SUSANNAH: I said her bein' quiet's the worse sin of all. I damned her to Hell, Gertie. I cursed her, and then she died a speakin' in the Lord's tongue.

GERTIE: Susannah, maybe you had it right. Maybe she did know, and she couldn't stand the truth a bein' throwed up to her like that.

SUSANNAH: It don't make no difference whether she knowed or not. She's dead! I cursed her, then she died. Satan's a talkin' through me like he was when Eve said, "Here, Adam. Take a bite a this apple for me." She wouldn't a died if'n I hadn't a had the power of the Devil wrapped up inside a me.

GERTIE: Maybe it was the power a the Lord. You ever think on that?

SUSANNAH: I couldn't pray with her. She begged me to kneel and pray so's she could save my soul. I didn't even think on it. You know the handmaid of the Devil cain't pray. I cursed her. She died a prayin' while'st I couldn't do it.

GERTIE: Hush now, Susannah. [*Hug.*] You're wrong 'bout all a this. You ain't got the power of the Devil inside a you. What happened to Waincey and Sister Rankin, well, that's just the Lord a movin' in mysterious ways like they say. [**GERTIE** *tries to embrace her, but* **SUSANNAH** *pushes her away.*]

SUSANNAH: Don't touch me! You cain't never touch me again, Gertie. I'm damned for eternity, and if'n you touch me again, you's a goin' to be damned, too.

GERTIE: I ain't! Susannah, I love you. I truly love you. We ain't sinners. [*Grabbing her hands.*] Come on, girl. Take a deep breath. Take a deep breath a me and tell me that's a sin. It ain't, Susannah. [**SUSANNAH** *succumbs momentarily, but then pulls aggressively away.*]

SUSANNAH: You know what we's a doin' ain't right, Gertie. You know it same as me, and you's a lettin' the Devil speak through you, too.

GERTIE: You think I'm scairt a some Devil? I ain't scairt a nothin'— Demons or God or what anybody's a goin' to say when I tell 'em I love you. I'm ready to tell it, Susannah. I love you so much, I'm a ready to tell anybody what wants to hear it—I'm a goin' to town right now and start a testifyin' everthing to anybody what'll listen. [**GERTIE** *begins exiting.*]

SUSANNAH: [*Defeated.*] You cain't do that. You cain't bring shame on yourself like that. I ain't worth it. You're a good girl, Gertie. You cain't tell nobody nothin' 'cause you don't know everthing.

GERTIE: What don't I know, Susannah?

SUSANNAH: I'm a goin' to have a baby.

GERTIE: A baby? How long you knowed?

SUSANNAH: A month.

GERTIE: How far along are you?

SUSANNAH: Two months.

GERTIE: But you been with me three. [*Pause.*] Whose is it? Who's the daddy? Is it Harlan? Has he snuck up here a botherin' you? I'll kill him.

SUSANNAH: It ain't Daddy's.

GERTIE: Whose is it, then?

SUSANNAH: Brother Rankin's.

GERTIE: But you told me he never touched you there. You said he made you take it in your mouth.

SUSANNAH: The first time.

GERTIE: You said it was only the once't.

SUSANNAH: I never, Gertie. I just didn't say it's more'n once't. You didn't ask. Delmer had me come to town after ever Sunday service. He told me it's so's we could save my soul—he said if'n I told anybody 'bout it or didn't show up, the Lord would strike me dead. I had to go four times for Waincey married me. I been twice't since I been here.

GERTIE: Why? How could you do that?

SUSANNAH: 'Cause he knows 'bout you and me, and he said he'd tell if'n I didn't come.

GERTIE: How could he know?

SUSANNAH: Junior saw us one a those days down by the crick. He saw us, and then he went and told Delmer all 'bout it.

GERTIE: Why didn't you tell me?

SUSANNAH: I's afeared a losin' you, Gertie. Satan had a hold on me, and I's a tryin' not to listen to the Lord. I wanted you. I wanted you to be with me forever. I listened to Satan when he said, "Take what you want, girl. Take what you want. You ain't never a goin' to feel this good again." I did it, Gertie. I went to town in the night, and I did whatever he told me so's I wouldn't have to give you up.

GERTIE: You cain't be blamed for a tryin' to protect me. You cain't be blamed for that.

SUSANNAH: I can, Gertie. Everbody's a goin' to see it when this baby starts a showin'. Everbody's a goin' to know that I'm a sinner. I ain't worried 'bout God forgivin' you 'cause you's so good, but people's not that forgivin'. They don't got to know nothin' 'bout you, though. They don't got to know nothin' 'bout the two a us together.

GERTIE: What're we a goin' to tell Waincey?

SUSANNAH: We ain't a goin' to tell him nothin'. I'm a goin' to tell him 'bout the baby, and wait for his reckonin'. You're a goin' to act like nothin' happened. You're a goin' to forget the sin we done committed. You can still be clean, Gertie.

GERTIE: I cain't do that. You're a part a me now. I cain't let you go just 'cause you's a tryin' to keep me from harm.

SUSANNAH: You got to, Gertie, or it's all a goin' to be for nothin'. You got to let it go. I ain't a goin' to sin no more. I'm a goin' to talk to Waincey, and then I'm a goin' to stay or leave whatever he says, but I aint' a goin' to lay with you in his house no more. If'n he wants me to stay, a knowin' 'bout the baby, it's time I started actin' like a wife to him.

GERTIE: You cain't do it, Susannah. How're you a goin' to give me up and us all a livin' in the same house? How're you a goin' to look at me ever day and not touch me? How'm I a goin' to watch you a goin' off to bed with my brother? I love you. We cain't do it. I cain't do it. You love me, Susannah. The sin's a goin' to be in denyin' that you love me. You cain't do it.

SUSANNAH: [*Coldly.*] I don't love you no more, Gertie. Not like that.

GERTIE: Lyin's a sin, Susannah.

SUSANNAH: That's why I don't do it.

GERTIE: You love me. You said you's never a goin' to stop lovin' me.

SUSANNAH: Well, I did. You stop it now, too, Gertie. Stop it. Do it for yourself. Save yourself. I'm a goin' to.

GERTIE: You cain't do it—we got names—I'm Gertie and you're Susannah. We ain't a story some old man done wrote and snuck into the Bible. We're REAL. This story is real. We ain't daughters no more. We's full-growed women that love each other. You're Susannah, and I'm Gertie, and we love each other. You cain't hide us on this mountain and make us do whatever they tell us is right. You cain't hide us like a secret; you cain't make us blank. We got names. We got faces. You cain't do it. I'm a goin' to find Waincey right now and tell him the truth! [**GERTIE** *runs off.*]

SUSANNAH: Don't, Gertie! You cain't. Please . . . don't.

GERTIE: We got names—we got faces! I love you, Susannah.

SUSANNAH: Gertie! GERTIE! [**SUSANNAH** *stands there sobbing. She slowly calms down and begins to remove her shoes and dress until she stands there in only her shift. She leaves her clothes lying on the stage and exits toward the creek.*]

Scene 4

Three days later. Dim morning light rises to hilltop graveyard. There is a new stone. **GERTIE** *crosses to family plot. She stands staring at new stone for a long beat.*

GERTIE: I ain't used to a preachin', Susannah, but I come to do it for you. I couldn't let Brother Rankin lay you to rest. I ain't a goin' to ask you why you done it. It ain't a question I guess you can answer. I want to tell you the story, Susannah. The story that's true and right. [*Pause.*] Once there was a man named Lot who had himself four beautiful daughters and a lovin' wife. Two a them daughters was married and a livin' off in the town of Sodom with their men, but the other two's still at home. The Lord decided to destroy that town 'cause some a them men had lost themselves to pleasure without love. God talked on it with Abraham, and Abraham asked the Lord to save his cousin, Lot. Two angels came to tell Lot to leave the town so's he wouldn't be destroyed. Lot gathered up his wife and his two daughters, but the daughters what had husbands had to listen to their men when they told Lot he's touched. The angels warned Lot's wife not to look back when they's a leavin' 'cause she couldn't stand the sight a God, but when she heard the rumblin' and the commotion, she's worried 'bout her flesh and blood. She couldn't handle the Lord's destruction, and so she perished like her daughters left behind in the fire. Lot and his daughters wandered through a little town that was deserted where they found food and wine. They took the food they needed, and Lot was right set on takin' the wine, too. Days later when Lot had been a drinkin' steady, the Devil sat on his shoulder and whispered in his ear, "Even the Lord couldn't a survived the struggle left behind you. Take what is your'n to do with as you can." Now everbody knows a body who's been drinkin' will listen to the Devil. Lot took his daughters both, and they got to be with child. They's daughters, Susannah. Thou shalt honor thy father and thy mother. They did what Lot told them to do. When there was signs that they wasn't the only people left, Lot changed his story. I reckon he's too shamed a walkin' into town after he'd been by himself with those girls so long, and his daughters was swelled with big bellies. He said they got him drunk, and somebody told somebody else and somebody wrote it down that way. If'n the daughters had told the story, we'd know their names. We'd know their momma's name. That's the true and right story, Susannah 'cause God would a punished them if they'd got their daddy drunk and made him sin. Ain't no sign a punishment for Lot's daughters in the Bible, though. Their sons Ben Ami and Moab would rise to rule two new tribes in Israel as honored men. Lot is the abomination, Susannah, not them nameless daughters. [*She stands for a moment crying softly, then kneels.* **WAINCEY** *enters now using a cane.*]

WAINCEY: [*Softly.*] Gertie? We got to go. [*Pause.*] Gertie? We're a goin' to miss the train.

GERTIE: [*Kneeling. Angry.*] You shouldn't a done it, Susannah. You shouldn't a went to the crick. [*She breaks down sobbing.*]

WAINCEY: Gertie, honey? We got to go.

GERTIE: I have to finish this, Waincey. It ain't done till I finish it. [*Pause.*] I wrote it out for you. [**GERTIE** *pulls out a scrap of paper from her pocket.*] It says, "Susannah." I wanted you to remember. I want you to always remember your name. You cain't forget it now. It'll be here with you always. [*She begins digging in the earth and burying the scrap of paper. Pause. She stands.*] I come to testify, Susannah. I want the story to be right and true. [*Fade to black.*]

THE END

it is no desert

DAN STROEH

I walked in a desert.
And I cried:
"Ah, God, take me from this place!"
A voice said: "It is no desert."
I cried: "Well, but—
The sand, the heat, the vacant horizon."
A voice said: "It is no desert."
— *Stephen Crane*

About the Playwright

Dan Stroeh's work has been seen by audiences in New York, Boston, Washington DC, Los Angeles, Salt Lake City, Milwaukee, and Cincinnati. His other plays include *The Fundraiser, 10 a.m. Signing, The Second Advent, The Artist's Way, Law-V-Bow-em,* and *Her.* He is currently the company playwright for Boston's Alarm Clock Theatre. Dan has been a visiting artist at the Sundance Theatre Lab, the O'Neill Playwrights Conference, the Kennedy Center, and the Mark Taper Forum. Dan was a contributor to *Monologues for Men by Men, Volume 2* (Heinemann Press) and *Audition Arsenal, 101 Monologues by Type, 2 Minutes & Under, for Men in Their 20s* (Smith & Kraus). His prose and poetry have been published in *Kairos, The Wittenberg Review of Literature and Art,* and *The Florida English Journal.* Also an enthusiastic educator, Dan has guest lectured at Wittenberg University, State University of West Georgia, and numerous high schools and young writers' conferences. *it is no desert* won the 2001 Michael Kanin National Student Playwriting Award for the Kennedy Center's American College Theatre Festival.

Production History

it is no desert was originally performed by the playwright from March 30–April 2, 2000 in Blair Hall Theatre on the campus of Wittenberg University. It was produced by Josh Keiter; the stage manager was Rafael Villamil and the lighting was designed by Emily Upperman. It was revived on October 28 and 29, 2000 in Wittenberg University's Chakeres Memorial Theatre for participation in the Kennedy Center American College Theatre Festival. It was directed by Steven C. Reynolds and produced by Josh Keiter; the technical director was James Humphries, the assistant stage manager was Karl Miller, and the lighting was designed by Emily Upperman.

Characters

DAN STROEH

COACH

TEACHER

MIKE

MARK

JOHN

DAVE

DR. DRUMMOND

DR. EDWARD BENNETT

MOM

ORTHOPEDIST

DR. KINNETT

ALBERTA

DR. CHANG

JONATHAN'S MOM

KRISTIN

PROFESSOR

TONY

JOHN WILKES BOOTH

ICU DOCTOR

FRIEND

Notes

it is no desert is to be performed by a single actor. During sections of dialogue, distinctions between characters primarily should be made vocally, through the pitch and tonal quality of the actor's voice, as well as through accents. For example, in the original production, Dr. Bennett spoke with a British accent and Tony was from Brooklyn; Alberta's voice was soft and maternal while the orthopedist was loud and abrasive. Slight movement (a shift in body weight, a turn of the head) can also be used in these sections. These, of course, are only examples and the actor should not feel limited by them; he should explore his own methods of differentiation.

ACT I
Part 1

*The audience arrives to find a dimly lit stage. Bare, except for three units: UR,
a wheelchair; UL, a hospital bed and a nightstand with a phone on it; DC,
a table with a closed journal and a pen on it, and a desk chair.*

Lights up on the bare stage. From UC, **DAN STROEH** *enters. He is thin,
clean-cut. He uses a cane, and throughout the play he walks with a slight limp
that comes both from pain and weakness, but cannot be attributed necessarily
to either leg. He also wears braces on both legs, just below his knees, supporting
his ankles. These are mostly hidden underneath his pants. He walks forward to
the table, deposits his cane, where it remains for the length of the play, sits, opens
the journal, and leans forward a bit, addressing the audience.*

DAN: Every night I dream of running. One of those spirit-propelled sprints
that I remember from my childhood. Wind rushing past my face, the trees
around me blurring into green streaks. One of those childlike runs that is
really half-falling, which is the beautiful part, because you're on that delicate
line of losing control. I'm half-falling down a hill at speeds only a little boy
could achieve and I'm gleeful and glorious and angelic and unstoppable.

I wish I could share that feeling. The only way I can describe it is this: I
have a friend who drives an Acura Integra—a sportscar with a sunroof—and
in high school I used to climb up and sit on the roof, my legs dangling down
into the car and held by the other passengers. Kraig would start her up and
we would tear through the vacant streets of his neighborhood. I swear he'd
hit speeds of sixty or more and my eyes would water and I'd have spit spilling
out the side of my mouth creeping back towards my ears, the rushing wind
forcing my face into a contortion of joy, spit and tears streaming backward
on my face, laughing and screaming. . . . That's almost the way it feels to run
in my dreams.

When I first started having this dream it surprised me. It wasn't so much
the fact that I was having a dream about running, which, in truth, even when
I was healthy I despised. It was the utter simplicity of it. Just me hurling
down a grassy hill. I think, at the time, I expected myself to be having a more
interesting, visceral dream. I was very aware of my condition, and relatively
comfortable with it. And at the same time, I was aware of my limitations and
all the things that I could no longer do. I suppose I expected myself to dream
of stage combat, say, or hiking . . . or soccer. Now there you go. Soccer. If I
was going to dream of *running,* I should have been dreaming of soccer.

I was captain of the soccer team in high school. I played stopper. I ran the
tightest defense in Cincinnati. We called it the HURT-MAIM-KILL defense.
One season we went EIGHT GAMES without a shot on goal.

Now, I loved the game and I played year round, but there was one thing about it I absolutely *hated*. And that was the running. Pre-season conditioning, laps before practice, the sprints before games. I could have done without 'em. Now I'm not saying that if a striker from the other team broke loose toward our goal I'd stop and say, "Aw, man, now I gotta run to catch this piece of crap." No, that wasn't the case at all. That made sense. That had a goal. Run. Catch up to the guy. Stop him. There you go. Makes sense. But lap after lap of huffing and puffing just pissed me off. I did it anyway, of course, but I grumbled through every minute of it. The worse thing about it was the fact that I could never get ahead. No matter how early in the summer I started running, or how hard I worked on my own, or how well I thought I'd kept myself in shape, when that first day of pre-season conditioning came I was worthless. I was crap. Coach would say,

COACH: Come on, Stroeh! Step it up! What kinda captain finishes runs back with the goddamn freshmen, huh?

DAN: [*To* **COACH.**] I just don't want them to feel left out, Coach. I'm an INCLUSIVE captain.

COACH: Screw that, Stroeh. You get your ass in gear.

DAN: [*To the audience.*] And I tried. I tried to get my ass in gear. But it didn't work. I never understood it. I always figured I just wasn't a runner.

I decided to change all that junior year. Our coach had implemented a new policy: each day, before "official" conditioning started, we were to meet at the high school track and run a mile and a half. We were to do this mile and a half in eight minutes. Once we achieved this time we could stop coming to these morning runs and just meet the team for regular conditioning. Now, a mile and a half in eight minutes for a bunch of high school soccer players is not easy. In fact, it's close to impossible. So essentially what Coach was doing was insuring that each of us ran an extra mile and a half at full sprint for him every single day. The only guys who had a chance of actually achieving the feat were the fastest guys we had who really didn't need to be running to keep in shape anyway and who were probably running cross-country as well, so a mile and a half in eight seemed like nothing.

But I decide, as the captain, and an individual who hates running, that I'm not going to put up with that crap. I'm not gonna fall into Coach's little trap. I decide that on the first day of pre-season conditioning at that high school track, I'm gonna push my body like I've never pushed it before, I'm going to abuse myself, I'm going to run like there's a Sycamore High School striker twenty yards from me charging our goal, and I am going to do that mile and a half in eight minutes. And the coach can just stand there and gawk.

So there we are. A late August Monday morning. Six a.m. Dew on the football field. The all-weather track looking foreboding under a slight haze of mist. Everybody's got their running shoes on. Gel-soles and Air-soles. I don't own running shoes. I'm wearing Samba Classics, my favorite indoor soccer shoes. Everyone's nervous. Some of the freshmen are puking already. The hotshot midfielders who (don't ask me how) absolutely LOVE to run are in a circle stretching and talking and looking at us defenders with smirks on their faces. I stretch. Psyche myself up. Set my Timex Ironman Triathalon watch. And line up with the others to await Coach's whistle.

[**DAN** *steps up to "the starting line." A beat, then, from backstage, a whistle.*]

And off I go. For the first few seconds I focus only on myself, my eyes fixed straight ahead of me, looking down periodically at the red track and the little white lines flying by. Then, hesitantly, I risk a look up and behind me. And, much to my surprise, I'm in the lead pack. I'm eating the midfielders' dust, granted, but behind me the rest of the team is sort of petering out in groups of four or five down to those last few guys who either should have been working harder on their summer break or just can't handle the pressure. And I realize, "Hey, I'm doing it! I'm actually doing it!" So I go back to focusing on myself. Trying to breathe the way my track-star friends had taught me. Trying to make my entire body move in one forward motion, no up and down, no side to side, just forward . . . forward . . . forward. . . . And I'm running! And I'm keeping up with those bloody midfielders and I can hardly believe it. Lap after lap, I follow them, trying to keep myself going and matching the rhythm of their feet which are slapping the track in those neon-covered shoes. And I'm *running*! I pass the coach and he screams,

COACH: Last lap gentleman, last lap and you boys have fifty-five seconds.

DAN: Then he yells it so everyone can hear:

COACH: Fifty-five seconds!

DAN: And I look down at my Timex Ironman Triathalon Watch and up at the midfielders who have taken off at this news leaving me far behind, and I'm starting to feel like myself again, and I say to myself, "Okay, Dan, you're gonna do this. Now go!"

And for a split second I imagine myself, streaking around the track, passing that finish line a half-second before eight minutes is up, falling to the ground, my body quivering, the coach standing above me saying, "Well I'll be damned, Stroeh, you did it!" And in that split second I envision my triumph. And I make up my mind that I am going to finish under time. Visualize and then go. If you can dream it, you can do it. And so I suck in a deep breath, gather my last bit of strength and strain forward toward victory. . . .

And then I hear a sound I've never heard before, and I find myself face down on the ground, making out with the all-weather track. And I can't move my leg. I lie there screaming and muttering as the rest of the team tromps by, and suddenly I'm looking up at my coach.

COACH: Which leg, Stroeh? Your right?

DAN: [*To* **COACH.**] Oh man, Coach, it feels like someone's trying to rip it off. [*To the audience.*] They have to carry me to the trainer. Who tells me that I've severely torn my quad muscle, and I'll be off ball for at least six weeks.

As it turned out, I was off ball for the entire season, because, for some reason, no matter how hard I worked in physical therapy or how sure the trainer was that the injury had healed properly, I just couldn't get my strength back.

[*A beat.*]

In fact, I haven't played soccer since. That was eight years ago.

But, at the time, it was no great tragedy. You see, I loved soccer, but my real passion—the passion I'd been feeding ever since childhood, the passion I wanted to dedicate my life to, the passion that seemed to eclipse everything else in my life—was . . . Acting.

Compared to theater, soccer was really only a distraction. I spent most of my high school career hearing my teachers say,

TEACHER: Dan, you are not here to do Drama!

DAN: Which was true, of course, but no matter what I did, it was on my mind. I even played Hamlet . . . . It was only the final scene, and it was only for a drama class, but still, it felt wonderful; even if it was only a couple of us theater geeks trying to show the football players who were taking Intro to Drama as a blowoff course that Shakespeare really was very exciting.

There were several of us, including the great triumvirate, the Three Musketeers: me and my best friends, Mark and Mike. Together we held a monopoly on all the best roles in Loveland High School Drama Club Productions and held the positions of power on the Thespian Society Executive Board.

So first there is Mike, a brilliant character actor who plays the villain with such freshness I was convinced, and remain convinced, that he could rank up there with Pacino and Nicholson. He is playing Laertes in a wondrously villainous, albeit inappropriate, way. And then there's Mark, a wholesome, redheaded pretty-boy and my best friend in the world since kindergarten. He is playing Horatio. I am the Prince, and I am on cloud nine.

With the help of some other Drama Club members we present the final scene—the fencing duel—which Mike and I choreographed ourselves.

There we are on the stage, presenting any actor's dream scene for a bunch of jocks, the set of *The Sound of Music* in pieces behind us, Mark staring on in horror, Mike foaming at the mouth and growling, myself bedecked in black and warding off his angry blows:

[**DAN** *fences.*]

DAN: [*As Hamlet.*] Give me your pardon, sir. I have done you wrong. Free me so far in your most generous thoughts that I have shot my arrow o'er the house and hurt my brother. [*To the audience.*] Mike lunges. Sweeps his sword. Glares at me through those deep, dark, angry eyes.

MIKE/LAERTES: I am satisfied in nature whose motive, in this case, should stir me most to my REVENGE!

DAN: [*To the audience.*] (He really did scream "revenge.") I step back, stare at him with that I'm-the-Prince-of-Denmark-and-I'm-giving-you-one-last-chance look in my eyes. Mike cocks his head. I smile. [*As Hamlet.*] Come on, sir.

MIKE/LAERTES: Come, my lord.

DAN: [*To the audience.*] And we're off—fencing all over the stage, down into the pit toward the bored audience of athletes who are whispering to one another and drawing pictures of us with breasts to match our Elizabethan tights. Mark is playing a concerned yet confident Horatio. Claudius is an anxious and sweaty sophomore whose nerves at performing in front of the Fighting Tigers works well to duplicate the uneasiness of the adulterous and murdering king. The queen—(who played the queen?)—Oh, it didn't matter. We are having the time of our lives. And in the midst of all this, I notice something strange. At one point in the scene, as the king is offering me a drink from the poisoned cup of wine, Laertes sneaks over to stage left. I am down right, in the pit, next to the audience, and we had decided that I would realize that he had snuck off, sheathe my rapier, sprint over to stage left and up the stairs, dramatically unsheathing my sword as I did, and charge him. I do this, but I realize, I'm not moving very quickly. I feel like I'm in slow motion. Strange. . . . But finally I get there and we're off again. We're fencing: "Hah! Ho! A hit! A very palpable hit!"

MIKE/LAERTES: Hah! Uh! A touch, a touch, I do confess 't.

DAN: And then Mike thrusts his poison-tipped foil, nicking my side. The queen is swooning, I'm concerned, I take Mike's foil and slice his thigh, "O villainy! Treachery! Seek it out!" Mike strains up from the floor, gasping,

MIKE/LAERTES: It is here, Hamlet. Hamlet, thou art slain. The king, the king is to blame!

DAN: I kill the king, the queen dies, Mike's Laertes falls off the edge of the stage into the orchestra pit, and I lie dying, somewhat histrionically, I'll admit, center stage. Mark, tears in his eyes—real tears—cradles me in his arms. [*As Hamlet.*] I die, Horatio. The rest is silence. [*To the audience.*] And

Mark looks up at our audience, who are now either asleep or making crude remarks as to the questionability of our sexual orientation. He tearfully sighs:

MARK/HORATIO: Goodnight, sweet prince. And flights of angels sing thee to thy rest.

DAN: And that was that. My fifteen minutes—literally—as Hamlet. And as foolish as it was, I felt so alive; so completely alive. That's how it always was for me. I mean, I was just a kid—untrained, naïve, overdramatic—but I was passionate. When I was onstage I couldn't imagine myself being happy anywhere else.

Like right now. To be up here, sharing myself with you. This is an exchange. A covenant. I agree to be honest. To be utterly vulnerable. And you give me two hours of your life. Two hours in which *I* am in control. In my world, a world driven by my need for control, and plagued by my continuing loss of control, that is a real gift.

Part 2

DAN: [*To the audience.*] Wittenberg University. Springfield, Ohio. August, 1996. I'd always known that I had a good life. But from the moment I stepped foot on that campus life. just. got. better. It was the most incredible thing I'd ever felt. FREEDOM exploded into my life like a burst of light. It was as if I'd never lived. I felt assured that I had been BORN to go to college. Now that was what I'd been seeking all along—utter independence, utter responsibility. I didn't even need a period of adjustment. I was THERE. I was ready. I felt like I could do anything. And I *tried* to do everything. By the time the middle of my first semester rolled around I barely had time to eat what with classes and meetings and rehearsals and auditions and I tell you I had never EVER been that happy.

And while some of my friends were still settling in, I'd already made Wittenberg my home.

In November I was in a show that was part of a one-act play festival and my brothers came to see me in it. I think I was just as excited about their *visit* as I was about the show itself. . . . You see, John's nine years older than me, and Dave is almost eight years older than me, so for as long as I could remember they were *the boys*. There were four of us kids—John (the oldest) Dave and Kristin (the twins) and me—but when my parents talked about their children it was Kristin and Dan and *the boys*. Mom and Dad would say, *the boys* are going sledding, *the boys* are off to a soccer game, *the boys* are going out to dinner with their friends. They were *the boys* and I was the Doozer. Even at nineteen, I was the Doozer. But, slowly since I'd been at Witt, through visits home, and talks on the phone, I started to feel like that uncrossable line that divided *the boys* from the Doozer was blurring. Disappearing. I started to feel less and less like an annoying younger brother and more like a peer. When we'd sit at home late at night, I would catch glimpses of what I had longed to feel for so many years: what it was like to be one of *the boys*. And so the show was just a good excuse to revel in it—to immerse myself in that unspoken fraternal love that's always there when we're together.

And so they arrive and it is indeed a great time. After the play I find them waiting outside my dressing room, smiling with their characteristic enthusiasm. John hugs me—hard—and then starts in with the noogies:

JOHN: Great show, big man. Really, really spectacular.

DAN: [*To the audience.*] Dave wraps his big hands around my relatively scrawny bicep and squeezes, shaking me just a little.

DAVE: You rocked it, Dooz, you rocked it.

DAN: [*To the audience.*] I just smile. Then John says,

JOHN: Well, bro. It's your night. What d'you wanna do?

DAN: [*To the audience.*] So we get some IBC root beer and junk food and head back to my dorm room. We stay up till three or four, talking and laughing. . . . The next day we get up and have breakfast at Perkins. They tell me stories about when they were students at Witt, we talk about camping trips and Christmases and books and profs and classes and women and beer and I really feel it then. For the first time in my life, I feel like we're all there together. The three of us . . . *The boys*.

After breakfast we take a walk around campus and we're headed up this long hill from the Student Center to the Chapel when John says,

JOHN: Hey, Dan, what's wrong with your leg, big guy?

DAN: [*To* **JOHN.**] What? Nothing's wrong with my leg.

JOHN: You're walking really weirdly.

DAN: I am?

JOHN: Yeah. Look at yourself.

DAN: [*To the audience.*] And so I do. And he's right. I guess I'd noticed it before but ever since my injury in soccer junior year I'd just gotten used to considering myself unathletic. So I hadn't worried. And at the time, I just blew it off.

JOHN: You should see a doctor, Dan.

DAN: [*To* **JOHN.**] Yeah, yeah. Whatever. [*To the audience.*] But they told my mom. And so a little over a month later, just after our Christmas in Cincinnati, I found myself at the family doctor.

One of the great phenomena of modern medicine is the diagnosis process. I mean, if you break your arm, and you go in and you say, "Doc, I can't move my arm and part of my bone is sticking through the skin," it's pretty obvious what's wrong. But if you go in and say, "Doc, my brothers came to see me in a play at school, and they say I'm walking really weirdly. What do you think is wrong?" From that moment on the strangest things can occur.

So, it's really at the insistence of my brothers and my mom that I go to Dr. Drummond at all. I'm assuming it's just the old soccer injury acting up—maybe it hasn't ever healed properly, I don't know. But I'm thinking he's gonna check me out, massage my leg a little and say, "Oh, yeah. Definitely. This never healed correctly. How long ago was this?" And he'll tell me what to do. Pills to take, exercises, whatever. Then he'll ask me about school and my shows like he always does, and I'll take off back to Witt for rehearsal.

So Mom and I are waiting in the examination room, talking about how nice Christmas was although I'm forlorn because we can't find the 78-speed record of my father singing "Oh Holy Night" as a twelve-year-old-soprano. After a while Dr. Drummond comes in, I hop up on the table, and he's talking to me as he begins his examination.

[**DAN** *sits on the table.*]

DRUMMOND: So how do you like college, Dan?

DAN: [*To* **DRUMMOND.**] Oh, I love it; it's just great— [*To the audience.*] He grabs my wrist and holds my elbow.

DRUMMOND: Don't let me pull you back. Good.

DAN: [*To* **DRUMMOND.**] —Yeah, I've always known that I'd like college but I didn't know I'd enjoy it THIS much. [*To the audience.*] He grabs the other wrist, holds the other elbow.

DRUMMOND: Same thing. Don't let me pull you back. Good.

DAN: [*To* **DRUMMOND.**] I'm in another show. It's directed by the chair of the theater department— [*To the audience.*] He holds my knee and grabs my ankle.

DRUMMOND: Now kick out against me. Push.

DAN: [*To* **DRUMMOND.**] Yeah, and classes are good too. I—

DRUMMOND: Push,

DAN: [*To the audience.*] he says again. [*To* **DRUMMOND.**] I am pushing.

DRUMMOND: Hmm. Okay. Other leg. Push . . . Hmm.

DAN: [*To the audience.*] He said *Hmm* a lot. And it wasn't a sighing hmmm. It was a sharp, spitting, burst of breath: *HM!* I found it disconcerting for some reason. I'd never noticed it before.

He tests my eyes. My ears. My hands. My feet. And soon, he's not interested in how I'm doing at school. He's not talking to us. At all. He's mumbling to himself and scribbling on his clipboard. And I'm sort of sitting there, feeling—strangely—like some school kid who's done something wrong and is sitting in the principal's office. He finishes scribbling and mumbling to himself, and stands for a moment, rubbing his clean-shaven chin and frowning at the floor.

Then,

DRUMMOND: Take off your shirt for me.

DAN: I do. Suddenly, out of nowhere, I begin to feel very conscious of all the idiosyncrasies of my body. The strange shape of my ribs, the way my collarbones stick out, the weird bumps on my shoulders. He puts his fingers on either side of my spinal cord and runs them down my back. Then he grips me around the waist, and squeezes.

DRUMMOND: Does this hurt?

DAN: "No," I say. "NO!"

DRUMMOND: Hmmm,

DAN: he says. Again. Chin-rubbing and frowning. Then, he leaves the room. [*To* **MOM.**] What was that? [*To the audience.*] Mom shrugs.

MOM: He's just checking you out, hon.

DAN: [*To the audience.*] Annoyed, and a little nervous, I go back to reading *Hunting and Fishing*, the only magazine that's been placed in this particular room. After a few minutes, Dr. Drummond returns. He looks at his clipboard. Rubs his chin. Then:

DRUMMOND: I'm gonna send to you to a neurologist.

DAN: [*To* **DRUMMOND.**] A neurologist?

DRUMMOND: Just so he can check you out. I can't find anything really wrong with you, but he'll be able—better suited—to tell you what's going on.

DAN: [*To the audience.*] So he sends me to a neurologist. [*To* **MOM.**] A neurologist? [*To the audience.*] I say to Mom in the car. [*To* **MOM.**] Why not a-whatever-a muscle guy-

MOM: An orthopedist,

DAN: [*To the audience.*] she says. [*To* **MOM.**] An orthopedist maybe but why a neurologist?

MOM: Who knows.

DAN: [*To the audience.*] So there we are. Dr. Edward Bennett, neurologist. The lobby, in a sad attempt to be cheerful, is made up with fish. Ocean painting on the wall, shells on the end tables, a fish tank. . . . If you made everything a little more cartoony, it could be a pediatric office. . . . And I'm thinking to myself, adults are suppose to be fooled by this crap? If you're going to go see a neurologist, I don't think that a couple of fish are going to cheer you up. I snicker to myself, imagining adult patients sitting there staring at the fish tank. Then I realize—I'm going to see a neurologist. And I'm staring at the fish tank.

I'm escorted into the exam room—it's six-thirty or so, which should have given me a clue since, I have now learned, only emergencies get seen at dinnertime. So Dr. Bennett goes through that whole process again. Checks my hands:

BENNETT: Don't let me squeeze em . . . Good.

DAN: And my arms:

BENNETT: Don't let me pull you back. . . . Good.

DAN: And my legs:

BENNETT: Push out at me. . . . Good . . .

DAN: He runs his hands down my back, and I'm feeling very self-conscious again, as if I had anything at all to do with the way my back curves or the way my ribs are shaped or the way my legs bend.

Then he has me take off my shoes and he pulls out something I have never seen before: a metal rod curved to a point at one end. Slick and sterile and sharp. . . . He takes this thing and he runs it down the sole of my foot. [*To* **BENNETT.**] OW! . . . Uh, ow. [*To the audience.*] I'm hesitant. I started out very hesitant. [*To* **BENNETT.**] Uh, that, uh . . . sorta hurts.

BENNETT: It does? Where exactly?

DAN: Well, uh, everywhere I guess.

BENNETT: Here?

DAN: [*To the audience.*] he asks and runs the bloody thing down my foot again. [*To* **BENNETT.**] Uh, yeah. There. Definitely there.

BENNETT: Hmm,

DAN: [*To the audience.*] he says. His *Hms* were a little less harsh than Dr.

Drummond's, but they were sing-songy, as if he were at some five-star restaurant trying to decide between *amuse bouche* and stuffed mushrooms for a pre-appetizer. *Hmmm.* In any case, he hmms his hm, and scribbles on his clipboard.

BENNETT: How about the other foot?

DAN: And he runs it down the sole of my other foot. [*To* BENNETT.] Ow!! Uh, yeah. That one too. And I paid attention this time—it's the whole foot for sure—you don't have to do it again . . . [*To the audience.*] Then he lifts this pointy thing up and I realize that it is disguised as a normal ol' doctor's hammer, and I sorta look at it with wide eyes and butterflies in my stomach and all, and he lifts it and bops me on the knee with the hammer part. Bop. Nothing happens. He does it again. Bop. Again nothing.

BENNETT: Try to relax, son.

DAN: And I try. But I can't forget that this thing has a sharp end that I've never noticed before and I'm starting to wonder how many other things about simple everyday doctor's instruments have I not noticed? And I start looking around the room and I'm cold and very self-conscious of my nine-teen-year-old body perched there on that exam table, my feet hurting and thinking that there might be a vast conspiracy of doctors creating torturous exam devices in the guise of normal old equipment. Needles comin' out of those popsicle-stick tongue depressors, and things like that. And he says,

BENNETT: Please, son, try to relax.

[DAN *takes a very deep breath and closes his eyes.*]

DAN: And he does it again—BOP—and the knee moves a little. Then he says,

BENNETT: Hop down for me. . . . Okay, now go stand by the door and walk towards me. [DAN *crosses to the "door" and does this.*] Now go back and stand on your toes.

DAN: "My toes?" I think. And I try. But—*what the heck?*—I can't. I must just not be trying hard enough. I focus. Take a deep breath. Lean forward and—I can't. "I can't," I say.

BENNETT: How about your heels?

DAN: [*To* BENNETT.] No. Not the heels either. [*To the audience.*] I try really hard, and fall against the door.

BENNETT: That's okay, son, just hop back up on the table for me.

[DAN *crosses to the table and sits on it.*]

DAN: And for a second, I start to get a little concerned. I'm already nervous about being surrounded by these torture instruments masquerading as normal doctor's tools, and now I realize that I can't stand on my toes or my heels. And Dr. Bennett scribbles something on his clipboard, excuses himself and leaves the room. With the doctor gone, the neuroses just float away. And how can I be worried, I've got my Mom there. [*To* **MOM.**] What's for dinner?

MOM: Oh, whatever you want.

DAN: [*To the audience.*] Typical answer. [*To* **MOM.**] Well, what do we got?

MOM: We could call Dad and go out somewhere if you want.

DAN: [*To the audience.*] How ya gonna turn that down? "Don Pablo's it is," I say. And the doctor returns. He looks at his clipboard, rubs his chin, squints.

BENNETT: I'm want you to have a CAT scan tomorrow morning. First thing, if that's okay. Nothing big, I just want to check some things out.

DAN: Alrighty. And off we go to Don Pablo's.
  The next morning Mom and I get up early for the CAT scan. I have never had a test like this before, and I'm interested in how it's going to work. Beyond that, though, is a certain anticipation. Up till now, I've just been going with the flow—humoring my parents and my siblings and my doctors. Suddenly I realize that something might really be wrong. . . . And it's strangely exciting. Maybe I'll need an operation or something. Or have to do special physical therapy. (I'm still convinced it's the quad.) The idea of having a story to tell and maybe getting a little sympathy from the ladies at school makes me almost *hope* for something to be wrong.
  So I go in and get scanned. We head home and Mom takes off to go shopping. And since Dad's at work and I'm tired from getting up so early, I go back to bed. [**DAN** *crosses to the bed.*] I'm napping when the phone rings. [*The phone rings.* **DAN** *picks it up. Into phone:*] Hello, Stroehs? [*To the audience.*] It's Dr. Bennett. He's calling to tell me what he's found on the scans. "Growths," he says. His voice is shaking.

BENNETT: Growths around your spinal cord down your back and into your pelvis.

DAN: [*To* **BENNETT.**] You mean tumors?

BENNETT: Yes,

DAN: [*To the audience.*] he says. And goes on to explain what the next course of action will be.

BENNETT: When your parents get home have them call me.

  [**DAN** *hangs up the phone.*]

DAN: I went back to sleep.

[*A beat.*]

I'm often asked what that phone call was like for me. That moment when all I knew was that there were *growths*. Was I scared? Was I angry? Did I cry? [*A beat.*] And the answer is *no*. No, I wasn't scared or angry. At least not at the time. It was just one of those things. I know this seems overly simple but it's the truth. Fear and anger are not really a part of my life. My life is guided by a higher power than doctors and nurses and *growths*.

[*A beat.*]

When I was a little boy, my family would go camping all the time, and we loved to hike. And my siblings always wanted to take these long, long hikes—miles and miles of hiking. Of course as a pudgy little six-year-old this was hard for me and I'd whine and pant and scream, "My legs aren't as LONG as yours!" We would never stop, though. We always hiked the whole trail—no matter what. But, when I got tired, when I couldn't go on anymore, when my fat little legs couldn't take another step, my family would carry me. They'd pick me up and put me on their shoulders, and go on hiking. Kristin would tromp along with me for a while and when she got tired she'd pass me to John, when he got tired I'd get handed off to Dave, then eventually I'd end up with Dad. They'd do this for the entire hike. Step after step, mile after mile, they'd carry me.

[*A beat.*]

You see, my life is guided by a higher power than doctors and nurses and *growths*. I know that God will never give me more than I can handle. I know that He will use this situation for good. He'll take care of me. If I know anything, I know that.

[*A beat.*]

The next day, the fun begins. It's sort of like being a twig dropped in rapids. You get handed down a long line of doctors each giving his or her take on the specific ways the quote—*growths*—unquote will manifest themselves. Neurologist to neurosurgeon to oncologist to orthopedist to pediatric oncologist to urologist to neuro-oncologist to geneticist. All these over-educated people poking and prodding me, discussing what it could possibly be. Back and forth through the hospital—east wing to west wing; west wing to east wing. The same strength tests. The same questions. MRIs, blood tests, urine samplings, and on and on. The next step was a needle biopsy, to take a sample of the quote—*growths*—unquote. Fortunately, that didn't end up being necessary.

What it came down to were these. [**DAN** *lifts shirt, points to dark spot* *on his stomach.*]

Café-au-lait spots, they call 'em. I always thought they were birthmarks, but actually, they're telltale signs of my disease. You see, the disease affects the glands that control the pigment of your skin. So, after a battery of tests and scans and exams and How-are-you-doing-today-Dan?—I'm—fine, I was diagnosed a hundred percent by a doctor who simply counted how many café-au-lait spots I had on my body.

Thus began my career as a patient and a subject of study.

Part 3

DAN *crosses US and stands, listening.*

VOICEOVER:

> March 19, 1997
>
> The Office of Howard M. Saal
> Head, Human Genetics
> Children's Hospital Medical Center
>
> Dear Colleagues,
>
> This is the initial Genetics office visit for Daniel Stroeh, 19 $^7/_{12}$ year old white male college student who was referred by Dr. Kerry Krone for evaluation of possible neurofibromatosis.
>
> Daniel has parathesias of the right lower extremity and the left lower extremity, more significant on the right side. MRI scan of the lumbosacral spine revealed abnormal paraspinal enhancing masses identified bilaterally extending from the carina superiorly to the sacral area inferiorly with the masses increasing in size as they descended inferiorly. Examination of the skin reveal fourteen café-au-lait spots greater than 0.5 centimeters in diameter, six of which are greater than 1.5 centimeters in diameter.
>
> ASSESSMENT: It is quite obvious that Daniel Stroeh is a nineteen and seven-twelfths year old male with neurofibromatosis type 1. Unfortunately, this young man presents with a very serious complication of multiple tumors extending through the neural foramina from the carina on down beyond the sacral region. His pelvis is filled with tumors and, unfortunately, this is causing some compression of the bladder and displacement of other surrounding organs. Fortunately, the patient is not symptomatic with regard to bladder or bowel function. However, this patient is significantly symptomatic from the standpoint of weakness in the lower extremities. This has been

progressive and presents a significant management challenge.

Sincerely,
Dr. Howard M. Saal

DAN: Neurofibromatosis. Neuro-fibroma-tosis.

Fortunately, the tumors aren't malignant—they're not cancerous—but because of their size there is real concern. They're causing nerve damage—thus the weakness in the legs and feet; thus the need for the cane and the braces. And, as I was to learn later, there's always a chance of benign tumors *this* large becoming malignant.

The disease is considered untreatable and incurable. And, with the tumors located where they are in my back, inoperable. So, the next question was: What to do?

While my doctors deliberated on this I went back to school, giving only scraps of information to my friends and professors. At the same time returning to Cincinnati regularly to take care of all the baseline testing. This was so the doctors could determine exactly how I was doing at *that moment* in time so they could trace accurately how much better—or worse—I got in the coming years. By the middle of the Spring semester I was a regular at Children's Hospital in Cincinnati, and when classes ended in May, more and more tests were ordered.

Some tests weren't so bad. Others . . . well, were. Bad. My orthopedist was a real jerk, but his tests didn't hurt. He just examined me and poked me and had me walk and talked to my parents and talked to me and then re-diagnosed it as NF and proceeded to pull out his microcassette recorder and compose a letter:

ORTHOPEDIST: Dear Dr. Drummond and Colleagues, I have completed the physical exam for—

DAN: [*To the audience.*] He looks at my chart—

ORTHOPEDIST: Daniel C. Stroeh [*Mispronounces name—Stroh.*]. Left lower extremity is at . . .

DAN: And he goes on like this for five minutes, just talking into his tape recorder and ignoring us and I'm looking at my parents and they're staring back at me and my Dad smiles cause he knows what I'm thinking and I almost laugh at this arrogant jerk who wants to display his utter command of medical terminology and spontaneous letter composition for me, his honored patient. He finishes and says:

ORTHOPEDIST: Thank you for sharing in the care of this patient. Sincerely, Signature.

DAN: And for some reason this really pisses me off and I want to steal his microcassette recorder and leave a little message for his nurse or his secretary or whoever transcribes these things:

"Tell your boss to stop being such a dick!"

But I can't do that, so I just have to sit there and take it.

My neurosurgeon, Dr. Kinnett, was a tall man—obviously a former athlete—with a warm smile and a calming voice.

KINNETT: Theater, huh?

DAN: he said when we first met.

KINNETT: My daughter's into theater.

DAN: I took to him immediately. He was a great guy. But looking back I don't know if it's better to have a big jerk administering painless tests or a really great guy administering tests that hurt like hell. The first time I had electric shocks sent down through the nerves in my legs I thought that I had discovered the world's perfect torture. But, like I said, he was a good guy, so I gripped the exam table, gritted my teeth, and tried to think happy thoughts. Dr. Kinnett did his best to make me as comfortable as possible, and—best of all—hasn't ordered any new tests since.

Now neurology was pretty bad. But nothing compared to urology. I will not go into the details of the specific tests themselves, but I will say that it is hard to be cheerful for any urological exam. Especially with the temperament of the nurses in that particular ward. I guess working with children all the time, and perpetually being at risk of being doused in pee makes one a little stern. I mean, the least they could have done would be to laugh at my jokes. One time, I'm lying there on an exam table, getting tubes inserted into places God-knows-they-shouldn't-go and I look down at what she's doing THEN smile up at her and say, "You know I was reading a great short story by Franz Kafka last night about a horrible device used for torture . . . Know what it was called? 'In the Penal Colony.'"

Yeah. You laugh. She wasn't amused. And it only took me a few minutes to lose any remnant of humor.

The tests went on until mid-June. It had been a surreal six months. I KNEW I was sick—or else, that I had a disease—but the symptoms were virtually nonexistent, so I could pretty much go on as I had before. Still, it was strange because I was spending a lot of time in hospitals, but nothing was getting accomplished. The doctors were getting a lot of information on me, but there were no solutions being offered. I guess they weren't sure what to do. Finally, in late June a decision was reached. I was accepted into a protocol chemotherapy program at the National Cancer Institute, part of the National Institutes of Health, Bethesda, Maryland.

[**DAN** *turns upstage, as if giving a tour.*]

The National Institutes of Health is located on an enormous campus, just outside of Washington D.C. Buildings everywhere—full of doctors and researchers and nurses and patients and anxious family members. The National Cancer Institute is located in Building 10—the Medical Center—which sits atop a hill, sort of overseeing the rest of the campus. It contains fifteen floors of clinics and hospital rooms. I was a patient on the thirteenth floor: pediatric oncology and HIV/AIDS. Just down the hill from Building 10 is The Children's Inn, which is essentially like a Ronald McDonald House, a sort of hotel with rooms for families of the patients of the thirteenth floor clinic. This was a place full of toys and games and very sick children from all over the world. It perpetually smelled of curry, and escaping to my room only meant escaping to the reek of betadine-washed sheets and the feel of uncomfortable beds. The chemo program I was admitted to required that I stay on the NIH campus—at the Children's Inn—for most of the summer.

My first day in the clinic I was put through all the typical tests—MRIs, blood tests, physical exams—it was nothing new. I did meet Alberta Aikin, though. She was the nurse practitioner who was in charge of the chemotherapy study I'd been accepted to and she was willing to sit with my parents and me for as long as we needed, answering any questions we had. I found myself relaxing a little. After a busy and exhausting day, something about Alberta calmed me. She reminded me a little of my mom. The skin of her face. The way that she smiled. Her hands.

She taught me some important things that afternoon. On our brief tour of the facilities, she introduced me to all the nurses and pointed out where the best candy machine was. Then she took me in to get an IV placed in my arm for the next morning's operation, and she taught me how to take a needle: look in the opposite direction, count to three, take a deep breath in your nose and exhale out your mouth. [**DAN** *does this.*]

When it was all over, she rode with us in the elevator downstairs, and walked us to the front door.

ALBERTA: Well, I'm so glad that you're going to be here with us. Hopefully we can help you. And remember,

DAN: she said, taking my hand,

ALBERTA: Whatever I can do to make you most comfortable, just let me know, okay? Now, any other questions for me?

DAN: [*To* **ALBERTA**.] Yeah. Where's a good place around here to get some dinner?

ALBERTA: O'Donnells. Down Wisconsin Avenue. Best seafood in town.

DAN: [*To the audience.*] And we headed off to dinner.

The next morning I checked into the hospital for the first time. The west wing of the thirteenth floor, or 13 West as it's called. The IV in my arm was still sore as I signed the admission forms and prepared to head to my first appointment. I was really uncomfortable. And grumpy.

So, my first stop of the day is down in the basement, in the bowels of the Medical Center, for the insertion of my *Hickman catheter.* NIH always seems to be remodeling something, and my parents and I walk through a labyrinth of halls; walls stripped of paint, ceiling panels missing, wires hanging down, till we arrive at our destination. We step around a ladder into a dimly lit hallway. A sign on the wall reads "Special Procedures." We're in the right place. But no reception desk. No waiting room. Further down the hall to our left is a little man, a doctor, selecting something from a shelf. He turns. He seems surprised to see us at first. Dad waves. "Is this Special Procedures?"

CHANG: Daniel Stroeh? [*Mispronounces name—"Stroh."*]

DAN: [*Correcting him—"Stray."*] Stroeh. Dan Stroeh. Yes, that's me.

CHANG: I'm Dr. Chang. I'll be inserting the Hickman today. Do they want one lumen or two?

DAN: [*To the audience.*] I look back at him blankly. [To **CHANG.**] Lumen?

CHANG: The openings. One or two?

DAN: I don't know. [**DAN** *crosses to the phone on the nightstand. To the audience.*] He grumbles something about "those doctors upstairs" and picks up the phone to call and check it out. And I'm starting to wish for someone a little less abrasive to do the procedure.

"Dual Lumen," he says as he slams down the phone. "Ready?" [*A beat.*] I am. My parents are escorted to a waiting room somewhere else in the maze, and I'm brought into a large, bright room, full of x-ray equipment, and instructed to remove my shirt.

[**DAN** *pulls off his shirt and removes a Hickman catheter from his pocket.*]

So *this* is a Hickman catheter. Essentially it is a long-term IV. The doctor, using needles and x-rays, inserts it in your chest here [*He points to a scar just to the right of his sternum.*], runs it under the skin to about here [*He points to another small scar just under his collarbone.*], and then sends it deep into your body into one of your larger veins. This spot [*He points again to the scar next to his sternum.*] is called the exit site—the place where the tube actually exits the skin. You have to keep it very clean and well-bandaged to avoid infections.

So once the Hickman's inserted, it just sort of dangles there, and you just hook up your chemo or your antibiotics or whatever and it pumps right on in. I always thought that if I wasn't fundamentally opposed to drug use I could have done smack or something, you know? There'd be no lines.

[*He sits.*]

I'm led over to the operating table and a red-bearded technician rolls up and starts scrubbing down my chest with betadine. The schloppy wetness of the huge cotton balls, the way he's sort of dabbing, and the fact that I'm lying there helplessly makes me suddenly think of *The Princess Bride*. I feel like Wesley in the Pit of Despair.

I go from being uncomfortable to being a little freaked out. Doctor Chang finally enters and explains the procedure to me, emphasizing that "those doctors upstairs" *should have* explained all of this to me yesterday, but since they didn't he's taking his own time to do so now, for my benefit, so nothing will be unclear during the operation.

Then he gives me something in the IV in my arm "to calm me" and pulls out a syringe to numb my chest. For a moment I grow tense, looking at the length and girth of that needle and then, suddenly, almost unexpectedly, I'm "calmed."

[*He is very "calm."*]

Oh, what a wonder drugs are. Now I love the Beats, but I'm no William Burroughs. I don't drink and I don't do drugs, so I have no point of reference, but this—this is good stuff, let me tell ya.

So, I'm sorta hovering there, dreaming of riding in a boxcar with Jack Kerouac talking about Zen Buddhism and grass mats and saki and I'm feeling this weird pressure on my chest, pushing . . . pushing . . . pushing. . . .

What the heck is that? Pardon me for a sec, Jack.

And I open my eyes a little and look down.

Dr. Chang is perched above me, instruments in both hands. He looks strangely like he's carving a turkey. He is surrounded by his assistants. The red-bearded technician holds a swab covered with blood. I try to be cool.

"Hey, uh, Dr. Chang, dude, can I have, uh, some more of that stuff? Please?" I ask as politely as possible because, for some reason, I'm suspicious that they won't want to give it to me.

But, Dr. Chang nods. A nurse turns, and I'm back in the boxcar.

Part 4

[*Lights up on **DAN** lying in the bed. His shirt is back on.*]

DAN: [*To the audience.*] Later that day, as I'm slowly recovering in my room upstairs, watching *The Simpsons*, Alberta appears with my first dose—my test dose—of my new chemotherapy, *phenylacitate*. "How are you feeling?" Alberta asks.

ALBERTA: Still a little woozy?

DAN: [*To* **ALBERTA.**] A little bit.

ALBERTA: Well, this won't take long. This is just a small test dose.

DAN: [*To the audience.*] They make it a practice of sending in a test dose to see how the body reacts to the drug before they pump in five hundred milliliters of the stuff. And because the Hickman has just been put in, I'm still sore, and other complications that I don't really understand, the chemo is to be pumped into the IV in my arm, which, good God, they have not yet removed despite my protestations.

I look at her. And she smiles. She knows what I'm thinking. (Something I will learn about Alberta is that she *always* knows what I'm thinking.)

ALBERTA: I know,

DAN: she says as she hooks the chemo tube to the IV.

ALBERTA: You want that thing out of your arm. We'll take it out as soon as we're done here. I promise.

DAN: [*To* **ALBERTA.**] Thank God.

ALBERTA: Now, this is the phenylacitate,

DAN: [*To the audience.*] she says, holding up a little bag with clear fluid inside it.

ALBERTA: Of course, your normal bag will be much bigger, but the pump is the same as the one you'll have.

DAN: And she pushes a few buttons, checks that the tubes are all tightly connected, and says,

ALBERTA: Now this may sting a bit there in the arm area. Some patients have found that it does sting a bit.

DAN: Another of the great phenomena of modern medicine is the tendency of doctors and nurses to understate the truth about a particular situation. That initial infusion did, in fact, sting a bit in the arm area. As I watched the pump click away and the chemo bag slowly empty, a burning pain traveled up my arms and into my chest, inside my veins. I just sat. And tried to think of something else. When it was finally over, Alberta took everything apart and removed the IV from my arm.

ALBERTA: Better?

DAN: she said. [*To* **ALBERTA.**] Yeah. Thanks.

ALBERTA: I'll be back to check on you in an hour or so.

DAN: [*To the audience.*] Then she smiled at us and headed off to her other duties.

I was exhausted. I felt invaded. All these things that should NOT be going be going into my body—plastic tubes, burning chemicals, pieces of metal—were being forced in by medical professionals.

The next day they hooked me up for good. I was given a little black hip pack to strap around my waist. This hip pack contained a five hundred milliliter bag of phenylacitate and a pump. It also had a little hole for the tube that carried the chemo out of the bag, through the pump, and up into the Hickman (and thus into my veins—goody, goody!) The chemo pumped in twenty-four hours a day, for twenty-eight days at a time. Every night, Alberta explained, the pump would beep at me to tell me that the bag was almost empty. This is when I would change the bag, replace it with a full one. After the twenty-eight days on the drug, I had fourteen days off, at the end of which I was to return to NIH for check-ups and scans, and then—if everything was okay—I would be put back on for another round of twenty-eight days. Twenty-eight days on, fourteen days off. Twenty-eight days on, fourteen days off. This would go on for a year.

My drug, phenylacitate, was originally developed for brain tumor patients who hadn't had success with other chemotherapy. You see, I needed a really potent treatment because—unlike other tumors—NF tumors never shrink. So, the only hope in my situation is to halt any growth.

Of course, I wasn't thinking about tumors at the time. *I* was thinking how humiliating it would be to have to walk around wearing a hip pack all the time. But, I was lying in a hospital bed then and didn't have to worry about that much yet.

I stayed sore for several days, and even as the swelling went down I was far from used to having a tube sticking out of my chest. It was very surreal. To think that it was supposed to be there. To think that it had essentially been forced, *plunged* into my body so recently and there it was. And it wasn't going anywhere.

Finally, after the required hospital time for recovery, they released me to the Inn, which, granted, was not my favorite place, but was certainly better than an automatic bed in a hospital room. Mom and I planned some day trips down to D.C., and I was looking forward to seeing some plays and catching some movies.

Dad left to get back to Cincinnati for work. I got sick.

[**DAN** *leans back. He is delirious with pain.*]

Oh! God! Oh! It feels like my body's turning inside out. My head is so tight, and I'm so so cold, and I have these chills, and I'm shaking all over—uncontrollably. I try to stop it, but it takes all my concentration. My fever's up around 104, 105. I can't get comfortable. Mom is concerned. She tries to help, to do whatever she can to soothe my pain but—*God, don't touch me . . . Oh! All I want to do is sleep!* But I can't, no matter how I position myself on the bed my head pounds and my back hurts and my legs throb, and I shake and shake and shake. It's like nothing I have ever felt before.

Mom calls the Medical Center to see if I can get some medication, and I can, but the pharmacy requires that I come to get it myself. *That makes a lot of sense.* She's ready to get a wheelchair and take me up there, but I say no. *No, I just—I just want to sleep. To sleep.* Finally—slowly—I calm down enough to find a position that works. I'm as comfortable as possible and I'm just drifting off to sleep when— [*The phone rings.*] Oh! [*The phone rings again.*]

It was the Medical Center calling to say that the cultures they had taken before they released me had come back and I had a staph infection, which meant that I was required to go back to the hospital and check in.

[**DAN** *crosses slowly to the wheelchair and sits.*]

And so I was on my way up to Building 10 after all. Mom got me into a wheelchair and we headed up.

I just sat there, shaking and glaring and all I could do was pray. Pray that I got a single—that I didn't have a roommate. I couldn't handle a roommate. I couldn't handle hearing his TV. I couldn't handle hearing his parents talk to Mom. I just couldn't handle it.

Finally we get to 13 West and I'm rolled down to the end of the hall into the last room on the left. . . .

[**DAN** *stands and slowly crosses to the bed.*]

Not only do I have a roommate. But it's obvious that he has been here for a while and he has no intention of leaving. Posters on the walls, stuffed animals everywhere, a family around the bed, and this little guy—eight or so—nestled there and squeezing a stuffed monkey. The monkey has a Hickman. I just let the nurse help me into bed and close my eyes. Mom gets acquainted with the roommate's family and the nurses start hooking me up to things; antibiotics dripping in one tube alternating with saline for hydration. Doctor's orders: after the antibiotic is out, keep him hydrated, but don't stop the chemo, for the love of God!

And so I lay there listening to my roommate's mother dominate the conversation:

JONATHAN'S MOM: Jonathan—

DAN: —the roommate, I guess—

JONATHAN'S MOM: —has been in for several weeks. He spends a lot of time in hospitals but he's a good sport. And what does your son—Dan, is it?—what does Dan have? Oh, really. No, I haven't heard of it, interesting . . .

DAN: And here I am, racked with pain, and I wish these people would just SHUT UP and let me sleep, that's all I want to do, my gosh . . . If you had any idea how this feels. . . . And then I hear Mom ask what Jonathan is being treated for . . . Don't perpetuate the conversation, I think! Let me sleep! I'm sick here! Man!

JONATHAN'S MOM: Oh, Jonathan has leukemia and HIV.

DAN: Jonathan has leukemia and HIV. "How old is he?" Mom asks.

JONATHAN'S MOM: Fourteen.

DAN: The little guy in the bed beside me, with his teddy bears and kitten posters and his Oscar the Grouch comforter and his monkey-with-the-Hickman is not eight. He's fourteen. And he has leukemia *and* HIV. I suddenly feel like a whiner. I suddenly feel lucky. And a little ashamed. And then, I sleep.

[*Lights slow fade to BLACKOUT.*]

ACT II
Part 5

Lights up on the bare stage. Same as before. **DAN** *stands next to the bed, looking at the spot he occupied at the end of Act I. A beat, then he addresses the audience.*

DAN: Eventually, the infection ran its course, my fever subsided, I started feeling better, and—once again—I was released to the Inn.

At first, everything was a discovery. I'd lie there in that uncomfortable bed and take inventory. A distinct mental separation between pain, aching, weakness, tingling, etc.

It was difficult for me to determine the exact sources of all the strange inconsistencies in my body. In my head I equated everything bad about my illness with my presence at NIH—I had never been symptomatic before and now I felt like a real patient. It was as if things had exploded the moment that phenylacitate hit my veins. Suddenly, the weird walk my brothers had noticed in November became a real LIMP—I tripped and fell all the time. The cane I had bought in May on an I-may-need-it-someday whim became a necessity. I couldn't move my toes. The soles of my feet tingled and were very sensitive. I had headaches all the time. My legs and back tensed up to the point that I could never find a comfortable position to sit in. Essentially, I was miserable and not at all in the mood to venture out into the common areas of the Inn to run into my little pediatric neighbors, or smell the food their parents were whipping up, so I spent most of my stay in my room; trying to get comfortable, trying to get used to carrying around that hip-pack, trying to get used to the pain, trying to get used to my new life. I was very unhappy. There's not much more to say.

Even a visit from Kristin couldn't cheer me up. Here she was—the woman who had always been my favorite sibling as a child; the woman who had read me stories and taken me to Disney movies and sat patiently watching puppet shows—here she was, visiting from Indiana, that same enthusiastic smile on her face (there were very few people who could have made me happier), and all I wanted to do was sleep.

KRISTIN: Come on, bud,

DAN: she said.

KRISTIN: Let's call a cab and go downtown. We'll go to a play. I'll take you to a play, how about that?

DAN: But it took all of my willpower just to force myself up long enough to go down the street to dinner at Ruby Tuesdays. . . . That was the high point of the month.

After that first round in Bethesda, all I wanted to do was go home. I knew that everything would be so much easier once I got home. Back to my room, back to my bed, back to my bathtub, my family, my friends, my *CAR*, back to freedom. It had been an awkward month and I was only beginning to get used to my new lifestyle.

The rest of the summer went by rather quickly. I had people to see and things to catch up on. There were some rumors to be dispelled and some nerves to calm, so I did a lot of visiting, despite the fact that I really had no desire to do so. . . .

Everywhere I went it was the same. These were people that I had known for years, and the old *things like this don't happen to people I know* seemed to hang in the air around my little town. I was always greeted in the exact same way—a tilt of the head, a drop of the neck, a raise of the eyebrows, a slight nod, and "So, how ya doing?"

And, of course, I had the stock response, "Oh, I'm okay. Considering the circumstances things are ideal. I'm just looking forward to going back to school. Thanks."

By mid-August I flew back to NIH for the first of my check-ups and scans, and started back up on my second round of phenylacitate. Soon afterward, school began again. I moved into a little one-bedroom apartment, stocked the closets with medical supplies, filled the pantry with easy-to-make food, and prepared for the long haul.

Chemo and school, chemo and school. Looking back, I'm not quite sure how I did it, but at the time it seemed like the rational thing to do—there were no other alternatives. My doctors said there probably wouldn't be a problem so I went ahead with it. And it *was* tough, yes, but at least I was living. Being sick is one thing, but the worst thing in the world is being cut off from your normal life—from the things that you want to be doing.

Being on chemo sank me into a murkiness that was impossible to get out of. The rounds started off badly—like a brick wall—fatigue, nausea, extra pain, you name it. . . . And it got worse from there. By two weeks in I was really out of it; the world was a haze, and I couldn't think straight about anything. I slept for fourteen, fifteen, sixteen hours a day. Headaches, no appetite, (I won't go into the intestinal effects.) It all hit hard and worsened daily till the end. By the last day I didn't want *anything more* than to be off that crap. And suddenly it would be over, and I would have two weeks off. Each time I got to unhook myself at the end of a round, put away the last chemo bag, turn off the pump, and store the hip-pack, it felt like a little triumph.

And, oh, the two weeks off. My head never completely cleared, but mental state aside, it was just spectacular not to have to lug that hip-pack around and change the bag nightly. Still it would take at least a week for me to start to feel better and by the time I was beginning to feel . . . good? . . . I was on a plane back to NIH for check-ups and scans and another round to begin anew.

Life on chemo was strange to say the least. Days, weeks flew by in sickening blurs. My life was an endless cycle of sleep-class-food-sleep-class-food-sleep-food-TV-sleep and on and on. I was living alone, which was good, because my misery doesn't prefer company at all.

Days became pretty typical. The pain kept me awake most nights, and usually I was up six or seven times to stumble to the bathroom and fill the tub to soak my legs and back in the hottest water I could stand. The day officially began either when it was almost time for class or when I hurt so much I couldn't go back to lying flat anymore.

So, when the day DID begin, after my wake-up bath (only subtly different from the go-back-to-bed-bath) I'd slowly pull on my pants and wince to strap on my brace and tie my shoes, and go shirtless into the bathroom for the ultra-annoying Hickman-catheter-site-cleansing-ritual.

[**DAN** *pantomimes the following section.*]

My box of medical supplies sat atop the toilet and I'd pull out the necessary stuff, peel off the sweaty cover bandage and scrub away: three alcohol swabs first, to wipe away the nastiness that had built up and suck up the sweat, making sure it *really was* VERY clean. Then, three betadine swabs, the third squeezed out so it wasn't sopping and would soak up the excess betadine.

All contact with the exit site was in a circular motion, starting at the actual site, at the tube, and swirling outward. Then, very carefully, I'd loop the tube around the site so that if it was accidentally pulled only the *excess* tube would move. Then I'd put on the cover bandage (yes, with one hand—pretty impressive, huh?)

When I was finished I would wipe off any betadine not covered by the bandage and throw all the wrappings away. This process took a good ten minutes—if I was doing it properly, which, I admit, sometimes I wasn't.

I think the Hickman was the strangest part of the whole experience. The knowledge that there was a little piece of plastic sprouting from my chest that led to the inner depths of my body. The skin around it was very fleshy, and red, and swollen sometimes, and it made me nervous. Especially in big crowds. I was always worried that it would somehow get torn out. I constantly had to fight off the image of myself in the middle of a chaotic crowd with strange hands grasping at my unprotected chest while I shrieked "God no! My Hickman. Please!" Then my shirt would flood with dirty redness and my life would spill out of the pea-sized hole by my collarbone.

[**DAN** *removes a piece of paper from his pocket and unfolds it.*]

An unsent letter to my brother Dave:

November 3, 1997

To My Adventurous and Scholarly Brother,

Upon His Matriculation in Hamburg, Germany:

Dear Dave,

Greetings from Wittenberg and from the hazily sleepy world of your
little bro. I miss you! How's Hamburg? How's the Hieffeweizzen? It
has been about a week since I've been off my chemo, and I'm really
feeling pretty good, although I still took a long nap today. I think my
body has really adjusted weirdly to the phenal*crap*itate and so when
I'm off I have extra energy to work off and no way to do so. The odd
thing is that I seem to always hit my energy high really late in the
day—around eleven thirty at night or so, that's even the case when I
haven't taken a nap . . . I start to feel really restless and, of course, there's
no cure because this is Springfield, Ohio and there's not a whole lot
to do; plus my friends are busy and working on school crap so I end
up doing nothing but chilling in the Commons or taking a drive.
Thus is life even *off* the stuff. . . .

In any case, life goes on. Classes are still very interesting and just
challenging enough, although, as you heard from Grandma, I had a
little freak out around midterms. I had my acting scene on Wednesday
and an exam in Lit on Friday, and I just tripped out and couldn't get
any studying done for the midterm—it was pretty horrible. I was
paralyzed. I can't even tell you what was wrong. Things seem so much
worse—this situation seems so much worse—when I have things to
do, and I just can't do them . . . I used to be such a good student. I
used to be so busy. Now I'm so exhausted all the time that all I do is sit
around my apartment. There's a mound of things surrounding my
La-Z-Boy, strategically placed so I don't ever have to get up once I'm
sitting down. Books, homework, food, garbage can, remote—all
within reach. It's sort of pathetic.

The other side to all this is the actual physical part—walking,
standing, bending over, things like that. It's not that I feel like I'm
necessarily getting worse, it's just that I keep noticing more stuff that
I can't do, and realizing how much I miss it. Can't move my ankles,
can't *feel* my toes. Can't lie down without pain, can't stand without
wobbling, can't walk without tripping, can't bend without falling
down. Certainly can't run or dance or do stage combat anymore.
I've been wearing my brace and I'm watching slowly as my right
calf muscle is getting smaller and smaller. Atrophy? Is that the word?
I don't know. I'm sick of medical terminology.

Despite how pathetic I sound, things here are as good as can
be expected. My friends look after me and I talk to Mom and Dad
almost every day. So, I'm all right. Don't worry about me, I just
thought I'd update you. Having you this far away when I have so

much to share with you is weird. I'm sure things are great on your end, but write soon.

Love,
Dan

And my life kept blurring by. Looking back is hard—not emotionally necessarily, but simply HARD: I can't remember much at all. I mean, I remember generalities, but everything is hazy: how my family and Mark moved me into my apartment as I stood idly by panting from the heat; how I struggled with even the handpicked twelve credit class-load I was taking even though I knew I needed sixteen to graduate on time; how impossible it was to keep up; underplaying the pain and difficulty of the situation for anyone who asked since I didn't want to worry them; getting my brace and learning to overcome my pride and WEAR IT; running into my friend John Cassell in the Commons periodically and receiving his estimation on how badly I was doing based on the size of the bags under my eyes; forgetting to pick up my chemo and having to enter the hospital through the emergency room to get up to the pharmacy; watching as life just sort of passed me by.

I felt like I was living in slow motion, and now my memories are in fast-forward. When I think back all I can remember are short flashes:

Class. I did my best. I took the best notes possible. I tried to pay attention. I never once fell asleep. I tried to keep up, but that was hard. Some of the worst possible times were when I had an assignment due and I just couldn't get it finished on time. Or, I just couldn't even get started on it. Pretty bad. The chemo tore at the edges of my brain all the time. No matter what I did I was easily distracted; I lost anything resembling tact. I essentially became a bumbling idiot. But there was this all-pervasive heaviness all the time. I felt like I was walking around in some invisible cloud that dulled my senses and made my body feel so heavy. Sometimes I would zone out and forget where I was . . . or at least forget that I was supposed to be paying attention . . .

DAN: [*In class.*] Hey, Sally. Sally! Do you have any gum?

PROFESSOR: Is there a problem, Dan?

DAN: Oh, no. No. Just asking Sally if she had any, uh, gum. [*To the audience.*] I didn't spend much time on campus. By the time my classes ended I was ready to go home for a nap. I spent the afternoon watching TV or trying to read. A lot of times I would lie in my La-Z-Boy and memorize monologues to deliver for myself.

"This can be no trick! The conference was sadly borne! They have the truth of this from Hero! Love me! Why! It must be requited!"

But soon the energy would run out and I would fall asleep, only to wake up in the early evening, with an insatiable craving for Chi-Chi's or Max Ly's

China Palace. And, of course, by early evening all of my friends had already eaten and were working on school stuff, so I was usually forced to go pick up some fast food or make some macaroni 'n cheese to eat in front of the TV. Sometimes my friends would come out with me even though they'd already eaten. They'd drink coffee and watch me eat, then pull away my plate when I hit the point of capacity.

"The point of capacity" is a term that I have given to the moment that I realize that there is no way that I can eat another bite without throwing up. It sneaks up on me. One moment I'll be devouring my chimichanga happily, then I'll raise a forkful to my mouth, put it in, and only then do I realize that if I swallow this, it's not gonna stay down. This is when I pull the napkin trick, and sip water till my stomach calms.

After dinner I would usually sleep and watch more TV, but some nights— when I was feeling *really* energetic—I would sneak into rehearsals for upcoming plays. I'd sit in the back and just watch. And it made me happy. It made me feel connected; at least a little bit.

I don't date much. I sometimes imagine myself on a first date, sitting in some really nice restaurant across the table from a beautiful woman and hitting that point of capacity unexpectedly. She stares at me in horror as I try to control my breathing, concentrate on not vomiting all over her, repeating all the time in short gasps, "I'm okay—really—it's okay." And then, once I'm passed the point of danger, simply explaining, "It's just the tumors, you know, shrink the size of my stomach." How does a girl react to THAT?

Obviously, my romantic life was much worse while I was on chemo. Granted, everything was worse while I was on chemo, but this especially. How does a guy pick up ladies with a Hickman catheter dangling from his chest, or a hip-pack full of chemo strapped around his waist? You get 'em home, put on some Barry White, pour some cognac, light a few candles, sidle over to her, strip off your shirt—"Ignore the hideous white tube, love. You can just lick around it . . . Oh yeah." What woman wouldn't run screaming? I mean, even without a stark rubbery tube sprouting from a puffy, pus-covered hole in my chest, I'm not the sexiest man alive. You can count my ribs. Even with all that aside, it's hard to seduce someone when you reek of phenylacitate. So, most of my evenings were spent alone.

And, really, what I wanted from a woman was not going to come as a result of a few dates. I wanted someone just to be there. Someone to read to me. To hold me. To run her fingers through my hair and tell me that everything was going to be okay. I guess I wanted someone to take care of me. Late at night in bed, when campus was silent, and all I could hear were the distant cars and the occasional passing train, I would long for her. I would lie there in the dark, trying to get comfortable, and WISH for someone— someone I was in love with—there to help me through this. And I'd look around my dark, empty room, with the silence crowding in around me, and

I'd think to myself, It's *idiotic* to feel lonely. I have an incredible family, and innumerable friends, why should I feel lonely?

But I did. And I couldn't deny it. That loneliness became as familiar as the pain in my legs. And soon, I'd sleep.

It was during that year, starved for artistic fulfillment, that I discovered writing. I was in a creative writing class taught by a poet named Greg Fraser, and I was shocked at how much I learned. Of course, I'd always *enjoyed* writing—puppet shows when I was a kid and angsty teenage poetry—but never like this. I never REALLY knew what writing was. And what I learned that semester was that I loved to write! I wrote and wrote and wrote—poems and essays and short stories. It was all crap, but still, it felt so good! Writing became almost an addiction, but I could only feed it in spurts. Like so many other things, the stupid drugs made it nearly impossible. During the four weeks on chemo, my mind barely functioned well enough to get through the day—there was no way I could churn out decent work. But I journalled as best as I could and spent the two weeks off in a desperate race to get stuff down before my mind sunk into the chemo-haze again.

I found that writing was what I had needed all along. Feeling trapped inside that apartment, inside my body, I was so helpless, and that led to a certain apathy. But when I found writing, I didn't feel so lazy anymore. I suddenly felt like I was *doing* something again, and not just watching my life go by. I had "my work" and it felt good. I documented my illness. I recorded my thoughts. I encouraged myself. . . . I wrote down dreams:

[**DAN** *removes a piece of tattered notebook paper from his journal and unfolds it.*]

I dreamed last night

of a freer me.

Running, sprinting, racing

down a grassy slope

under blue and sunny skies.

My legs,

pumping with inhuman energy,

SLAMMED against the earth,

pushing it away.

That CONNECTION was made.

ME with the EARTH.

blood, bone, muscle,

meeting

rock, soil, root

with every tromp of my Adidas.

And I felt everything.

impact—slightcushionofsole—musclescontract—jointsshift—
and,again,pushoff.

The world around me mumbled into the rhythmic
fomp—fomp of rubber on sod.

I was an immaculate machine of flesh,

hurling with childish glee into oblivion.

Then I awoke to the drop—drop

of guttered rain on my mailbox

and I limped to the kitchen to make a pot of tea.

It was a freedom and a release I had never experienced before. The more I
wrote about my situation, the more I could admit that I was, in fact, in that
situation. I grew more comfortable with asking for help. I answered honestly
when people asked how I was. I started telling my friends the truth.

I was sick. And that was okay. I was okay with that.

Part 6

DAN: [*To the audience.*] As good as the two weeks off were, the inevitable
always hung in the air around me everywhere I went, and—before I knew
it—I'd be on my way back to NIH for my check-ups and scans and, of
course, more chemo.

Coming back to the Inn is always an interesting experience for me.
Everything reminds me of that first miserable month: the magazine racks,
the stuffed animals, the smell of the sheets, the feel of the towels, the sterile
sameness of the rooms, the clump-clump of little shoes on highchairs, the
whines of children who have EVERY RIGHT IN THE WORLD to whine
all day and all night if they chose to do so.

But, I think, above all, it's the sickness. The reality of all-encompassing
ILLNESS that pervades the place. It floats in the air, rests in the stares of the
stuffed Mickey Mouse and Raggedy Andy dolls, hides behind the caring
smiles of the volunteers, nestles in between the pages of the magazines, settles

like dust on the TV, is dispensed with my animal crackers from the vending machine, rides with me in the shuttle up to Building 10, stares back at me from the mirrors and the windows and the fish tanks. Back home, at my parents' and at Witt, surrounded by my family and friends, it's easy to forget that I am sick—believe it or not, it is. But at NIH, no matter how hard they try, you stop being *a person* and you become *a patient.*

All of this aside, two-day visits were nothing compared to that summer, and I could usually get myself feeling almost cheerful, even though I knew that I'd spend my entire time there searching for a decent place to hang out.

As desperate as I was to get things finished and get out of there, days at the Medical Center were long and tedious for me: waiting for the MRI machine then waiting for the scans to develop then waiting for the doctor to come off rounds for my check-up. If I could scrunch all the actual office-visit and physical exam time into a single lump I'm sure it wouldn't amount to more than three or four hours. And so, in the downtime I constantly found myself searching for a place to relax without a lot of other patients or worried family members around. The Medical Center contains two cafeterias, a coffee shop, and what seems like hundreds of lounges. Then there are the waiting areas. During that year on chemo I tried many of these, sitting and reading or scribbling in my journal or watching the TVs bolted to the walls.

Eventually I took to hiding away in a lounge next to the Medical Center library. It was a very comfortable place—free from TVs and little children, and it made me feel less like a patient than the clinic waiting rooms did.

On my fourth trip back, after a somewhat unsatisfying sleep at the Inn, I climbed on the shuttle to the Medical Center early, hoping to finish all the required tests (and all the necessary waiting) by mid-afternoon. After signing in at my clinic and learning that the MRI scanner would be occupied for at least two hours, I slinked off to the Medical Center library lounge, hoping to get a little reading done and finish the poem I'd been working on.

So, I'm sitting down to open *Dharma Bums* when I hear someone enter the room. Expecting a medical student, I glance up. He's about my age. He's wearing pajama pants, a Phish T-shirt, and a camouflage sun hat pulled down over his eyes. I can see that under his hat he's bald.

"Hey," I say. He nods and moves across the room to ease himself into a chair.

DAN: [*To* **TONY.**] Are you a patient on the thirteenth?

TONY: You a med student?

DAN: No, a patient . . . on the thirteenth.

TONY: Really?

DAN: Mm-hm.

TONY: Yeah, I wondered about the cane. Yeah, man, I'm a patient on the thirteenth. But they have me admitted right now. Sucks.

DAN: Been there, done that.

TONY: Yeah, dude. You stayin' in the Inn?

DAN: Yep.

TONY: Cool. My family's there.

DAN: I'm only here for the day. Hopefully.

TONY: What're you in for?

DAN: Neurofibromatosis.

TONY: Hell, yeah.

DAN: How about you?

TONY: Carcinoma. On my wrist.

DAN: How's it going? Are you on chemo?

TONY: Yeah. You know the thirteenth, they keep the juice flowing, man. I just started a new drug. That's why I'm in.

DAN: Geez, why do they insist on keeping us admitted when we start a new drug?

TONY: Well, dosage and shit like that. Toxicity.

DAN: That makes sense, I guess. I'm Dan.

TONY: Tony.

DAN: Nice to meet you.

TONY: You too.

DAN: [*To the audience.*] Tony pushes himself up out of the seat and moves across the room towards me. He's wearing a bag strapped around his waist— his chemo. [To **TONY.**] Don't you love the little bags? I call mine my I'M-NOT-hip-pack. [*To the audience.*] Tony laughs and plops down in the chair next to me.

TONY: Only a day, huh?

DAN: Only a day.

TONY: That's pretty sweet. How do you manage that?

DAN: I'm a monster. I'm pushy. They know how I work . . . they know I wanna get the heck outta here as soon as possible. [*To the audience.*] Tony reaches down, pulls up the leg of his pajama pants and scratches at a long, deep scar on his ankle. [*To* **TONY.**] Whoa, dude, what did you do?

TONY: Climbing. I fell.

DAN: And your ankle got cut up on the rocks?

TONY: No. My ankle got wrapped up in my safety cable. Saved my life but hurt like hell.

[*A beat.*]

DAN: No crap. So you climb?

TONY: Used to. All the time. It was my gig, if you know what I mean. But now, you know . . .

DAN: [*To the audience.*] I know. Tony shakes his head.

TONY: Wouldn't you know it man. I mean, shit, if I had a tumor in my back or my neck or my ass or even my brain, I could still climb. But I have this little carcinoma on my wrist and it's over. For good.

DAN: I don't respond. There's nothing to say to things like that.

TONY: Shit, Dan, it's like the goddamn cancer has a brain. It knows just where to attack to destroy your fucking life. I mean, take you—with your cane and all—I bet you were really into running or sports or something; something where you had to use your legs.

DAN: I look over at him. [*To* **TONY.**] Acting. I was an actor.

TONY: There you go. No dance numbers for you no more, huh, Dan?

DAN: Nope.

TONY: There you go. Shit.

DAN: [*To the audience.*] It always amazes me how quickly patients connect with one another. Before I was sick, I would never have thought that a stranger could be so frank so quickly, but I realize sitting there with him that Tony and I live similar lives; lives full of doctors and nurses and clinics and hospital food and mind-numbing medicine.

TONY: It just fucking pisses me off you know. I mean, what the hell? A carcinoma! I didn't even know what the fuck a carcinoma was before. Now I'm gonna live my life in hospitals.

DAN: [*To* **TONY.**] Maybe not. Maybe things'll clear up.

TONY: Oh, c'mon, Dan, don't blow sunshine up my ass.

DAN: I'm not. But you gotta at least have some hope.

TONY: No I don't.

DAN: What I'm saying is, you gotta consciously fight the disease. You gotta wake up every day and say, "I thwart you!"

TONY: "I thwart you?!" Shit, you are a fucking actor.

DAN: My point is that you have to decide you're gonna get better, and make that your goal.

TONY: When d'you get diagnosed?

DAN: A year ago.

TONY: A year ago. I knew it. Boy, give yourself another year of this shit. We'll see where 'I thwart you' is in a year or so.

DAN: [*To the audience.*] I don't respond. I check the time.

TONY: So, when you go back on chemo?

DAN: [*To* **TONY.**] Soon.

TONY: Too soon, huh?

DAN: Yeah, well . . . it is the treatment. And everything's stable so far. At least it was until last month. I'll know more this afternoon.

TONY: Waiting for the MRI?

DAN: Yeah.

TONY: I wish they'd find a better way to organize that damn thing.

DAN: [*To the audience.*] I nod. Tony pushes himself up out of the chair.

TONY: Well, Dan, I'm gonna go puke. I'll see you on the thirteenth.

DAN: [*To* **TONY.**] See you later, Tony. It was nice to meet you.

TONY: Like hell it was.

DAN: No, really, man. I know what you're saying, I just—

TONY: Peace, Dan. Peace.

DAN: [*To the audience.*] And he's gone.

VOICEOVER: Dan Stroeh to MRI scanner three. Dan Stroeh to MRI scanner three.

[**DAN** *looks offstage.*]

Part 7

DAN: [*To the audience.*] Back home, I continued to write as much as possible. But as time went on, it got more difficult. That spring, as I was getting groggier and groggier even during the two weeks off, my brother John came for a visit. To celebrate, my parents and I decided to take him out to a play. I opened up the paper and was thrilled to find that a little theater company on the west side of Cincinnati was performing *Assassins*, one of my favorite musicals of all time. We got tickets. I had to do a little shopping so I took off in my Mom's car and met them there for show time.

I don't know what it is about *Assassins*. But ever since I first encountered it, I have dreamed about playing John Wilkes Booth. There's just something about that final scene—about the way he says,

JOHN WILKES BOOTH: The mass of men lead lives of quiet desperation.

DAN: The performance is incredible.

I limp out of that theater after the performance and I'm just sick with envy. I'm thinking to myself, if only this stupid chemo would end so I can get back to THAT! Mom and Dad head home in Dad's car and John decides to ride with me. Mom's car is new and really fun to cruise in. So we climb into the car; I'm talking excitedly to him about the directorial decisions, the lighting, my take on each actor's performance. I start it up and begin to back out. Unfortunately, a van has squeezed in beside me, and the parking lot is tiny, so John has to get out and guide me. When he thinks I'm in the clear he gets back in. I make a joke about my inability to drive. He laughs. I swing out to take off, and then—CRUNCH. The front of Mom's car grazes that stupid van. We get out and examine the damage. The van looks untouched, but in Mom's car there is a huge, hideous dent next to the passenger's side door.

It hits me like a two-by-four across the forehead. I just stare at it. I'm in shock. Shame, rage, utter frustration flood my head, and I just get in, yell at John to do the same and speed off.

JOHN: Dan, careful—don't get into another accident just cause you're pissed.

DAN: But I'm not pissed. I'm crushed. I have learned to deal with so much since the whole episode has started, but the hardest thing to face is my sudden ineptitude. More and more over the last few months I've felt that I can't do anything right. No matter how hard I try, there are things that I've lost control over. And now—NOW I can't even DRIVE. God, and Mom's car . . . How much have I messed things up for my parents in the last year? How many sacrifices have they made for me? How much of my SHIT have they put with? And now I'm coming home with Mom's perfect new car dented by my stupidity.

I drive home in silence. When I finally get there, I show it to my parents, who don't even seem to mind all that much, but it doesn't help. This feels like the bottom to me. This feels like the end. I sit on the porch and weep. For the first time since my diagnosis, I weep and weep and weep. The concrete at my feet grows wet with tears. I shake and snot and cry.

Every once in a while Mom comes out and says,

MOM: It's okay, honey, it's all right. Just come inside. It's cold out here.

DAN: But I don't budge. I just keep crying and shuddering. And I look up at the stars in that deep, dark sky above my neighborhood, and I realize, I can't ACT. Who am I kidding? I can't even DRIVE, how can I act? If I think that I could actually run around that stage and do those dances like those actors up there tonight, I'm deluding myself. I can't play John Wilkes Booth. Not anymore. Not like this. Not the way I am.

And it just feels too hard. It's as if the inside of my head has filled up with chemotherapy and my brain has become submerged in phenylacitate. I've lost control of my body. I've lost control of my life. And it's never going to end.

So I just sit there for hours, weeping over the person that I had become.

[*Long beat.*]

And then, almost suddenly, the year on chemotherapy is all over. I put away the last empty bag, turn off the pump, and hide it all away. Two weeks later I fly back to NIH to get the Hickman removed. After MRIs and some blood work, plus my physical, it's approved from on high that the thing can finally be taken out of my chest. I have a surgery scheduled for several days later, but while I'm sitting there, waiting for a meeting with my doctor, Alberta walks up and says,

ALBERTA: They have an opening NOW. You can get it out now . . . if you want.

[**DAN** *smiles.*]

DAN: So she takes me down to the tenth floor and then through another labyrinth of halls to the ICU where a youngish, ex-jock of a doctor treats me like I'm twelve.

ICU DOC: [*Ultra-masculine.*] Well, hi there.

DAN: I lay down on a surgical table while he pulls out one of those huge syringes and starts hitting me with local anesthetic all around the site. I look to Alberta. [*To* **ALBERTA.**] No, uh—Nothing in the arm this time? [*To the audience.*] The doctor answers for her.

ICU DOC: No, not necessary. This'll only take a second, sport.

DAN: [*To the audience.*] Sport? Alberta smiles at me and shakes her head. Sort of the way she would if we were laughing together at the hijinks of a child. The doctor makes conversation as he allows time for my chest to numb.

ICU DOC: So are you a student?

DAN: I nod.

ICU DOC: What do you study?

DAN: "He's an actor," Alberta says proudly.

ICU DOC: Really? Would I have seen you in anything?

DAN: "Do you think you used enough local anesthetic?" Alberta asks.

ICU DOC: Oh, he'll be fine. Won'tcha, sport?

DAN: [*To* **ICU DOC.**] I guess. [*To the audience.*] And after he's poked my chest a few times to make sure that it is, indeed, numb, he pulls out a scalpel and starts cutting the Hickman free. At first, I'm fine. After a moment, though, I realize. This hurts. A lot. I'm not totally numb. I'm lying there grimacing and he's leaning over my chest, doing his thing, talking how his motorcycle got stolen from in front of his house, so he had to buy a new one, and then that one got stolen, and so he's on his third motorcycle and he's worried it's gonna get stolen and he's wondering who the hell's stealing his motorcycles. I say, "I'm not sure if I'm totally numb."

He doesn't look up from what he's doing. He just says, "This'll take just another sec or two."

And I start taking deep breaths, trying to relax myself, and I look over to Alberta and he's still scraping and cutting and I'm grimacing, thinking to myself, "It's cool. It's cool. It'll all be over in a minute." But he's still working.

ICU DOC: Doesn't seem to want to loosen up. The skin's grown around it a lot.

DAN: I'm gritting my teeth, squinting my eyes, trying not to look, trying not to move. Alberta's holding my hand. "Why don't you give some more local?" she says.

ICU DOC: No, he's fine.

DAN: And then Alberta's voice changes. For a brief moment, the sweet, gentle Alberta disappears and I hear her say,

ALBERTA: Give him some more local.

DAN: And he looks at her. And looks at me. And then turns to find the syringe of anesthetic. Finally, after more needle pricks and more waiting and more scraping, he says,

ICU DOC: All right. We're ready. Take a deep breath in. Now—

DAN: [*Sucks in a deep breath.*] And he yanks, and the Hickman, all sixteen inches of it, slides out of my chest.

[*A beat.*]

So I return to campus in the fall Hickman- and chemo-free, with my head slowly getting less cloudy, but things are still hard. My desire to return to acting is almost overwhelming, but it seems hopeless. The first mainstage that goes up is *The Glass Menagerie*. And I audition. Don't get called back. And I realize, you can't cast an actor with a limp opposite a character whose most distinguishing feature is her limp. I live in constant pain; everything I do *hurts*. I can't dance. I can't fence. I can't bend over to pick up a book or to tie my shoes. I can't walk smoothly—I can't run. I can't even sit on the floor—not gracefully, at least, and not if I want to get up again. This institution that has buttressed my life is being pulled away. And the walls are a-tumblin' down. I have always said that things were okay—as long as I can keep going, things are okay. Now, I don't have anywhere to go, I don't have anything to do. There this hole somewhere in me that only theater fills—only *acting* fills—and now it seems like it will always remain empty.

I stop referring to myself as an actor.

I know I need somewhere to go, and I turn to the page. Being off chemo means that I'm functioning better and better and so I dive into what is to become my new passion: I start writing as much as I possibly can. The more my head clears, the more I write, and the more I write, the more in love with it I become.

And suddenly, that world inside that I had only glimpsed while on chemo starts to pour out and flow all over the page. I find that I have so much to say, I can hardly contain it. I get to the point where I'm writing for countless hours every day. My friends yell at me because I'm constantly forgoing a night on the town to sit in a coffee shop with my journal and laptop. They hate it. But they don't understand. They don't understand what a healing it is.

You see, I fight all the things I hate about the world, about society, about the past, about the present, about the future, about my problems, about MYSELF on the *page*. I exalt the things I love, I dissect myself, I immortalize my friends, I puke out my fear and aggression and apprehension. I write about women of whom I am enamored. I feel connected in a strange way to this bizarre ghostly group of some of the greatest people in history. I do things on the page that I could never do myself. I take risks. I cuss loudly. I make love. I'm insane. I'm mean. I'm irresponsible. . . . I'm healthy. . . .

With everything going on in my life—the internal struggle, the battle with my body, the acceptance of inevitable evils—I love the feeling that I have somewhere to turn. Those blank pages staring up at me are like open arms.

[*A beat.*]

And look. It has led me back to the stage. Such a journey life is.

[*A beat.*]

A few weeks ago one of my friends asked me if I was dying. Of course, being the sensitive and caring individual that she is, she couldn't come right out and say it, so she had to beat around the bush a little bit.

FRIEND: When you write, what do you write about?

DAN: [*To* **FRIEND.**] Oh, I don't know—myself, my life, my thoughts . . .

FRIEND: Do you write about the future?

DAN: Yeah, I guess. Sometimes.

FRIEND: Do you write about YOURSELF in the future?

[*A short beat.*]

DAN: Are you asking me if I'm dying?

FRIEND: Yeah. I guess I am. Someone told me that you said you were, and . . .

DAN: Well, we're all dying . . . [*To the audience.*] The answer is no. I'm not dying. But I want to be living as if I were. I want to revel in every day. I want to open books and devour every single word. I don't want to take the simple things for granted: when I wake up early and step out of my apartment and stare up at the sky above the city, the fresh crispness of morning hitting my face; in the afternoon, hanging out with my buddies in the park, drinking coffee and talking; back at home, surrounded by my family, holding my little nieces, overwhelmed by that love; late at night with Mark and Mike, sitting on the stoop, reciting Ginsberg and Monty Python.

No, I'm not dying, but I am on the brink. My condition ensures that I will be on and off meds for the rest of my life, and I've had my break. Soon, I will go back on chemotherapy—which is a good thing, because I need it—but, I will once again become that bumbling idiot that I so hated. I will sink into the murkiness that made it virtually impossible to write or to perform . . . or to live life outside of my La-Z-Boy.

It's a race. I'm not running, like in my dream, but it *is* a race. A race to get it all down. To get everything that's in here [*He taps his forehead.*] down here [*He lays a hand on his journal.*] before it all starts again—the sickness, the exhaustion. Soon my brain will once again sink into that chemo-haze, and my ability to think—my ability to WRITE—will slip through my fingers. But, until then. . . .

[*He turns in the journal to a blank page, removes the cap from a pen, and begins to write. Very slow fade to BLACKOUT.*]

END OF PLAY

Yemaya's Belly
QUIARA ALEGRIA HUDES

And what if someone said:
'Be careful of the ocean deeps:
Or its depths will be your gravestone.'
Would it be wise to take a boat
And set out from harbour in the middle of a storm?
— Calderon, *Life is a Dream*

About the Playwright

Quiara Alegria Hudes' ritual-theater epic *Yemaya's Belly* was honored with the the 2004 Paula Vogel Award in Playwriting and the Latina Playwriting Award for the Kennedy Center's American College Theater Festival, the 2004 Clauder Prize (best play by a New England playwright), and has been produced around the country at Portland Stage Company, Miracle Theatre, Signature Theatre, and Detroit Repertory. Quiara has been commissioned to write a "family version" of the play which will premiere at People's Light and Theatre Company for audiences aged seven and up. Quiara is the librettist for *In the Heights,* a musical about the Latino community in Washington Heights that blends hiphop, salsa, and merengue into a youthful new sound (music and lyrics by Lin Manuel Miranda). *In the Heights* has been developed at Manhattan Theatre Club and the O'Neill Music Theatre Conference and will open Off-Broadway in 2006. *Elliot (A Soldier's Fugue)* is Quiara's drama about Latino men in the United States military in Iraq, Vietnam and Korea and will open next season at the Culture Project in New York and Miracle Theatre in Oregon.

Quiara is also the creator of Barrio Grrrl!, a young Latina superhero from "el barrio." The theatrical version, *The Adventures of Barrio Grrrl!,* has been produced in New York's Summer Play Festival and at Portland's Miracle Theatre. Quiara is now working on a comic-book version of this rougharound-the-edges kick-ass real-life superhero.

Quiara received an M.F.A. in playwriting from Brown University and is a resident playwright at New Dramatists. She attended Philadelphia public schools, where she wrote her first play.

Production History

Yemaya's Belly was developed in 2002 at Brown University in workshop with Paula Vogel. It was presented in a staged reading at South Coast Repertory in July 2003. It was subsequently presented in readings at Signature Theatre in April 2004, New Theatre in August 2004, and Repertorio Español in November 2003. *Yemaya's Belly* was first presented in a professional production at Miracle Theatre Group in February 2004. *Yemaya's Belly* world premiere equity production was produced by Portland Stage Company on March 1, 2005, under the artistic direction of Anita Stewart. The production was directed by Peter Sampieri, the set design was by Anita Stewart, the lighting design was by Byron Winn, and original music was by Shamou. The production featured the following cast:

JESUS/MULO ....Alexis Camins

YEMAYA/MAYA ....Stephanie Beatriz

JELIN ....Joaquin Torres

TICO..Gilbert Cruz

LILA/MAMI ....Brigitte Viellieu-Davis

Characters

JESUS/MULO, a boy, 12 (*hay-soos, moo-lo*)

JELIN, Jesus's uncle (*hay-leen*)

TICO, a man who hacks open coconuts (*tee-ko*)

LILA, owner of a grocery store, and MAMI, Jesus's mother

MAYA, a girl on a boat, and YEMAYA, a young festival performer

Time

Recent history.

Setting

The ocean. It may be miles away, a distant whisper. Or we may be underwater. We are always in relation to the ocean. A thousand shades of blue moving in waves. Sometimes the motion is soothing. Other times it is violent. The wind influences the ocean.

Real items float to the surface. Dominoes. A duck feather. A Coke bottle. A coconut husk. Rice. Shovels. A machete. Things that tell us where we are.

Rituals

Some actions are designated as rituals:

> *RITUAL*
>
> **JESUS** *holds the bottle of Coke in one hand. When the cold starts to burn, he switches the bottle to the other hand and shakes out the burning hand for relief...*
>
> *END RITUAL*

A ritual involves a body and an object, together in a moment of possession. Rituals are crude, physically exaggerated. They make the body raw.

1

A mountain farming town on an island. It is accessible by one narrow road that winds up the side of the mountain. Just when it seems the road couldn't possibly go any higher, there is Magdalena. Sunrise on a mountaintop farm. The wind blows ferociously. **JESUS** *is alone.*

JESUS: Red white and blue
Sugar and gin
My story begins

Once there was a boy. It was Sunday and church was over. The boy wanted to buy a cookie so he asked his papi for a penny. "Oh, papi . . ." But before the boy could finish his papi yelled, "No!" The boy said, "But papi . . ." And the papi yelled, "No!" So the boy turned away and whispered, "Stiiingy." "Repeat it louder, so I can hear," the papi said. So the boy repeated it. "Stiiiiingy." And then the boy heard a growl come from inside the papi's belly. It sounded like the beginning of a hurricane. The boy took off running so the papi wouldn't smack him with the belt. He ran all the way to the top of the coconut tree. And he spent the night up there and he didn't come down for dinner, even though his mami had made pork chops. That night, the wind was so strong that he flew away. [*He spreads his arms to fly.*] He flew over the farm. He flew over the mountain. He flew over the ocean. He flew all the way to America, and he landed in the house of the President of America. He told the story about his stingy papi, and the President of America gave the boy a penny to buy a sugar cookie.

Red white and blue
Sugar and rum
My story is done

[**MAMI** *enters with a coffee cup.*]

MAMI: Jesus! What are you doing? Bring your father his cup of coffee.

JESUS: I already brought him one.

MAMI: Grownups need at least two cups.

JESUS: Papi doesn't know how to have a conversation.

MAMI: He works too hard. All his breath is used up planting and digging.

JESUS: I ask him a question, he doesn't even bother to look at me.

MAMI: Then do what I did. Stop asking him questions.

JESUS: I said why it's so windy and he said to leave him in peace.

MAMI: It's windy because St. Peter opened up the gates of heaven to let someone in.

JESUS: They must be some huge gates.

MAMI: Any other questions?

JESUS: Can I have a penny for a cookie after school?

MAMI: Hurry. Bring him the coffee before it gets cold. Your slacks and shirt are on the table. And be careful with the wind. Don't spill it.

> [*The wind blows in* **JESUS***'s face.*]

2

Tico's bar stand at the roadside. An old produce crate is enjoying a second life as a retail counter. On the counter are some bottles of rum, a pile of coconuts with the green husk still on, and a machete to hack open the coconuts. Behind the crate sits **TICO***, an old dude.* **JESUS** *is at the counter.*

JESUS: I'm broke. Papi wouldn't give me a penny.

TICO: If you want to do a job for me, you can earn a drink.

JESUS: Okay.

TICO: You're going to do my inventory. When you own a business, you always keep track of how much stuff you have. That's your inventory. It's a list. You say the item first, then how many you have.

JESUS: Coconuts, six. Bottles of rum, two. Beer, four. Straws, three. Machete, one.

TICO: That's it. A full day's work.

JESUS: What else is there to do?

TICO: You sit and wait for someone to come along. You just earned yourself a coconut. [*He demonstrates a coconut.*]

JESUS: Can I open it?

TICO: No. That's a job for experienced men only.

JESUS: How do you get experience?

TICO: Your father teaches you how to do it.

JESUS: Papi doesn't like to show me things.

TICO: Let me see you make a muscle. [**JESUS** *does. There's no muscle.*] This machete is heavy.

JESUS: I'm strong.

TICO: If you swing it the wrong way, there goes your pinky. Hold the coconut down with one hand. Swing the blade back and forth like this. Concentrate. You want to be precise. [*He demonstrates a smooth hacking motion.* **JESUS** *tries this. He hacks at the coconut chaotically and works up quite a sweat.*] It's not a pork chop. You don't nibble at it. You give it a good cut. [**JESUS** *tries using more force.*] Careful! You'll cut off your hand and the damn thing still won't be open. Watch how I do it. [**TICO** *takes the coconut. In four precise strokes through the air, he creates a hole in the top. He slips a drinking straw into the hole and gives it to* **JESUS.**] It takes practice before you get good.

> [**JELIN** *enters and plops down into one of the chairs. He punches* **JESUS***'s arm and ruffles his hair.*]

JELIN: Hey! Little Jesus! Shouldn't you be in school? You always want to be where the action is, don't you? Always hanging around with the big boys. You'll learn more from us anyway. What do they got to teach you in school that we don't already know? [*To* **TICO.**] Did the bus come through yet?

TICO: You got plenty of time. That thing always comes late.

JELIN: I'm heading down to the city. Take care of some business.

JESUS: Have you ever been in the city before?

JELIN: What do you think?

JESUS: What's it like?

JELIN: [*To* **TICO.**] So I heard you got in some trouble this weekend.

JESUS: Grownups can't get in trouble.

JELIN: [*To* **JESUS.**] Shh.

TICO: It's those damn Pentecostals. Baldomera is always dragging me to her Pentecostal meetings over at her brother's farm. You should see them. Out on the hill, singing and clapping. Speaking in tongues. So this weekend it's raining and thundering. Mud everywhere. She still makes me go. Everyone there is wet head to toe, praying like fools. When we arrive at the meeting, hwa! I slip in some mud and land flat on my ass. Right in the middle of everybody. I yell out at the top of my lungs, "God damnit!"

JESUS: You're not supposed to say that.

TICO: Silence. Everyone stops in their tracks and turns around and stares at me like I'm the devil. They said I'm never allowed back to another meeting.

JELIN: A happy ending! Why don't you pull out those dominoes?

TICO: I don't have anything to bet. [**JELIN** *hands* **TICO** *a couple bucks.*]

JELIN: You still owe me from last time. [*He sets up the dominoes.*]

JESUS: I'm in.

JELIN: You got any money to put on the table?

JESUS: No because my papi's stingy.

TICO: Let the kid play. He doesn't have to put any money down. [*To* **JESUS.**] Make up a bet.

JESUS: If I win, I go to the city with my uncle.

JELIN: Oh no. I'm going for grown-up stuff.

JESUS: I'll be good.

JELIN: Your father wouldn't approve. You know how he is.

JESUS: He's working. He won't find out.

JELIN: What do I care? It's not like the kid is going to beat me at dominoes.

TICO: I've been giving him lessons.

JELIN: All bets are on the table.

> [*Their domino game begins. It should be choreographed like a macho ballet. Shuffling:* **JELIN** *pours the dominoes on the table and swirls them around. They make clicking sounds as they are shuffled. He deals each of the players their pieces.* **JELIN** *moves: he slides the domino on a teasing, curvy path along the table. Just before playing it, he lifts it and flicks it down in its place.* **TICO** *moves: he blows on the domino, then slaps it down with quick force.* **JESUS** *moves: no special move. Each player takes another turn. After* **JESUS***'s second turn, the men pause.*]

TICO: Did you see that? Who taught him that strategy? Tell me what kid has a game like that?

JELIN: Strategy only goes so far. You have to teach him how to look intimidating when he makes a move.

TICO: He plays it innocent. He makes you think he doesn't have a plan.

JELIN: [*To* **JESUS.**] Watch your uncle and learn. You have to create your own kind of move. If you want to be dictator of dominoes, you have to have style. [*He slides the domino across the table and then, with decisive force, flicks it down.*]

3

An old port city on the island. A bustling square in the middle of town, lined with historic buildings. JESUS *wanders on, followed by* JELIN.

JELIN: I told you to stay where I could see you. Don't go running off.

JESUS: How come they got so many people here?

JELIN: What kind of a question is that?

JESUS: Look at these signs. We need signs like this in Magdalena. Ours are embarrassing, all scribbled and made out of old cardboard. We need some neon signs. We need some fancy stuff.

JELIN: Check it out. It's a tattoo parlor. In the window, you can watch them drawing tattoos on people. They take a big needle, put some color on the tip, and, pah!, stick it under your skin. If you get lucky, maybe they're putting one on a woman's ass.

JESUS: Ew.

JELIN: You'll appreciate that one day.

JESUS: Papi has one on his nalga. But don't tell him I said that.

JELIN: I was there when he got it put on. He cried like a baby.

JESUS: Mami said it's a sin to have a tattoo. She said if you have one, you can't be buried like a normal dead person. You can only be buried in shame.

JELIN: That woman is always telling stories. God doesn't have time to be bothered with the small stuff.

JESUS: Sure he does.

JELIN: He has to keep the whole world running. You think he cares about a cheap tattoo on your father's ass?

JESUS: You're probably right.

JELIN: Of course I am.

JESUS: [*Pointing.*] Look at that sign. It's made out of gold.

JELIN: That's El Castillo.

JESUS: El Castillo.

JELIN: It's the oldest building on the island. It used to be a convent where all the nuns lived. But now they made it into a five-star hotel. The rooms have enormous beds. The pillows are bigger than your whole body. When you eat there, they give you a separate fork for your salad, your meat, and your rice.

JESUS: Do they get real important people staying there?

JELIN: Only the rich. They make sure of that.

JESUS: What about the President?

JELIN: We don't have a President.

JESUS: Why not?

JELIN: Because we have a dictator.

JESUS: I don't mean us. I mean the President of America.

JELIN: Sure. He stays in the Presidential Suite.

JESUS: You watch. I'm going to stay there one day. I'll bring mami, so she can sleep on the big bed. You can come too. You and me will go to the bar, buy some beers, curse about politics.

JELIN: Is that how grown men behave?

JESUS: We'll comb our moustaches. Drive up in fancy cars.

JELIN: And how do you plan to become one of the rich people?

JESUS: I'll get some money from papi.

JELIN: He doesn't have that kind of money.

JESUS: You don't know.

JELIN: Who's older, you or me?

JESUS: You.

JELIN: Then I know.

JESUS: I saw his money. He hides it in the rice barrels.

JELIN: What's he got? A barrel full of rusty old pennies?

JESUS: Once he opened one and showed me how to count to a hundred. He always says, don't spend it. Don't touch it. Don't look at it. Don't tell no one about it.

JELIN: You're telling me.

JESUS: I can trust you with my secrets.

JELIN: Anyway you can't dip into your father's stupid rice barrel. Real men have to earn their own money.

JESUS: I can be like Tico and open a store.

JELIN: Or be a farmer like me and your father.

JESUS: No. I want a sign with my name. A neon sign or a gold sign.

[*A carnival performer emerges. It is* **YEMAYA.** *She is young, heavy, and breathtakingly beautiful. Her skin is the richest shade of brown. She wears a regal blue dress adorned with cowries, silver lace, and duck feathers. Underneath the full skirt, her large hips sway like waves. She approaches* **JESUS** *and* **JELIN.** **JELIN** *is aroused.*]

JELIN: Good afternoon, señorita.

JESUS: Whoa. Look at her.

JELIN: Shh. [*To* **YEMAYA.**] Don't mind him.

JESUS: Is there a carnival?

JELIN: Use your brain. What do you think?

[**YEMAYA** *plucks a duck feather from her dress and ruffles it in* **JESUS**'*s hair.*]

YEMAYA: You like carnivals?

JESUS: [*Fixing his hair.*] They're okay.

YEMAYA: Oh. Then maybe I should go perform somewhere else.

JELIN: He loves carnivals.

YEMAYA: [*Placing a cup before her, for collecting tips.*] *For the spirits.*

[**JELIN** *and* **JESUS** *put some change in her cup.* **YEMAYA** *performs.*]

Remember me like you remember your ancestors

memory more vast than your human years

search back to the treasures in your birth

and find me there

Many of your ancestors were buried in my belly

blue eyes lie blind in my water

brown eyes lie blind in my water

in my dark water they are all the same,

the eyes of your ancestors

Do not forget me

come back to me

and I will slay your enemies

I will crusade for your comfort

I will swallow those who spite you

I will leave your enemies crying in shame

Then when death comes

you will see through the eyes of your parents

you will see through the eyes

that saw before you

you will speak through an eternal voice.

> [*Touching* **JESUS** *with the feather on "my children."*]

My children move in broad strokes

across this mortal world

just as my tide travels the large surface of the earth

But my tide is regular

and returns to the same shores

So do the hearts of my children

return to me

to the breast of Yemaya

> [*Her performance is over. She takes her change cup. Just as she exits,* **JESUS** *follows her and snatches the duck feather from her hand.*]

JELIN: Jesus, how dare you! Why the hell . . .? Don't you ever touch a woman like that. Do you understand me? I'm talking to you.

JESUS: Yes, tio.

JELIN: You want to be a rich man? You want to stay at El Castillo? Then you better learn to behave like a gentleman, not a stupid-minded little boy. What do you say?

JESUS: I'm sorry. I won't do that again.

JELIN: Give it to me. [**JESUS** *hands* **JELIN** *the feather.*]

RITUAL

JELIN *holds the feather. He puts it to his nose and, with a large nasal inhale, he smells it. That's how a woman smells. He puts it back to his nose and sniffs four staccato inhales in a row. Fruit. Fish. Saltwater. Blood. He touches the feather to his nipples, tickling and teasing them. He drags the feather down his torso and finally to his crotch, where he brushes the feather.*

END RITUAL

[**JESUS** *interrupts* **JELIN**, *imitating a very loud sniff.*]

JESUS: What does it smell like?

JELIN: Fruit. Fish.

JESUS: Ew.

JELIN: None of your business. If you're anything like your uncle, you'll get it one day.

JESUS: I think she liked you. She was giving you the eyes.

JELIN: Now I'm late for my meeting.

JESUS: Let me hold it. [**JELIN** *hands him the feather.*]

JELIN: Don't lose it.

JESUS: It's mine anyway.

JELIN: I'll be done soon. Don't leave the square. And keep your hands to yourself. [**JELIN** *exits.* **JESUS** *smells the feather, searching for what it is that* **JELIN** *had found there.*]

4

Later. **JESUS** *walks into Lila's Grocery on the square, feather in hand. There is a food counter with some stools.* **JESUS** *checks out the place, takes a seat.*

LILA: Hello there little man. What can I do for you?

JESUS: Nothing. Thank you.

LILA: Need a snack?

JESUS: Just looking around.

LILA: This is a grocery store, not a museum.

JESUS: Is this your place?

LILA: You see that sign out there? What's it say?

JESUS: L-I-L . . .

LILA: Lila's Grocery. That's me.

JESUS: Impressive sign.

LILA: It was the cheapest one I could find.

JESUS: Then I bet you didn't look in Magdalena. Believe me, where I come from they make them much cheaper.

LILA: You going to buy something?

JESUS: You keep it pretty clean in here.

LILA: Hey, you going to buy something?

JESUS: I'm waiting for my uncle.

LILA: If you're not going to buy something then wait for him outside.

[*Pause. He demonstrates the feather.*]

JESUS: I don't have any money. You want this?

LILA: Cash only.

JESUS: [*Bargaining.*] It smells like fruit.

LILA: Let me have a look. But no promises. [*He hands her the feather. She inspects it meticulously, messing around.*] I don't know. It's missing some fluff right here.

JESUS: It's from the dress of a queen.

LILA: The queen of what?

JESUS: Shoot. I didn't ask her.

LILA: Then how do you know she was a queen?

JESUS: If you smell it, it'll put you in a trance.

LILA: [*Smelling the feather.*] Wait a second . . . Hmmm . . . Hmmmmmmm . . . Hmmmmmmmmmmm. . . . Nope. No trance.

JESUS: I think she was the queen of the ocean.

LILA: The whole ocean, or one rinky-dink beach somewhere?

JESUS: The whole thing.

LILA: This will get you one drink. How's a Coke sound?

JESUS: Yes please.

LILA: Coming right up.

JESUS: I'm planning on opening a grocery store.

LILA: A man with an agenda.

JESUS: I'm going to make enough money to stay at that hotel. El Castillo.

LILA: You think I have that kind of money?

JESUS: You don't?

LILA: None of your business.

JESUS: I want a sign like yours except with my name. In my store if the kids are good, they get a free cookie.

LILA: That's no good. Let me give you some advice. You have to think like a businessman.

JESUS: You mean a business lady?

LILA: Rule number one. Nothing is free. Never give something for nothing.

JESUS: You've been in the business a long time, haven't you?

LILA: I've got an official business proposition for you. But only if you're serious about owning a grocery store. [*Pause.*] Well?

JESUS: I'll listen to your proposal.

LILA: When you're all grown up, come back and find me. You can buy this store from me. You get your sign. I take off to a secret location where no one can bother me.

JESUS: I like this store. I would definitely consider buying it.

LILA: [*Putting a bottle on the counter.*] Here's your Coke.

JESUS: Thank you. [*He picks up the bottle, but startled, he drops it on the ground.*] Ow!

LILA: What happened?

JESUS: It stung me!

LILA: What? [*She starts to clean it up.*] What a damn mess.

JESUS: It stung my hand when I touched it.

LILA: Honey, a bottle of Coke can't sting you. Look, I'm touching it and it isn't stinging me. Now feel it and tell me what's wrong with it.

JESUS: [*Feels the bottle, then pulls his hand away.*] Why does it feel like that?

LILA: You mean cold?

JESUS: Oh.

LILA: It's straight out of the refrigerator.

JESUS: I didn't drop it on purpose.

LILA: Have you ever had a Coke before? [*Pause.*] Do you know what a refrigerator is?

JESUS: Of course I do.

LILA: What is it?

JESUS: It's a thing that makes things sting.

LILA: Do they have electricity where you're from?

JESUS: I don't know.

LILA: So you don't drink your milk cold?

JESUS: Ew! Cold milk?

LILA: Let me fill you in on a little secret. Everyone outside your no-name town drinks their milk cold and their Coke cold.

JESUS: Magdalena.

LILA: What?

JESUS: That's the name of my town.

LILA: I bet you don't have running water.

[*Moment.*]

JESUS: Does the President of America drink things cold?

LILA: He would never drink a warm Coke.

JESUS: I still like it better the normal way.

LILA: It's the country boys like you that turn into stubborn old mules.

JESUS: My papi says that people who live in the city are backwards and twisted.

LILA: Look at me and tell me where I'm twisted. [*He looks at her. Nothing* *is twisted.*] Your father doesn't know everything. You learn the important stuff on your own, when your parents aren't around. I bet your father never showed you how to buy a Coke with a feather. Right? [*She sniffs the feather again. She retrieves another Coke bottle.*] Here. But drink it outside. If you drop it, you're on your own.

JESUS: But you said, rule number one, never give something for nothing.

LILA: Nothing? I got a feather and a good laugh.

JESUS: Can I still come back?

LILA: For what?

JESUS: To buy the store.

LILA: A deal's a deal.

JESUS: Let's shake on it. [*They shake.*]

LILA: Little Mulo. The stubborn one. Be very careful. The bottle's cold.

5

A minute later. **JESUS** *stands outside of Lila's Grocery. The bottle of Coke is in his hand.*

RITUAL

JESUS *holds the bottle of Coke in one hand. When the cold starts to burn that hand, he switches to the other and shakes out the burning hand for relief. He puts the bottle to his lips. He pulls it away. He sticks his tongue into the rim of the bottle. He licks the rim of the bottle. He sticks his tongue against the side of the bottle. He puts the bottle back to his lips and takes a gulp. He swishes the soda around rapidly in his mouth, puffing out his cheeks, and then swallows. His eyes widen. A smile slowly forms across his face. He starts gulping down the Coke.*

END RITUAL

[JELIN *enters.*]

JELIN: Where the hell were you?

JESUS: I went into the store.

JELIN: I said don't go anywhere.

JESUS: I got a refrigerator Coke.

JELIN: Put it down and let's go.

JESUS: It was free. I just gave her the feather.

JELIN: The bus leaves in a few minutes.

JESUS: You want to try?

JELIN: It's time to go home.

JESUS: But what about the signs? You said the movie theater has the best sign.

JELIN: Listen to me. Magdalena is having a fire.

JESUS: What's on fire?

JELIN: Some houses. They need water.

JESUS: My house is on fire?

JELIN: Some farms. I don't know. A lot of things.

JESUS: The fire's everywhere?

JELIN: No more questions.

JESUS: What about mami and papi?

JELIN: Did you hear me?

JESUS: The bus takes too long. It took us all morning.

JELIN: [*Referring to the Coke.*] What the hell is this?

JESUS: A refrigerator Coke.

JELIN: Put it down! [**JESUS** *doesn't move.*] Goddamnit, give it to me! [*He rips the bottle from* **JESUS**'*s hand and throws it to the ground.*]

JESUS: There was still some left.

6

Weeks later in Magdalena. After the fire. A dark place. **JESUS**'*s mother lies on the ground, still.* **JESUS** *sits beside her.*

JESUS: I got some oil to rub your skin. Does it still hurt here? [*He gently massages her side.*] Yesterday you made noises when I touched you here. Why don't you make some noises now? [*He pokes at her side, seeing if she'll make a noise.*] It's aloe and some other kind of stuff. Special stuff for the burns. Doña Aye made it for you. You put in on the skin, then you move your fingertips in little circles. Like you used to when I was sick. You would rub that tingly stuff on my chest. You would move your fingertips in little circles. It stunk, and then I would fall asleep and dream like I was flying over the mountains.

Can you hear me?

Are you still dreaming about ghosts?

Do you just dream at night or are you dreaming all the time now?

You should eat. [*He tries feeding her. There's no response.*]

I'll sing you a song. How about the one we used to sing on the farm and try to bother papi while he worked. When he was grumpy. [*He sings a lullaby.*]

I'm going to the sea
To meet my secret love
If she remembers me
The sun
The sun
The sun

> [*At the tune,* **MAMI** *rises from the floor. She sings along. They have a little dance they do when they sing this song.*]

MAMI: I'll sing her all my songs
And as the words are sung
They'll dance within her waves
The sun
The sun
The sun

JESUS and **MAMI:**
The sun lives at the edge of the sea
The sun said she would wait there for me
The sun . . .

MAMI: I'm going to the sea
To argue with the rain
And when the clouds are gone
The sun
The sun
The sun

> [**MAMI** *twirls offstage.*]

JESUS: Mami? [*He looks at the spot where she had been lying on the ground.*] I think you're dreaming all the time.

7

Night in Magdalena. Darkness. **JESUS** *and* **JELIN**, *digging graves.* **JESUS** *picks at the dirt with his shovel.* **JELIN** *is strong, an experienced digger.*

JESUS: I hate this place.

JELIN: God damnit. What did I just say?

JESUS: You're not supposed to use that word at a cemetery.

JELIN: That's right. I'm sorry.

> [*Silence as they dig.*]

JESUS: You're not supposed to use that word anywhere.

JELIN: At a funeral you are quiet. You respect the dead.

> [*Silence as they dig.*]

JESUS: This isn't a real funeral.

JELIN: You bow your head down and say goodbye.

> [*Silence as they dig.*]

JESUS: You're supposed to read from the Bible and the dead person is in a nice wooden box. And they already dug the hole ahead of time. And the men carry the box through town so the people can see and say goodbye.

JELIN: That's not how everyone does it. That's for lucky people.

> [*Silence as they dig.* **JESUS** *starts picking at the dirt oddly.*]

JESUS: Look. There's worms and bugs all over the place.

JELIN: Bugs only like the dirt. They don't touch the dead people.

JESUS: Yes they do.

JELIN: They're afraid of them. They won't touch your mother.

JESUS: Mami would say this kind of funeral is a sin.

JELIN: To her everything was a sin. Breathing was a sin. Eating was a sin. Smiling, being alive.

> [*Silence as they dig.*]

JELIN: Dig! Watch what you're doing and pay attention! Don't play with the dirt. You've hardly gone six inches. We'll be out here all night.

JESUS: It hurts my arm.

JELIN: Look how I do it. You hold the shovel one hand on top, one in the middle. Put it in the dirt. Push it in with your foot. Turn the shovel and throw the dirt behind you. [**JESUS** *follows the instruction.*]

JELIN: That's right. Be precise and strong. Don't pick at it like chicken feed. You have to learn to use your strength. [**JESUS** *digs more precisely.*]

JELIN: Good. That's the way it's done. [**JESUS**'s *digging becomes more focused and consistent.*] When my mother died, your father and I dug the grave. Our father, your grandfather, he tried to help but he was crying the whole time. He dug with his back to us so we couldn't see. We could tell. His eyes were red and puffy. When he died, your father and me dug the grave. Just the two of us. We didn't march through town. We didn't have money to pay the priest. Then after the fire, I buried your father alone. But I thought you should be here for your mother. She would like that. [**JESUS** *digs with increasing focus and precision.*] Sometimes you have to be like my father was. You want to cry but you turn your back and hide it. You don't let the world see. [**JESUS** *digs.*] When we're done, you can say something nice you remember about her. A story or something. That can be your prayer. [**JESUS** *digs stronger.*] Tomorrow we'll make a cross for the graves. We'll write their names on it. Okay? [**JESUS** *digs stronger.*] Answer me! [**JESUS** *digs stronger.*] Answer me or I'll whack you! [**JESUS** *hurls the shovel at his uncle. He lunges at* **JELIN** *and shoves him violently.* **JELIN** *stumbles.*] Go home.

JESUS: Where is that now?

8

A new day. Dark morning in Magdalena. **TICO** *sits at his crate. His shirt looks charred and ashy.* **MULO,** *formerly* **JESUS,** *enters. He is dragging a barrel behind him using a piece of rope.*

TICO: Good morning, Jesus. We missed you around here.

MULO: Don't call me Jesus. It's not my name anymore.

TICO: Oh yeah? What are they calling you these days?

MULO: Jesus is the name my parents gave me and I decided to change it.

TICO: I see.

MULO: You can call me Mulo now.

TICO: That's a weird name.

MULO: It's what a nice woman called me one time.

TICO: I don't think she was being nice if she called you a mule.

MULO: You weren't there.

TICO: So, Mulo, what's with the barrel?

MULO: I'm going to the city on business.

TICO: The bus doesn't come around until sunset.

MULO: As long as it comes.

TICO: It looks like you packed enough stuff.

MULO: It's money.

TICO: All right! I love money! Any in there for me?

MULO: No.

TICO: Let me get you a drink.

MULO: I'll have a coconut. And I'll open it myself.

TICO: Careful. [**TICO** *hands* **MULO** *a coconut.* **MULO** *holds it down with one hand. In four perfect, precise strokes, he creates a hole in the top.*]

TICO: You did it. You've been practicing haven't you?

MULO: I need a straw. [**TICO** *slips a straw into the hole.*]

TICO: If you can open a coconut, you can drink a little rum with it.

MULO: Really?

TICO: Just a drop.

MULO: I thought you're only supposed to drink at night.

TICO: Who told you that? It's never too early. [**TICO** *pours some rum into the coconut and hands it to* **MULO.** **MULO** *gulps and makes a face like it tastes strong.*] So how long are you going to be away on this big business trip?

MULO: Forever. I'm moving to the city.

TICO: Do you have family there?

MULO: I don't have family anymore.

TICO: Hey. Don't you ever say that. I'm your family. This town is your family.

MULO: [*He's drunk.*] This town? Before, the sun would rise and I would bring papi his cup of coffee. Now it's dark in the morning. The sun doesn't bother. The roosters don't know what time of day it is. Everyone's dead.

TICO: What about your uncle Jelin?

MULO: Your wife is dead.

　　　[*Moment.*]

TICO: Hey, you want to hear a story?

MULO: No.

TICO: It'll cheer you up.

MULO: So?

TICO: Baldomera used to drag me to her Pentecostal meetings over at her brother's farm. Those damn Pentecostals.

MULO: I heard this one.

TICO: The one where—

MULO: I'll have some more. [**TICO** *pours some more rum.*]

TICO: You're my only competition at dominoes. If you leave, then what am I supposed to do?

MULO: You can still play Jelin.

TICO: He's an idiot who thinks he's hot shit. I need a challenge or it's no fun.

MULO: Come visit me in the city and we can play dominoes there.

TICO: Hell no. Those city people don't play dominoes the right way. They have backwards rules. They play that you can match up a double piece with any piece you want. It doesn't matter what number it is.

MULO: No one plays like that.

TICO: I refuse to play dominoes with anyone in the city.

MULO: I'll teach them how to play right when I get there.

TICO: And they don't have good coconuts like I sell them here.

MULO: A coconut is a coconut.

TICO: They have shriveled coconuts with hardly no milk in them. You crack them open and sand pours out. They're always bringing in things from the outside. All they drink is Coke.

MULO: I like Coke.

TICO: Sure you do. You're a boy. But let me tell you. Coke is not on the same level as coconuts and dominoes. It never can be and it never will be. It's the natural hierarchy of the world.

MULO: I'm not a boy.

TICO: Jesus, you're not old enough to take care of yourself.

MULO: It's Mulo.

TICO: We have a responsibility to remember the beauty of Magdalena. What about the river? You used to spy on the girls swimming. And the mornings? I was there the first time you counted to ten.

MULO: Ten morning stars.

TICO: You would run around scaring the tree frogs.

MULO: They peed in my hand.

TICO: What about those mornings on the farm when you brought your father coffee?

MULO: I don't remember that.

TICO: I remember it for you. The city has no memories. Did you think about where you're going to stay? How are you going to eat? Things aren't free.

MULO: I have money.

TICO: Things are more expensive there.

MULO: This barrel has all my papi's savings.

TICO: Open it up and let me see.

MULO: I can't get it open. The fire made it stuck closed.

TICO: Give it to me. [**TICO** *pries open the barrel, looks inside.*]

MULO: Let me see my money.

TICO: Jesus.

MULO: Mulo.

TICO: Why don't you stay with me for a few days? I'll give you a job here at the stand. You already know how to do my inventory. You can be my assistant.

MULO: You want to steal my money.

TICO: It's not money.

MULO: Give it to me.

TICO: The barrel is full of rice.

MULO: It's hidden under the rice. Did you look under the rice?

TICO: It's all rice.

MULO: Liar. [**MULO** *reaches his arm into the barrel. It's all rice.*] Every night you go to sleep, you lay down on your family's ashes. When you breathe, it's your wife. When you walk you can feel her under your feet. You don't know what's a burned blanket and what's your wife's skin. You can't tell if it's the ashes from a book or your wife's hair.

TICO: Don't talk about Baldomera that way.

MULO: You breathe her in. You walk on her. You sleep on her. You go to the bathroom on her.

TICO: Go and wait for the bus somewhere else.

MULO: Look at this place, there's ashes everywhere. Ashes on your footprints. Look at your shirt. People's ashes on your shirt. It could be hers.

TICO: Get out of here.

MULO: Fine. [*He starts to leave.*]

TICO: Wait. Give me some rice to pay for your drink. You're a man. You learn to pay. [**MULO** *scoops some rice into the coconut husk and hands it to him.*]

MULO: There.

TICO: The bus stops another mile down the road. [**MULO** *drags his barrel off.* **TICO** *speaks after him.*] You should consider yourself lucky. At least your mother had a body. She had a burial. You should thank God for that. You don't know the difference between a blessing and a curse. [**MULO**'*s gone.* **TICO** *speaks to himself.*] This rice is my wife's ashes. I'll remember her voice that way. Her cooking. Her beautiful skin. Her dark skin. Her mulata hair in braids. She is not ashes. She is rice. I'll speak to her through the rice. Here's her heart. It can be so soft and so hard. Here's her body, and she doesn't have to be buried. I can carry her by my side.

RITUAL

He holds the coconut husk over his head and turns it upside down. Rice pours down over his head, shoulders, and falls to the ground. Then the husk is empty. He kneels to the ground and touches the rice around him. He lies on the ground, on top of the rice. He spots one grain of rice, puts it in his mouth and swallows it whole.

END RITUAL

TICO: Baldomera.

9

Lila's Grocery. **LILA** *is sweeping rice off the floor.* **MULO** *enters dragging the barrel.*

LILA: Hello there little man. That's quite a load. Is that a barrel on a rope? [**MULO** *doesn't know what to say.*] Why don't you have a seat? It looks like your feet could use a rest. [*He doesn't know what to say.*] What can I get for you today?

MULO: I came to buy the store.

LILA: Speak up honey. I'm not going to hurt you.

MULO: I came to buy the store.

LILA: What was that?

MULO: You don't remember me.

LILA: Don't take it personally. I get so many faces coming through here. In and out. So what's with the barrel?

MULO: It's full of money.

LILA: So I got a rich man in my store.

MULO: That's right.

LILA: What is it, rusty old pennies? Toy money?

MULO: And some rice.

LILA: You want some beans to go with that rice?

MULO: My house had a fire.

LILA: [*Moment.*] You're not from Magdalena? Where they had that big fire?

[*Moment.*] You're the boy who got burned by the soda bottle. See, I couldn't forget a face as sweet as yours. What happened to your family?

MULO: My mami had bandages on her face.

LILA: Come here and I'll give you a hug for her. [*She takes* **MULO** *into her arms.*]

MULO: Do they play dominoes here in the city?

LILA: They play right outside in the square.

MULO: But do they play with weird rules?

LILA: We play by the normal rules.

MULO: I like the rules my uncle taught me.

LILA: Was your uncle hurt in the fire?

MULO: Do you sell coconuts here?

LILA: We got some right over there.

MULO: You have to cut a hole in the top for a drink. That's how they do it in the country.

LILA: Listen, what's-your-name, this isn't a shelter.

MULO: [*Clears his throat.*] I'm following up on our deal. All I have is this rice but I would like to buy your store.

10

Sunrise at Lila's Grocery. **MULO** *is asleep on the floor. A girl shouts from outside.*

MAYA: Good morning! [*She taps on the door.*] Hello? [*She bangs on the door.*] Hey, on the floor. Are you open? [*She imitates the morning call of a rooster.* **MULO** *pops awake and lets her in.*]

MULO: How did you do that?

MAYA: Knocking didn't work.

MULO: I thought you were a rooster.

MAYA: Why are you sleeping on the floor like a stray dog?

MULO: It's my new bed.

MAYA: It's not a bed. It's the floor.

MULO: I used to sleep in a hammock, but they're not so great. You can tip over and fall out of them. On the floor you can't fall down.

MAYA: You can't fall down if you're already at the bottom.

[*Moment.*]

MULO: Hello and welcome to Lila's Grocery. How can I help you?

MAYA: I need two cases of Spam.

MULO: Let's see. [*He peruses a sheet of paper.*] According to my inventory, we have less than one case in stock. Do you want to place an order?

MAYA: As long as I can get it by the end of the week.

MULO: I have to check with my boss. What is that Spam anyway?

MAYA: It's meat in a can.

MULO: What kind of meat?

MAYA: American meat.

MULO: Is it as good as a refrigerator Coke?

MAYA: What?

MULO: A refrigerator Coke. It's a cold drink. It stings you and tastes good at the same time. It's like pleasure and pain all mixed up in your mouth. [*He retrieves a Coke bottle.*] You want one?

MAYA: You mean, a refrigerated Coke.

MULO: You want to feel it?

MAYA: No, just the Spam.

MULO: Don't you get sick of meat-in-a-can?

MAYA: My mother used to have it on her boat.

MULO: She was a fisherman?

MAYA: I don't like boys who ask a lot of questions.

MULO: It's important to be friends with my customers.

MAYA: It's top secret. She took people on boat rides to America. She took Spam because the meat never spoils.

MULO: Did you go with her?

MAYA: Sometimes.

MULO: So you actually went inside of America?

MAYA: They have a hundred kinds of Coke there.

MULO: What? I thought there's only one kind.

MAYA: They have a thousand kinds of meat-in-a-can.

MULO: Have you tasted them all?

MAYA: You could live there all your life and you still wouldn't have enough time to taste everything.

MULO: I'd eat a different kind of meat-in-a-can every day until I had tasted every single kind. And I'd drink a different kind of Coke each time to wash it down. Do they have Coke flavored like a coconut?

MAYA: I don't think so.

MULO: If there's a hundred flavors one of them has to be coconut. It's one of the basics.

MAYA: The flavors are different than the kind we have here. They have dark cherry. Lemon. Orange. Blueberry. Chocolate. Vanilla. Flavors like that.

MULO: Coconut Coke. Coconut coca-cola. Coco-cola. Cocola. Cola-coco. Cona-loco. Coca-nola. Co. Ca. No. La. Coca-nola! I'm going to invent it. The President of America is going to love it better than any other flavor.

MAYA: Maybe you'll make a fortune and you won't have to sleep on the floor anymore.

MULO: I'll sleep in fancy hotels. [**MAYA** *sees the duck feather displayed on the counter.*]

MAYA: What's this for?

MULO: It's from the queen of the ocean.

MAYA: I'm not impressed. [**MAYA** *picks up the feather. She inspects it. She smells it. In a teasing, sensual manner, she puts it down her shirt and under her bra.*]

MULO: That's stealing.

MAYA: Are you going to tell on me?

> [**LILA** *enters.*]

LILA: You opened the store without me?

MULO: We had a customer.

LILA: I'm sorry. What can I do for you?

MAYA: The little boy was helping me.

MULO: She put in an order for two cases of Spam.

MAYA: I need it by the end of the week.

LILA: That shouldn't be a problem.

MAYA: What's the price?

LILA: Ten cents a can.

MAYA: They used to be less.

LILA: They're twice as much down the street.

MAYA: Only one case, then. I'll be in on Friday to pick it up. [**MAYA** *exits.*]

MULO: I had my first customer. Here's the order slip. One case of Spam by Friday. High priority.

LILA: You don't open the store unless I'm here.

MULO: I could barely sleep last night. The neon is really bright. The men were playing dominoes in the square. When are you going to teach me the city rules?

LILA: We have more important things to take care of.

MULO: I stayed up and made lists of everything you sell. It's called inventory. [*He pulls out a piece of paper and reads from it.*] Bottles of Coke, twenty eight. Eleven in the refrigerator, seventeen on the shelf. Egg cartons, eight. Cans of pigeon peas, nineteen. You're low on bread. Only four rolls.

LILA: Slow down a minute.

MULO: Cans . . . of . . . green . . . peas . . .

LILA: Let me see. [**MULO** *hands her the inventory.*] Half these things aren't spelled right.

MULO: I wrote it late. I was tired.

LILA: It doesn't matter how many pigeon peas we have.

MULO: My friend Tico runs a business and he said you have to keep track of things.

LILA: Is he from Magdalena?

MULO: Why?

LILA: Was he hurt in the fire?

MULO: I don't know.

LILA: This weekend the two of us will take a drive to Magdalena and pay him a visit.

MULO: We should stay here so I can see what the weekend business is like.

LILA: We'll go on Sunday when the store is closed.

MULO: Now that you have me here, we can stay open on Sunday.

LILA: Does your uncle know where you are?

MULO: I don't have any uncles.

LILA: You said you did.

MULO: We should sit down today and discuss our deal. How much I have to pay you for the store. When we can add my name to the sign. How we'll split the work. Unless you want to retire all together.

LILA: Mulo, I could barely pay you in pennies.

MULO: How many pennies?

LILA: You can't just sleep on the floor. Magdalena's only a few hours away.

MULO: I have to wash the windows.

LILA: Not on Sunday you don't.

MULO: I have to get things ready for Monday.

LILA: Your uncle's probably looking all over for you.

MULO: I have to stay here and clean the refrigerator. I have to polish the sign. What will people think if the windows aren't clean on Monday?

LILA: I'm not bargaining with you.

MULO: Fine. If you want to cheat and break your deal. You want to send me back to the ashes. There's still burned dogs in the street. And bugs in the dirt. You can leave me with the bugs.

LILA: We're finding your family.

MULO: Worms in the dirt.

[*Moment.* **LILA** *gets the dominoes.*]

LILA: How about I teach you those city rules now?

[*Moment.*]

MULO: I was very good at the country rules. If it's anything similar, I'll probably beat you.

LILA: First thing, you make a bet. In the city, we only play when there's money on the table.

MULO: All I have is rice.

LILA: [*Hands him some pennies.*] Here's some pay for taking care of the inventory.

MULO: Can you bet things other than money?

LILA: You can bet whatever.

MULO: If I win, we don't ever go to Magdalena. I open the store on Sunday and you get a day off.

LILA: And if I win, we go find your uncle.

MULO: I also bet three pennies. Soon my barrel will be full of money.

[**LILA** *deals out the dominoes.* **JESUS** *goes first. He now has a "move."* *He puts the domino on the table face down and quickly flips it over, revealing his play.* **LILA** *moves. She holds the domino in the opponent's face and then slams it on the table. They continue to play in silence.*

Sunrise in Magdalena. **TICO** *is asleep on the floor under his bar. The coconut husk that holds his wife's rice is curled in his arms.* **JELIN** *walks in and slowly, without disturbing* **TICO**, *peeks into the coconut husk.*]

JELIN: Service! Service! [**TICO** *wakes up.*] Can a man get some service around here?

TICO: Closed for business. How many times do I have to tell you?

JELIN: You can't be closed on a day like today. We have to celebrate.

TICO: I was asleep. It was peaceful.

JELIN: The government farm scientist guy came through.

TICO: Let me guess. They're not giving us any aid.

JELIN: Next year at this time, our farms will be doing better than ever. The fire burned away all the crappy old dirt. The dirt underneath is more fertile. It's nutrient-rich.

TICO: Next year? I'm hungry now. I can't wait a year to eat a yam.

JELIN: Pull out the dark rum and let's have a toast.

TICO: You finished off my dark rum yesterday.

JELIN: We only need a drop.

TICO: The bottle's dry.

JELIN: How about some light rum, then?

TICO: It exploded in the fire.

JELIN: Did all your beers explode, too?

TICO: You want a bottle or a can?

JELIN: Bottle.

TICO: No more bottles.

JELIN: Well then a can.

TICO: All out of cans.

JELIN: Bullshit. I know you got something back there. You owe me ten bucks from dominoes. Give me the beer and I'll reduce your debt to five.

TICO: What beer?

JELIN: You can't lie to save your life.

TICO: I've got the best poker face around.

JELIN: Oh yeah? Let's see. [*He looks* **TICO** *in the eye.*] Based on your brilliant poker face, I say you've got one . . . bottle . . . of lager behind the bar.

TICO: Don't do this to me.

JELIN: That's some poker face!

TICO: Who do they think they are to come and tell us the fire was a good thing? They walk into a widow's home and say, you're very lucky woman. It's an excuse not to give us any aid.

JELIN: We'll play dominoes. If I win, I get the beer. If I win twice in a row, I get the beer and the rice.

TICO: What rice?

JELIN: The rice you got hidden in that coconut. You were hugging it like a baby. We'll have a beer and rice feast!

TICO: It's not rice for eating.

JELIN: What's it for then?

TICO: For having around.

JELIN: I'm a master at cooking rice.

TICO: If it was for eating, I would have had it a week ago when I ran out of food.

[**TICO** *pulls out the dominoes. He deals and they begin to play. Their play overlaps with* **MULO** *and* **LILA***'s game.*]

TICO: Any word from Jesus? [**JELIN** *moves.* **TICO** *stops playing.*]

JELIN: It's your move. [**TICO** *holds his domino, waiting for an answer.*]

TICO: Go find him.

JELIN: Are we playing dominoes or discussing my personal matters?

[*The men play in silence.* **LILA** *makes her winning move.*]

MULO: That's not fair.

LILA: See, it's not so different than the country rules.

MULO: If it was country rules I would have won.

LILA: We go find your family.

MULO: One more game.

LILA: You learned your first real lesson in the city. Never bet high unless you know what you're doing. [*She takes his pennies from the table.*]

11

Lila's Grocery. The end of the week. **MULO** *and* **MAYA** *are in the store.*

MULO: One case of meat-in-a-can.

MAYA: How much does it cost?

MULO: How much does it cost to go to America?

MAYA: I said, what do I owe you?

MULO: Please. I need to go on the boat with you. I have to leave soon.

MAYA: Will you be quiet? Don't just blurt it out so everyone can hear. You can't use the words boat or America.

MULO: I'm good at keeping secrets.

MAYA: It costs a lot of money. You have to plan it in advance.

MULO: The woman who owns this place says I'm a stray dog. She's going to make me sleep on the floor forever.

MAYA: The ocean isn't so good for sleeping.

MULO: America is.

MAYA: Don't say that word.

MULO: In that place, there's a hammock waiting for me.

MAYA: They sleep in beds there.

MULO: There's a fancy hotel where I'm going to stay. I'll give you the Spam for free.

MAYA: You mean you'll steal it? What if you're trying to rat me out or something? Maybe you're going to run and tell the police.

MULO: I swear on my mother's spirit. I didn't tell on you for stealing the feather.

MAYA: What happened to your mother?

[*Moment.*]

MULO: Two cases, for free.

MAYA: We need drinks.

MULO: Free.

MAYA: Tonight at midnight. There's a blue house at the end of the pier. Light a stick of incense. When you see my signal, return it. That's how fishermen talk to each other at night.

MULO: What about fisherwomen?

MAYA: All the original fishers were women.

MULO: Maybe that's why men like the ocean so much.

MAYA: Men don't like the ocean. They're scared of it, and they like being scared. You don't know about what men like.

MULO: Sure I do. I am one.

MAYA: Then you can bring all the Spam with you tonight so I don't have to carry it. Remember, how fishers talk to each other.

MULO: So no one else can hear.

12

Midnight. Sounds of water lapping. Darkness. A light flickers on and off. Another flicker. A signal.

MAYA: Who's there?

MULO: It's Mulo.

MAYA: You got the food? [**MAYA** *flicks on a light just long enough to reveal the Spam, Coke, and* **MULO**'s *barrel.*]

MAYA: What's in the barrel?

MULO: That's my personal stuff.

MAYA: The boat's too small. No personal stuff allowed.

MULO: It's my papi's savings.

MAYA: Stuff like that is dangerous on the ocean. The pirates come looking to steal whatever you have.

MULO: Pirates? Are you kidding me? [**MAYA** *flicks on the light and looks inside the barrel.*]

MAYA: Pennies and rice? Even the pirates wouldn't want this. Roll it in the water so it floats away and doesn't blow our cover.

MULO: It's good rice.

MAYA: I'm in charge. Understand? Now, are you coming or should I leave you here with your rice? [*We hear a splashing sound as the barrel is dropped into the water.*] Follow close behind and stay quiet. If you have to cough or sneeze, bunch up your shirt and cough quietly into the fabric. Once you get on the boat, I'll give you a fishing rod. You have to sit upright and carry it like a fisher. When you get tired, we trade and you rest a little.

MULO: I can't see.

MAYA: Hold on to me.

MULO: Do you think my barrel will sink or float? Where will it float to?

[*Water splashes nearby.*]

MULO: Someone's coming.

MAYA: Calm down. It's the water. Are you ready?

[*A voice cuts through the night. An echo that is too close.*]

MAMI: Jesus! [**MULO** *stops.*]

MAYA: What are you doing? Come on.

MULO: Did you hear that?

MAYA: It's the frogs. They sound like that at night.

MAMI: Jesus! Come and bring your father his coffee. He said you never brought him the second cup.

MULO: Mami?

MAYA: You're too young to come.

MAMI: Jesus! Did you bring him the coffee? Or were you lazy instead?

MULO: Maya? Where are you?

MAYA: Shh. We're almost there. Now touch the dirt and say goodbye.

13

Sunrise on the ocean. Blue water splashes against the boat. **MAYA** *opens a can of Spam.*

MULO: Does it sting when you eat it?

MAYA: No. For the tenth time.

MULO: Does it have little air bubbles?

MAYA: Here you go. Smell it first. [*He smells the meat.*]

MULO: Does all American meat smell like that?

MAYA: You get used to it. It says here, "Ingredients: Pork with added ham." Scoop some with your fingers. [*She hands him the can. He scoops some out with his fingers and tastes it.*]

MULO: It doesn't taste like refrigerator Coke.

MAYA: Not refrigerator Coke. Just one word. Coke.

MULO: It's not as good as mami's pork chops.

MAYA: But it never goes bad. [*They eat together.*]

MULO: How long til we get to America?

MAYA: It depends. A couple weeks usually.

MULO: What color do they paint the houses? Blue?

MAYA: It's not colors. It's brick.

MULO: What about hotels? What's the name of the fancy hotel?

MAYA: It's like Coke and meat-in-a-can. There's too many for me to name them all.

MULO: Did you ever meet the President of America?

MAYA: No more talking about America. Talk about the water. On a boat you tell water stories.

MULO: I don't know any water stories.

MAYA: Here's one. My mother is a water spirit.

　　　[*Pause. Long pause.*]

MULO: And?

MAYA: Her spirit lives at the bottom of the ocean. When there's a storm, I can hear her voice saying my name.

　　　[*Longer pause.*]

MULO: That's it?

MAYA: It's impressive.

MULO: That's not how you tell a story. You have to start at the beginning and say a lot of stuff that happens. And you have to give good details. Start over. From the way beginning.

MAYA: There was a woman who lived by the water. A fisherwoman.

MULO: Wait. What kind of fish did she catch?

MAYA: I don't know.

MULO: Make it up.

MAYA: Jellyfish.

MULO: Ew.

MAYA: And she cleaned off the slimy part and cooked arroz con jellyfish.

MULO: Ew. That's good.

MAYA: Her boat was called The Decision. On her boat, she took people to far away countries and continents. Out on the ocean, she caught fish with her bare hands. She scaled and prepared the fish with her strong teeth. Then she lay the fish on her warm belly to cook it. She fed many journeyers this way. On one trip, a man loved the flavor of the fish so much, he fell in love with her. He touched her belly and they kissed. Like this. [*Pause.*] They made a baby on the ocean. The baby grew inside the woman's watery belly, and then was born. She grew to be a gorgeous young woman. Sometimes she went on the boat with her mother. Sometimes she stayed back home by herself and waited for The Decision to appear on the horizon. One time, the girl waited more days than usual. Then more weeks than usual. Every night she stood with her ankles in the sand, waiting. It started to rain. Rain fell in the sand, in the waves. In the rain, she heard her mother's voice calling her name. "Maya! Maya!"

MULO: What happened to the mami?

MAYA: She sprouted seaweed for hair.

MULO: And the papi?

MAYA: She never met him. She drifts off in a boat to try and find him.

MULO: I think she'll find him.

MAYA: Don't say mami and papi. Say mother and father.

MULO: Mother and father.

MAYA: Now you tell a water story.

MULO: Red white and blue
Sugar and gin
My story begins

MAYA: What?

MULO: That's how I start. Say it with me.

MAYA and **MULO:** Red white and blue
Sugar and gin
My story begins

MULO: When I was a kid, we lived at the top of the highest mountain in the whole world. It was so high up, you could feel a breeze when St. Peter opened Heaven's gates to let someone in. Before the sun rose, my father left to water the farm. It was still dark out. The stars were like a thousand blinking eyes. See? [*He blinks his eyes like stars.*] I walked across the farm to bring him coffee. I waited for him to finish, to bring the empty cup back to my mother. Sip. Wait. Sip. Wait. While I waited, I looked at his feet. They were dirty and sweaty. All around his ankles, the tiny leaves were covered with little drops of dew. Mixed with the dirt. I used to believe his sweat was part of the dew. I thought, that must be how all these plants grow, from my father's sweat.

Now here's the end part. Say it with me.

MAYA and **MULO:** Red white and blue
Sugar and rum
My story is done

MAYA: Why were you looking at his feet?

MULO: He didn't really talk. I just stood there waiting. Never mind, you don't get it. [*Suddenly,* **MULO** *goes to the side of the boat, feeling sick.*] The Spam gave me a stomach ache.

MAYA: You're seasick. The waves are bad right now. It goes away after a couple days.

　　[*Light rain.*]

MULO: Listen. It sounds like tree frogs.

MAYA: It sounds like a storm.

MULO: Can you hear your mother? [**MAYA** *listens.*] Do you ever wish you could sink all the way to the bottom of the ocean and see her again?

　　[*Harsh rain erupts. It sounds like tree frogs. The ocean becomes violent.*]

MAYA: We have to scoop the water out of the boat.

　　[*The storm intensifies.* **MULO** *rises and walks to the edge of the boat. He leans over, feeling the storm push and pull at his gravity.*]

MAYA: Stop fooling around and come help me.

MULO: Don't you want the water to cover you?

MAYA: Grab the food!

MULO: [*Yelling over the storm.*] Hello! Hello! Hello!
Red white and blue
Sugar and gin!
Red white and blue
Sugar and rum!

MAYA: Don't stand there! A wave could hit!

　　[*Layers of blue thrash in every direction. A blue wave rises and covers* **MULO**'*s body. He disappears.*]

14

Underwater. **MULO** *plummets through layers and layers of blue. Down, down, down. Tumbling through bubbles and blue. In the blurry distance, at the ocean* *floor,* **MAMI** *sits at a table and plays dominoes alone. She sings to herself. Every so often, she moves, kissing the domino and then placing it down.*

MAMI: I'm going to the sea
To meet my secret love
If she remembers me
The sun
The sun
The sun
I'll sing her all my songs
And as the words are sung
They'll dance within her waves
The sun
The sun
The sun

> [**MULO** *continues to plummet. Slowly, a sign comes into view. It is El Castillo, the hotel underwater.* **TICO** *is the concierge. He approaches* **MULO.**]

TICO: Excuse me, sir, are you lost?

MULO: Which way is it to America?

TICO: Right this way, sir.

MULO: Is it to the left or right?

TICO: If you follow me I'll be happy to assist you. [*He leads* **MULO** *into the hotel.* **MAMI** *is in the lobby, playing dominoes with herself and humming quietly.* **MULO** *sees her.*]

MULO: Who is she?

TICO: Welcome to El Castillo hotel. How can I be of service on this fine day?

MULO: I guess. . . . I would like a room for one, please.

TICO: Wait. I'm sorry. Are you Señor Mulo? Of course. I'm Tico, the main man. We already have your reservation. The Presidential Suite. At the risk of being bold, I must tell you. The President of America was furious when he found out you reserved his suite. But what could I do? Señor Mulo, of course, is the preferred guest. And how long will you be staying with us?

MULO: A hundred days.

TICO: I'll mark you down forever, just in case. Otherwise the President may try to book your room for a later date. Your payment was wired to us, in rice and pennies. Your luggage has arrived and it's quite handsome. [*He points to the entrance, where* **MULO's** *barrel is propped.*] I'll have a porter bring that down to you.

MULO: That would be excellent.

TICO: I have a message for you. An Uncle Jelin is waiting at the bar.

MULO: Send word I'll see him soon.

TICO: Of course.

MULO: [*Points to* **MAMI.**] Who is she?

TICO: Just a lady who plays dominoes.

MULO: Where is she from?

[JELIN *enters.*]

JELIN: Hey! Señor Mulo! I've been waiting forever. This place is horrible without you. There's nothing to do. I got all our preparations together. They got our drinks ready at the bar. They got our moustache combs. They got forks, knives, and spoons.

MULO: Do they have the big pillows?

JELIN: Wait until you see them. They're enormous. But I have to warn you. The President of America had a tantrum after the Presidential Suite fiasco.

MULO: Tell him to join us at the bar for some drinks.

JELIN: He's refusing to talk to you.

MULO: Did he try Coca-Nola yet?

JELIN: Rumor has it he can't stop drinking the stuff. His advisors say he has one with every meal, plus a fourth as a late-night cocktail.

MULO: Send him a bottle from my personal collection, along with an invitation to join us at the bar. He can't refuse that.

JELIN: Perfect. He's a sucker for expensive gifts. [*He exits.*]

TICO: Here's your key. Make sure you don't lose it. They're nearly impossible to duplicate down here. [*He hands* **MULO** *the coconut husk.*] To get to your room, take the grand staircase. Follow it down, down, down. As far down as it goes. Your door is the last one on the bottom. That's the penthouse. The presidential suite. It has the most stunning view.

MULO: Down, down, down. As far as it goes.

TICO: As a matter of fact, I'll lead you there. [*They begin to exit.* **MAMI** *looks up from her dominoes.*]

MAMI: Mulo. Want to play a hand?

MULO: You know my name.

MAMI: Mulo the dominoes legend. They say your strategy can beat anyone.

MULO: Do I know you?

MAMI: The only boy I know is named Jesus. Should I deal you in?

MULO: I don't have any money to put down. My papi was stingy.

MAMI: We don't play for money down here. Ocean rules. It's the jungle or the desert. Life or death. Wind or water. Kiss or stop breathing. Which one are you betting on?

MULO: How do you decide?

MAMI: Blue green and gold
Yucca and corn
Your memory is born

TICO: Sir? Your room's waiting.

MULO: [*To* **MAMI.**] I have to get settled but I'll be back later. After I meet the President of America. Wait for me.

[**TICO** *disappears down the staircase.* **YEMAYA** *enters the hotel.*]

YEMAYA: Remember me like you remember your ancestors.

MULO: Excuse me! I have to comb my moustache.

YEMAYA: Brown eyes lie blind in my water.

MAMI: Kiss or stop breathing.

YEMAYA: You will see through the eyes of your parents.

MULO: I have to go all the way to the bottom.

YEMAYA: You will speak through an eternal voice. [*They kiss.*]

15

A minute later on the boat. **MAYA** *performs CPR on* **MULO.** *The ocean is still. His shirt is gone. His body is limp.*

MAYA: Hello? Mulo? Cough once if you can hear me. [*Pause.*] If you don't cough then you're dead and the sharks will come eat you. [*She holds his nose shut. He coughs.*] How many fingers am I holding up?

MULO: Blue green and gold
Yucca and corn
Your memory is born

MAYA: Saltwater twists the way you see things. You had saltwater coming out of everywhere. Out of your ears and nose. You were spitting it up.

MULO: I went to heaven.

MAYA: No, our Spam did. And our water did. Our compass. Everything went overboard.

MULO: It's at the lowest part of the ocean. Where no one's ever been. That's where they keep all the cans and the pork chops. I was about to go to the bottom but then you came and kissed me.

MAYA: It wasn't kissing. It's what you do when people stop breathing.

MULO: I saw the domino woman in the hotel.

MAYA: Oh God. Do you know what happens to people who starve on the ocean? Your stomach twists tighter and tighter until it snaps. And what we have to do for water?

MULO: She said you're pretty and you should kiss me.

MAYA: Hey! There's no hotel! There is no heaven!

MULO: That's how they kiss in America. Big wet kiss. [*He coughs.*]

16

Many days later. **MULO** *lies limp on the floor of the boat. He is weak, his body is shivering. He is moaning happily, deep in the midst of a sexual dream.*

MULO: Ahh.

MAYA: Mulo.

MULO: Ah. Ahh. Ahhh.

MAYA: Oh God.

MULO: Mmmm.

MAYA: Mulo! Wake up!

MULO: Look at her! [*He wakes up.*]

MAYA: You're talking in your sleep again.

MULO: Oh. What an amazing dream.

MAYA: By the sound of it, they've all been pretty amazing lately.

MULO: Poof. Into the air. I wish I could get it back. All men should sleep on the ocean.

MAYA: You're dehydrated and you're having wet dreams.

MULO: Did I miss anything exciting?

MAYA: Some clouds looked like a pineapple. A bird took a shit.

MULO: No American boat came to our rescue?

MAYA: A huge pack of jellyfish floated by. That's what our Spam looked like when sunk in the storm. All those cans like silver jellyfish falling through the waves.

MULO: I feel like a refrigerator. As soon as I wake up I feel my stomach again. [*He moves to the side of the boat, queasy, but nothing comes out.*]

MULO: There's nothing inside me.

MAYA: The sun won't go away.

MULO: You want to rip this part of you out. [*She feels his forehead for a fever.*]

MAYA: You have to think of something else. Why don't you tell me what your dream was like?

MULO: A man doesn't tell his secrets.

MAYA: You're not a man yet.

MULO: That's what you think.

MAYA: Then tell me about your manly dream.

MULO: Only if you tell me a secret in return.

MAYA: That's childish.

MULO: Then no deal.

MAYA: Okay, okay.

MULO: In my dream I was walking through the city. Kind of the city, except it was underwater. A woman came up to me. She had these amazing, enormous hips.

MAYA: What was she wearing?

MULO: A blue dress.

MAYA: Oh. I though she might not be wearing anything.

MULO: Her hands looked normal at first. But then I realized, instead of fingertips she had little seashells. She started to touch me with her seashell fingertips.

MAYA: Where?

MULO: I don't remember.

MAYA: I bet you do.

MULO: It felt smooth. Like the skin of an orange. Like the edge of a penny. You know when you cut open a coconut, if you run your finger inside the white part? That's how it felt. Do you think in America the women are beautiful like the woman from my dream?

MAYA: No. They're only that beautiful when you're lost at sea.

MULO: Then I'm glad I'm lost.

MAYA: Am I as beautiful as she was?

MULO: Maybe.

MAYA: Have you ever had a woman touch you?

MULO: Now it's your turn.

MAYA: The way the woman in your dream touched you?

MULO: You have to tell me a secret now.

MAYA: I've touched like that before. With boys on the boat. Show me how she touched you.

MULO: My fingers are all rough. See? [*She touches his fingers.*]

MAYA: I'll pretend.

MULO: I can't do it as good as the woman in my dream.

MAYA: Try. [*He leans his hand out to touch her. She grabs his hand and holds it still.*]

MAYA: Wait. Am I as beautiful as the woman in your dream?

MULO: Maybe.

RITUAL

MULO *reaches his hands out and touches her. His fingers slide up and down her body, making the motion of waves. As he does this, he makes whooshing sounds through his teeth.* **MULO** *puts his fingers to her breasts and pops his fingertips like sea foam.* **MULO** *reaches under her shirt and slowly pulls the out feather from between her breasts. He puts the feather to his nose and smells it. That is how a woman smells.*

END RITUAL

MAYA: What does it smell like?

MULO: Fruit. [*Inhale.*] Fish. [*Inhale.*] Saltwater. [*Inhale.*] Blood.

17

In the boat. Bright sun. Tired skin. Dry lips. **MAYA** *and* **MULO** *sit lethargically, little energy left.* **MAMI** *sits on the surface of the water.*

MULO: Hmm?

MAYA: What?

MULO: Don't fall asleep.

MAYA: I'm tired.

MULO: What if you don't wake up?

MAYA: Leave me alone.

MULO: What happens if you don't have a funeral?

MAYA: I don't know.

MULO: I think your soul wanders around and you can never rest.

MAYA: That's what's going to happen to us. We're not getting a funeral. We're going to float forever. Lost.

MULO: No. In America everyone has a real funeral.

MAYA: Wander around forever. Lost and lost and lost.

MULO: Did your mother have a funeral?

MAYA: We never found her body.

MULO: That's why you hear her voice when it rains. Maya. We have to give our mothers a funeral.

MAYA: You can't have a funeral without the body.

MULO: Pretend like the feather is their body. [*He holds up the feather.*] See? It's soft like her hair.

MAYA: Like her belly was.

MULO: Welcome to the funeral of our mothers. We don't have their bodies but this feather stands for them instead.

MAYA: Say their names. Gloria Perez.

MULO: Teresa Morales. [**MAMI** *rises and stands before the feather.*] Now we will say our prayers. Saint Peter, I hope you let my mother into heaven. Give her a green tree to sit under when she does the sewing. And give her some pork chops to fry, you won't regret it. And she likes her coffee with no sugar. Amen.

MAYA: Yemaya, Queen of the Ocean, let my mother speak through a seashell. Like the ones you hear on the beach. That way she can whisper like she used to after I went to bed. But she used to yell a lot, too, so give her some storms and hurricanes every once in a while. Amen. Now what? [*They hold the feather in the air. The wind blows in circles and spirals around them. Water splashes against the boat.*]

[*Magdalena.* **TICO** *is at his bar stand, holding the coconut husk.*]

TICO: Baldomera. Forgive me. Pouring you over my body, imprisoning you in the palm of my hand, clinging to you at night like a child. They said to plant whatever we have and it will be the best harvest ever. I'm no farmer, but what else can I do? The stand is down the drain. After the fire, no one's buying. Just making ends meet. I am going to plant you. Grain by grain. I will come and farm and talk to you and water the earth. You will become the mountain. [*He tosses rice onto the ground like seed.*]

[*The cemetery.* **JELIN** *stands before* **MAMI**'s *grave with a Coke bottle.*]

JELIN: It's been three weeks now. I found a woman in the city who saw him. She even took him in for a few nights, but she said he disappeared. A young boy, alone in the city. I searched all over. I took to the street. "Have you seen this boy? Please, have you seen my nephew?" Look. I wrote your name on it. "To Teresa, love your son Jesus." Tico said he liked Coca Cola. I promised Jesus I would put a cross on your grave but this is even better. [*He places the Coke bottle at the head of the grave.*]

[*The ocean. The air blows in circles, whistling and spinning. Water and wind all around.* **MULO** *and* **MAYA** *hold the feather in the air. They let go.* **MAMI** *catches the feather as it twirls through the air. She walks*] *on the surface of the water, waving the feather as she goes.* **MULO** *and* **MAYA** *watch as the feather glides into the distance.*]

MAYA: I think it worked.

MULO: They heard us.

[*The wind blows in circles and spirals. Water splashes against the boat.*]

MAYA: Mulo, look. Really far away.

MULO: It's the feather.

MAYA: Squint your eyes.

MULO: A mosquito? A horsefly sitting on the water.

MAYA: Red white and blue.

MULO: A fisherman? A rescue boat.

MAYA: Sugar and gin.

MULO: A little bit of green. White dots where the waves are crashing.

MAYA: Our story begins.

MULO: It's land.

[*They move through the wind and the water.*]

END OF PLAY

One-Act Plays

Supernova in Hamlet
KRISTINA LEACH

About the Playwright

Kristina Leach attended the Kennedy Center American College Theatre Festival as both a playwright and an actor. In 1999, she traveled to Washington, D.C. as an Irene Ryan Scholarship hopeful representing Region VIII. In the year 2000, *Supernova in Hamlet* won the 2000 John Cauble Short Play Award for the Kennedy Center's American College Theater Festival. In 2002, Kristina returned to the Festival again as the first runner-up for the David Mark Cohen Award for her play *Grasmere*. After she graduated from Cal State Fullerton, Kristina went on to write plays for all ages, most recently the play *1212* commissioned for South Coast Repertory's Young Conservatory Program. In March 2005, she was awarded the Orange County Weekly Theatre Award for Best New Play for *The Medea Project*, a modern retelling of the Greek myth. Kristina's work has been seen on stages in Los Angeles, Orange County and New York. In addition to writing and acting, Kristina is an accomplished director. She also teaches playwriting at the Orange County High School of the Arts and Basic Fundamentals of Acting at South Coast Repertory where she currently works as a literary assistant.

Production History

Supernova in Hamlet was first produced May 10-11, 1999 in the Cal State Fullerton Arena Theatre. It was directed by Christopher Younggren; the lighting design was by Michele Peterson Jones; the sound design was by Christopher Younggren; the production coordinator was Terry Walcutt; the cast was as follows:

DEREK	Alessandro Trinca
EMILY	Aimée Guichard
WILL	Jason Lythgoe
LYNN	Janine Renae Christl

Characters

EMILY, a woman on the wrong vacation; smart, witty, hopeful

DEREK, a guy who just wants to read; good-hearted, true, a bit unflappable

LYNN, a woman in love with the wrong man; sexy, intelligent, a little stuck

WILL, a man with obligations elsewhere; charming, casual, unaware

All characters are, at the very least, in their late twenties, flawed, and on the verge of something else.

Time

Late afternoon, the present.

Place

A room somewhere.

Notes

The set can be as realistic or representational as needed—a bed, a chair, and a small table, perhaps. Whatever the set, the couples share the space freely, unaware of each other's presence. There is a window that all four actors should be aware of; however, its placement whether there is an actual "frame" is subjective to production. The dialogue should be performed heatedly, relentless— as love will sometimes cause.

AT RISE: There are two couples. **LYNN** *and* **WILL** *are busy being as couples are—cuddling, teasing, or being dreamy are all appropriate choices for these two. On the other hand,* **DEREK** *sits reading a* Sky & Telescope *magazine.* **EMILY** *is trying to get a radio station to come in. There is static.* **DEREK** *tries not to notice.*

EMILY: [*Under her breath.*] Shit.

DEREK: Um. You done?

EMILY: It's not—

DEREK: [*Over.*] I'm reading, here.

EMILY: —coming in. Shit. [*Pounding on the radio, then, turning it off.*] You going to read all day?

DEREK: Planned on it.

EMILY: I'm bored. [**DEREK** *ignores her.*] I said—

DEREK: [*Over.*] I heard you.

EMILY: I'm bored. [*A moment. Then, under her breath:*] I said "the beach," you said "no—mountains."

DEREK: Are we here already?

EMILY: I'm just saying—

DEREK: [*Over.*] I mean, it's four-thirty. And we're here.

EMILY: [*Over.*] we could've gone somewhere, you know—

DEREK: [*Over.*] One hour is all I ask.

EMILY: [*Over.*] warmer.

DEREK: One.

EMILY: Jesus. It's—what? Forty below.

DEREK: It is NOT forty below.

EMILY: It's practically snowing.

DEREK: It's fifty-five degrees outside.

EMILY: There's ice.

DEREK: It's frost.

EMILY: My vacation—

DEREK: There's a difference.

EMILY: and I'm freezing my ass off.

DEREK: One hour is all I want.

EMILY: There's no T.V.

DEREK: Em—

EMILY: No radio.

DEREK: Come on, babe.

EMILY: The world could end.

DEREK: Emily.

EMILY: We'd never know it out here.

DEREK: We're in Big Bear. It's hardly remote.

EMILY: Whatever.

> [*There is a moment.* **DEREK** *resumes reading.* **EMILY** *goes to the window and looks.* **WILL** *and* **LYNN** *have been enjoying each other.*]

LYNN: I got your messages.

WILL: Oh, yeah?

LYNN: Yes. They meant . . . a lot to me.

WILL: It was the truth.

LYNN: I played them for Kay.

WILL: What?

LYNN: I played them for Kay.

WILL: Those are ours.

LYNN: I'm sorry. Are you mad?

WILL: Kind of. That's personal.

LYNN: You're mad.

WILL: I just won't leave any more messages.

LYNN: Really?

WILL: No. I'll just read your letters to Chris.

LYNN: Really?

WILL: No. Guys don't do that. Unless they're, like, sex letters.

LYNN: I could write you one of those.

WILL: I bet.

LYNN: Are you really mad?

WILL: Just embarrassed.

EMILY: Babe?

DEREK: Yes.

EMILY: What if it did? The world, that is.

DEREK: I'm sorry. Are you actually speaking English?

EMILY: What if the world suddenly ended?

DEREK: What are you asking me?

EMILY: What if the world suddenly ended.

LYNN: I just. I needed a witness.

DEREK: You mean, what would I do?

EMILY: Providing you lived, that is. What would you do?

WILL: What?

LYNN: I needed someone else to hear them so that people wouldn't think I was making you up.

DEREK: Are you with me?

EMILY: Why does it matter? No. Yes.

DEREK: Are we the only two left?

EMILY: Yes.

DEREK: I'd see how much food was left. I'd try to find other forms of life—wait—the world ended, right?

EMILY: Right.

DEREK: Then, is there no planet?

EMILY: Uh . . . it's just a big rock. You know, like, wasteland.

WILL: Your friends know I exist.

LYNN: Not the way I want you to.

WILL: Oh.

LYNN: They know you in name but not in application.

DEREK: No vegetation?

EMILY: No.

WILL: I don't understand.

LYNN: You're like this . . . imaginary friend.

WILL: A snuffleupagus.

LYNN: What?

WILL: Big Bird's best friend.

LYNN: The big orange elephant thing?

WILL: Yes.

DEREK: Animals?

EMILY: Maybe cockroaches, cuz, you know, the "studies."

LYNN: Yes. That's exactly right. When I was four, I had an imaginary friend named Jennifer. I used to ask for two cookies. One for me and one for her. That's what it feels like with you.

WILL: [*Laughing.*] Are you saving cookies for me?

LYNN: Forget it.

DEREK: And it's just you and me?

EMILY: Yes.

DEREK: I'd kill myself.

WILL: You want to talk about this?

LYNN: No.

WILL: Okay.

EMILY: What about me?

DEREK: I wouldn't kill you.

EMILY: No. What about me? You'd just leave me alone?

DEREK: Yes.

EMILY: Oh. Fabulous.

DEREK: Em. With a situation that bleak, a human must think of the better existence. Alone. Foodless. What options are there?

EMILY: But, see, that's where you're missing the big thing.

DEREK: What big thing?

EMILY: You world ENDED. You are left. No food or anything, but for some reason, you are still alive. Wouldn't you consider that a sign from SOMEONE? That maybe you were supposed to do something great? Like repopulate the planet?

DEREK: With just you?

EMILY: Or invent something that would, you know. Uh.

LYNN: Just tell me.

WILL: What?

LYNN: Tell me before I go insane.

WILL: I love you.

LYNN: And?

WILL: I've missed you.

LYNN: And?

WILL: I hate this.

LYNN: Okay.

DEREK: But it's a wasteland.

EMILY: See? That is what I am talking about. You have been chosen by the universal order of everything to be the only man left on the planet and your glass is half empty.

DEREK: What does the other half have if we live in a wasteland?

EMILY: There must be a reason why you were chosen.

DEREK: If I am chosen, then the universal order of everything is based completely on randomness, in which case, I am off the hook.

EMILY: How so?

DEREK: There would be no reason for the universal order to choose me because I am—wait—what the hell are we talking about?

EMILY: You're what?

DEREK: What?

EMILY: There would be no reason for the universal order to choose you because you are—what?

DEREK: I'm not adept.

EMILY: At what?

DEREK: Anything. It's like Darwin, right? Survival? I'm not the fittest of the species.

EMILY: Oh.

DEREK: Is all I'm saying.

EMILY: Got ya. [**DEREK** *resumes reading.*]

WILL: Did I miss anything?

LYNN: No.

WILL: You know all of this.

LYNN: I need to hear it. I go for days, you know? Okay. Then it hits. At night. In the late, early hours. And I think—fuck I was fine. What happened?

WILL: What happens?

LYNN: I miss you. I want to be with you. I need to see you.

WILL: Oh.

LYNN: And this? This is bullshit. This. When I'm with you, I think this probably wouldn't work if we were, you know—

WILL: Right.

LYNN: Legit. So. I hold onto that thought and it gets me through. It gets me home and asleep at a decent hour. It allows me to function on a daily basis with little or no discomfort upon thinking of you and I'm fine with it.

WILL: But doesn't it make you impossible to be around?

LYNN: Yes. But, at least I can eat. At least I can get out of my bed. Don't make me pathetic. Don't make me fucking co-dependent. Don't make me call you at two a.m. Don't make me drive by your house to see if your light is on. Don't make me wonder if you're having sex with her. I can't deal with that.

WILL: Got it.

LYNN: So. I think we'd be over in a minute if we were—you know—

WILL: Legit.

LYNN: Right. So. I'm fine. I take that inside. And I'm fine. Until I don't hear from you. For two days. No phone call. No page. No nothing. Then, I think, this is the one and I'm not allowed to call.

WILL: I know.

LYNN: You don't.

WILL: I do.

LYNN: Is your bed empty? Is it? Or do you have someone to fill the space? Someone to sit next to. Hold hands with in the car. Watch Letterman with.

WILL: I want that to be you.

LYNN: Good answer.

EMILY: You're not adept at anything?

DEREK: Not really . . .

EMILY: Come on.

DEREK: What?

EMILY: Everybody's good at something.

DEREK: Well. Sure. I mean, I can DO things.

EMILY: See?

DEREK: But nothing that should constitute me being the only man left on the planet.

WILL: I do.

LYNN: Prove it.

WILL: What?

LYNN: Leave her.

WILL: I can't. You know that.

LYNN: No I don't. I don't know that.

WILL: Come on, we've been here.

LYNN: Yes, I know. I have been here forever. So leave her. Take a chance.

WILL: What about what you were saying about us being "legit"?

LYNN: I was bullshitting.

WILL: What?

LYNN: Bullshitting. See, because, I don't want you to agree with me. I want you to take my hand and say, "You're the one."

WILL: You ARE the one.

LYNN: Then prove it.

WILL: I . . . [*He stops.*]

EMILY: What can you do?

DEREK: I don't know.

EMILY: Seriously, what?

DEREK: What can *YOU* do?

EMILY: I can start a fire from practically nothing.

DEREK: Really?

EMILY: Yep.

DEREK: How did you learn that?

EMILY: I had an uncle who was a bit of a purist. For real. He ate crickets and lived on the side of a hill.

DEREK: Was he a nut?

EMILY: No. Actually, he designed systems for some engineering firm or other. He was a millionaire. He just liked to live simply.

DEREK: And he taught you how to start fires?

EMILY: Mmhm.

DEREK: Well. That's—something.

LYNN: You are a coward.

WILL: What's the matter with you?

LYNN: I want something real just once.

WILL: This isn't real?

LYNN: What's real about it? Jesus. We have a code for phone calls. Ring once, I'm on my way. We don't acknowledge each other in public beyond general politeness. We don't sign cards. I keep the gifts I give you so she won't see them. I'm a myth. A figment. I don't exist in your material world. This is ridiculous.

EMILY: So what can you do?

DEREK: Let me think about it.

EMILY: This is really sad, hon.

DEREK: Thank you.

WILL: It's temporary.

LYNN: No it's not.

WILL: Yes. It is.

LYNN: Am I an idiot? Am I?

EMILY: I mean, to be totally inept.

DEREK: I didn't say I was totally inept.

EMILY: You said you weren't adept at anything. That makes you inept.

WILL: What are you asking me?

LYNN: I'm asking you if you think I'm an idiot.

DEREK: But you're making me sound like a boob.

EMILY: I am not making you sound like a boob.

DEREK: Yes, you are. I sound like a complete boob.

WILL: Uh. No.

EMILY: I was only repeating what you yourself said.

DEREK: I never said I was inept.

EMILY: You said you weren't adept at anything, that makes you—

DEREK: [*Over.*] No. Not being adept does not make me inept. It makes me, uh . . . it makes me . . . shit, what's the word?

LYNN: I must be—are we still talking about this?

EMILY: Gauche?

WILL: Looks like it.

DEREK: No, that's not it. Oh. Funny. No, it makes me average. Uh. Standard. It makes me . . .

EMILY: Typical.

LYNN: I can't talk about this anymore.

DEREK: Yes. Just that. [*He goes back to the magazine.*]

EMILY: Just.

WILL: Just what I was thinking. Let's screw.

LYNN: Perfect. The literal end.

WILL: Come on. It's what we do best, right?

EMILY: What are you reading?

LYNN: You push on my head. I hate that.

WILL: Excuse me?

LYNN: You PUSH. On my head when I'm blowing you.

WILL: I do?

LYNN: Don't play dumb, you know you do.

DEREK: An article.

EMILY: About?

WILL: I don't think I do.

LYNN: I have almost no gag reflex. So why is it when I'm blowing you, I gag?

WILL: Because I have a larger penis than you're used to.

LYNN: Are you fucking kidding me?

WILL: I don't think I push.

LYNN: Well, then, whom have you been inviting into bed with us?

WILL: I push.

LYNN: Yes.

WILL: And that's bad.

LYNN: What do you think?

DEREK: [*Becoming aware of* **EMILY***'s stare.*] Stars.

EMILY: Which ones?

DEREK: I don't know that this would interest you.

EMILY: Why not?

WILL: Anything else?

DEREK: It's nothing spectacular. It's just an article. In the "typical" sense.

LYNN: Just one thing.

EMILY: Come on, Derek.

DEREK: Why don't you just read it when I'm done?

WILL: Okay.

EMILY: I want you to tell me about it.

LYNN: My clitoris?

WILL: Yes.

LYNN: It is—and this is scientific, not opinion—it is a BALL of nerves. Got it?

WILL: Okay.

LYNN: So when you bite it. I feel that. Think about it.

WILL: Okay.

LYNN: Just. Basic anatomy.

DEREK: Why?

EMILY: Because, then it would be like we were doing something—you know, TOGETHER.

DEREK: Okay. So you know *Hamlet?*

EMILY: The play?

DEREK: Yes.

WILL: So biting is bad.

EMILY: Of course.

DEREK: Yeah. Well, there's evidence in this article that points to the fact that *Hamlet* may have been written after this supernova just appeared one night.

LYNN: I am in love with you.

EMILY: Supernova?

DEREK: Big, bright star.

EMILY: And no one had ever seen it before?

WILL: I love you, too.

DEREK: No. Well, listen, Bernardo, the night watchman—

EMILY: [*Over.*] Is he the "something is rotten in the state of Denmark" guy?

LYNN: What is the matter with me?

WILL: Nothing.

DEREK: No. That's Marcellus. And—

EMILY: He's a guard, though, right?

DEREK: It'd be great if I could get this one sentence out.

LYNN: Are you aware that you keep answering my rhetorical questions?

WILL: I do?

LYNN: Yes.

EMILY: Sorry.

WILL: How do I know the rhetorical questions from the real ones?

LYNN: Just listen. You can hear it.

DEREK: Yes. He is a guard. But, Bernardo says, "Last night of all, when yond star that's westward from the pole had made its course to illume that part of heaven where now it burns, Marcellus and myself, the bell then beating one . . ."

EMILY: And then what?

DEREK: The ghost enters.

EMILY: So. "Yond star" would be that supernova.

DEREK: Yes. And this article is loosely stating that perhaps Shakespeare was inspired to write *Hamlet* because of the appearance of this star.

EMILY: Wow.

WILL: I want you to be happy.

LYNN: Really?

WILL: Do you want me to answer that?

LYNN: Yes.

WILL: Yes. Really. How can I make you happy?

LYNN: Leave her. Marry me. Move to the mountains and make babies with me.

DEREK: Yeah. Because, I guess there were incredible religious implications surrounding it? And in 1572, a new star all of the sudden was a pretty big thing.

EMILY: I guess it would be.

WILL: I know you're kidding about the "babies" thing.

LYNN: Jesus *fuck.*

DEREK: So. That's what I'm reading.

WILL: What?

LYNN: Did you hear what I said?

WILL: It's hard not to sometimes.

LYNN: What does that mean?

WILL: You yell. You know that?

LYNN: I'm not yelling.

WILL: It's not in the volume. It's in the words. You use yelling words then you try to lower your voice to disguise it.

LYNN: Well. I'm sorry if I offended you, Mr. Sensitive.

WILL: And you're a bitch.

LYNN: Well you're an asshole.

EMILY: Imagine being that guy to discover it.

DEREK: What do you mean?

EMILY: To be staring up one night and out of nowhere this star is just there. That would be proof, I think.

DEREK: Of?

EMILY: Of some kind of order. Or plan. As if to say, "It's not over. I'm still up here creating." You think?

WILL: How did we get here? I thought we were going to make love.

LYNN: "Screw," I believe was the delicate term you chose.

WILL: I miss you just as much as you miss me, you know.

LYNN: [*Rolling her eyes.*] Ch—

WILL: That's why I haven't left her.

LYNN: What.

WILL: That.

LYNN: What?

WILL: You're patronizing me.

LYNN: I'm not.

WILL: You are, too. You aren't even aware of it.

LYNN: What did I say?

WILL: You didn't say anything. It's that noise you make. I mention that I may feel the same as you and you just write me off. Do you really doubt that I miss you?

LYNN: Yes.

WILL: It's your doubt. It keeps me in it.

LYNN: Don't you dare.

WILL: It's true.

LYNN: You haven't left her because I doubt that you miss me?

WILL: I haven't left her because you doubt me. Period. And patronize.

DEREK: I'm not sure I follow.

EMILY: That doesn't surprise me.

LYNN: So. It's me.

WILL: Not entirely. Somewhat. You're like this walking contradiction. You proclaim this kind of undying, unconditional love for me to your friends, then, when we're alone, you do this. You get mad. You yell, sorry, you use yelling words. I don't know which one of you is the real one. How can there be trust if I don't know you?

LYNN: Wow.

WILL: What?

LYNN: I don't know what to do.

WILL: You want to leave?

LYNN: I don't know.

WILL: You want to go to bed?

LYNN: I don't know.

WILL: I won't bite. Or—push.

LYNN: I don't know.

WILL: Think about it.

LYNN: I'm trying. It's just—

WILL: What?

LYNN: You keep fucking talking.

DEREK: What?

WILL: Sorry.

LYNN: I don't know what to do. You just told me it's me. And this whole time, I was sure—positive—it was you.

WILL: Not entirely.

LYNN: But it's me.

WILL: Somewhat.

LYNN: I'm stuck. I'm completely stuck.

WILL: I love you.

LYNN: I can't move my feet. All I want to do is run and I can't move my feet.

WILL: I love you. Stay.

LYNN: I heard you.

WILL: [*He goes to kiss her.*] Come on.

LYNN: Sure. Go ahead.

WILL: What?

LYNN: Fuck the shit out of me. When I'm lost in the last thing you told me. At this point, I can't leave. My eyes are wide open and I can't move. So. Go for it.

WILL: I wouldn't just fuck you.

LYNN: Why not? It's how we started this thing, isn't it? Let's just continue where we leave off.

WILL: We get so little time together, why ruin it?

LYNN: Because my time alone is ruined. It's without you. So, why not let it bleed into the time with you. It seems—what? Fair? I don't know.

WILL: You've stopped making sense to me.

LYNN: You've stopped speaking my language.

EMILY: I don't think we've ever spoken the same language, Derek.

DEREK: So. What, just because I don't subscribe to your outer limits thought process, we don't understand each other?

WILL: How do we cure this?

EMILY: Jesus that's sad. I make a comment on the state of our relationship and you mock me.

LYNN: Learn a new one.

DEREK: I wasn't mocking you.

EMILY: Come on, Derek. What are we doing up here?

DEREK: I thought we were vacationing.

EMILY: You're reading and I'm trying to get you to talk to me. We're a fucking case study.

DEREK: [*Finally setting the magazine down.*] We are not a case study.

EMILY: From one of those "men-are-from-some-planet-women-aren't" books.

WILL: I love you.

LYNN: The words are the same, but I can't understand them.

WILL: It's all you. I feel the same. I haven't changed.

LYNN: Then there is a problem. [*She notices the magazine, recently discarded by* **DEREK.**]

DEREK: You're making this much more of an issue than it needs to be, Em.

LYNN: Planning on stargazing?

EMILY: No, I'm not. If we can't spend twenty-four hours in a cabin together, what can we do?

LYNN: I didn't realize you were a closet astrologer.

DEREK: Emily.

EMILY and LYNN: Why are you with me?

DEREK and WILL: Why are you with me?

EMILY and **LYNN:** I asked you first.

[*A moment.*]

DEREK: You're what I'm good at. I'm adept at you.

[*A moment.*]

WILL: It isn't mine.

LYNN: [*As if she didn't hear him.*] What?

WILL: The magazine. It's. Not mine.

LYNN: I see.

WILL: What?

LYNN: Her. All over you.

WILL: It's just a magazine.

LYNN: It's evidence. It's proof.

WILL: Lynn?

DEREK: Emily?

LYNN: Don't do that.

WILL and **EMILY:** What?

LYNN: Don't start using my name now. It's my last defense against you. I think if I can get through a whole day without him saying my name out loud, I'll be fine. Then, you go and you say it.

DEREK: Why are you with me?

WILL: You don't want me to say your name?

LYNN: No. I want you to. I want you to say my name all the time. Just like you just said it. Say it again.

WILL: Lynn.

EMILY: I have no idea.

LYNN: Again.

DEREK: Is that a good thing or a bad thing?

WILL: Lynn.

EMILY: It just is. [*She looks toward the window.*] It's getting dark.

LYNN: I don't want you to ever say her name like that. Promise me you won't.

DEREK: See any stars?

EMILY: [*Still looking out.*] When I was little, all I wanted to be was twenty-two.

DEREK: What?

WILL: I promise.

LYNN: You're a liar. She puts up with you for the same reason I do.

WILL: And that is?

LYNN: The sound of your voice.

WILL: Are you going to leave me?

EMILY: It's true. All I wanted to do was be twenty-two. So that I could be an adult, you know? So that I could drive and go to work and be married with babies. Every time I played house I was twenty-two. That just seemed like the perfect age to me.

DEREK: Twenty-two?

LYNN: Yes.

EMILY: And I would dress for that age, in my mother's high heels and her fuzzy sweaters and wear pink lipstick and bracelets on my arms. And I knew everything. I knew what my husband looked like and that his name was Andrew and he worked in advertising.

DEREK: What happened?

WILL: What happened to us?

EMILY: I turned twenty-six.

LYNN: I started caring more than I should.

DEREK: Em?

EMILY: Yeah?

WILL: Yeah.

DEREK: Are you unhappy?

LYNN: And you couldn't care less. [**WILL** *starts to speak,* **LYNN** *stops him.*]

EMILY: I don't think so. I'm just waiting.

LYNN: Just let me believe that. It will be easier for me to hate you than to let you go. [*She reaches for his hand. He takes hers. They look at each other for a moment.*]

DEREK: For what?

EMILY: For a surprise.

DEREK: I want to surprise you.

EMILY: Don't throw words out like that, Derek. I'm aging way too fast for that kind of hope.

DEREK: Okay. I take it back. I am incapable of spontaneity. I mean it. There will be no mirth. Expect nothing but mediocrity and banality from here on in. I am fixed in my ways and have no desire to change. So. [*He smiles, goes to her, puts his arms around her.*] Get over it.

LYNN: Hm. This is exactly how it started, isn't it?

WILL: Yes. It is.

DEREK: Any stars yet?

EMILY: Not yet. [*Looking at* **DEREK**, *then out into the almost night sky, perhaps a smile.*] Soon, though.

> [*Lights fade slowly to black.*]

END OF PLAY

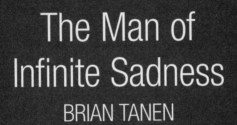

The Man of
Infinite Sadness
BRIAN TANEN

About the Playwright

Brian Tanen is a playwright and screenwriter, originally from Miami, Florida. He graduated from Yale University and received his M.F.A. in Dramatic Writing from New York University. He has studied playwriting with David Ives, Mac Wellman, Suzan-Lori Parks, and Toni Dorfman. His first play, *No Such Thing*, was workshopped at New York Stage and Film's annual Summer Series at Vassar College, directed by David Marshall Grant. His work has also been seen at the Cherry Lane Theater, Yale University, and NYU. *The Man of Infinite Sadness* was invited to the Region Two Festival of the KCACTF in 2005 as a winner of the regional one-act play contest for the Kennedy Center's American College Theater Festival. It was produced as part of NYU's Festival of New Works and was subsequently produced at SUNY-Potsdam.

Production History

The Man of Infinite Sadness was first performed in the Rita and Burton Goldberg Theater, at NYU in April 2004, directed by Kevin Newbury. The cast included:

HOLLY ....Heidi McAllister

WARD ....Michael Braun

MAYA ....Magin Schantz

CRYING MAN ....Cory Grant

CHARLIE ....Jared Coseglia

Characters

HOLLY, late twenties, thin, blonde, attractive. The kind of person who looks like she's got it together.

MAYA, late twenties, Holly's coworker/friend. The kind of person who looks like she hasn't quite got it together.

WARD, early thirties, attractive. Holly's boyfriend. Great on paper, less great in person.

CHARLIE, early thirties, chubby. Ward's friend. Kind but self-impressed.

CRYING MAN, a crying man. He wears a suit.

Setting

Various locales. The scene changes are achieved through minimal addition and subtraction of furniture, as well as changes to the lighting.

Holly and Ward's shared apartment.

A rooftop where Holly and Maya eat lunch daily.

A movie theater.

A restaurant.

Note About Fantasies

Throughout the script, the reality of the play is interrupted by moments of fantasy, indicated by the sound of chimes. The lighting can also be modified to clarify that these moments are imagined.

HOLLY *looks out the kitchen window of her apartment.* WARD *reads a newspaper. He laughs.*

HOLLY: What's funny?

WARD: Mmm?

HOLLY: Something funny? In the newspaper?

WARD: Ummmmm . . . no. Not really. Coffee's good.

   [*Pause.*]

HOLLY: I thought . . . something was funny. You laughed.

WARD: I did?

HOLLY: Yeah.

WARD: Sorry.

HOLLY: It's OK, you don't have to apologize.

WARD: Sorry. [*He sips coffee. She sighs.*] Still raining?

HOLLY: Yes. Ward?

WARD: Hmm?

HOLLY: Where'd you park the car last night?

WARD: Across the street.

HOLLY: It's not there.

WARD: Really?

HOLLY: You think it was towed?

WARD: It's not a tow-zone. I double-checked. [*He looks out the window.*]

HOLLY: You think it was stolen?

WARD: Hmm.

HOLLY: Ward?!

WARD: What?

HOLLY: Your car got stolen?!

WARD: Shit. I guess so.

HOLLY: What are you going to do?!

WARD: [*Chuckling.*] I don't know. Get a new one, I guess. [*He picks up the newspaper again.*]

HOLLY: Should we call the police?

WARD: Yeah. Good idea. Right after breakfast.

HOLLY: How will you get to work?

WARD: I guess I'll have to take the bus.

HOLLY: The bus?

WARD: Yup.

HOLLY: Won't that be inconvenient?

WARD: A little.

HOLLY: Doesn't the bus take forever?

WARD: Yeah. Probably.

HOLLY: Won't you be late?

WARD: I guess so.

HOLLY: Ward!

WARD: What?

HOLLY: Your car was stolen!

WARD: I know. But what am I supposed to do about it? [*Pause.*] C'mon booger, don't be sad. Have some breakfast.

HOLLY: I'm too upset!

WARD: [*Looking up from newspaper.*] Why? [**HOLLY** *walks out.* **WARD** *continues to read the paper. He laughs.*]

❊ ❊ ❊

HOLLY *joins* **MAYA** *on another part of the stage.* **MAYA** *sits on a bench.* **HOLLY** *places a little towel on her side of the bench before sitting. (She does this every time she sits outdoors.)*

MAYA: It's nice up here. I didn't even know this building had a rooftop.

HOLLY: I come up here for lunch every day.

MAYA: It's nice . . . Except for all the cigarette butts.

HOLLY: Yeah. Well.

MAYA: Good thing it stopped raining.

HOLLY: I know.

MAYA: The weather's been so temperamental lately. It's like, rainy rainy, rainy, and then all of a sudden . . . sunny. And then rainy.

HOLLY: I know. [*Pause.*] I feel like that too.

MAYA: What, moody?

HOLLY: A little.

MAYA: Are you getting your period?

HOLLY: Um . . . I don't really like to talk about that.

MAYA: Are you serious?

HOLLY: Mm hm.

MAYA: Really?

HOLLY: I just . . . I don't really understand the need to talk about . . . that.

MAYA: Your period.

HOLLY: That word.

MAYA: You would have died growing up in my house. Four sisters. It was period city. Period, period, period. Morning, noon, and night. We were all on the same cycle.

HOLLY: Please. Can we talk about something else?

MAYA: OK.

HOLLY: I'm in a terrible mood today. You've met my fiancé right?

MAYA: Ward?

HOLLY: His car was stolen this morning.

MAYA: Oh no! That's awful.

HOLLY: I told him to park it in the garage. It was raining though, and the garage is a couple blocks away.

MAYA: What are you gonna do?

[*Pause.*]

HOLLY: Get a new one, I guess.

[*Pause.*]

MAYA: That's life, right? At least you have a fiancé.

HOLLY: Oh. But I—

MAYA: [*Inspecting herself in a compact mirror.*] Do you think I have a fat head?

HOLLY: What? No.

MAYA: You don't think I have a GIANT head?

HOLLY: No.

MAYA: It's disproportionate.

HOLLY: That's not true.

MAYA: I look like Mrs. Potato Head. Just one enormous head with arms and legs sticking out. It's no wonder that I can't get a date.

HOLLY: I know plenty of men who would date you.

MAYA: Who?

    [*Pause.*]

HOLLY: I'll think about it. Maybe I can set you up. [*She opens her purse and removes a brown paper bag, its contents: a yogurt.*]

MAYA: Is that your lunch?

HOLLY: Mm hm.

MAYA: Just yogurt? [**HOLLY** *nods "yes."*]

MAYA: No wonder you're such a stick. What kind is it?

HOLLY: Huh?

MAYA: What flavor?

HOLLY: Oh, it's . . . peach.

MAYA: Can I try?

HOLLY: I only have the one spoon, sorry.

MAYA: That's all right. [**MAYA** *pulls out a set of plastic cutlery from her purse.*] I always bring extra.

HOLLY: Didn't you bring lunch?

MAYA: I ate it as soon as I got to work. [**MAYA** *helps herself to a taste.*] Maybe Ward could help you.

HOLLY: What?

MAYA: Maybe Ward could help you find someone for me to date. One of his friends, someone just like him.

HOLLY: Just like Ward?

MAYA: What? You don't think I could date someone like Ward?

HOLLY: That's not what I meant.

MAYA: I mean, obviously not as handsome as Ward, I'd feel too self-conscious. But an even match. An even match with me.

HOLLY: What do you mean?

MAYA: You know how you always see pretty women walking around with ugly men?

HOLLY: Yeah?

MAYA: Like women have to trade in expectations of attractiveness in order to get a guy with other good qualities, like being smart or nice?

HOLLY: Yeah.

MAYA: I just think it's amazing. Attractive women end up settling for ugly men all the time, but you didn't have to do that with Ward. You're really lucky. That's what I want.

HOLLY: You think we're an "even match" then?

MAYA: Definitely.

HOLLY: I've always thought he was the attractive one.

MAYA: No no, you're a stick! Guys love you. You're gorgeous.

HOLLY: Thanks. That's nice.

MAYA: It's true. You're a pencil.

HOLLY: Stop.

MAYA: Your eyebrows are perfect.

HOLLY: Stop.

MAYA: Seriously though, who does your eyebrows?

HOLLY: I do.

> [*In the background, a man enters wearing a suit. He hands cover his face, but it is apparent that he is crying. This is the* **CRYING MAN.**]

MAYA: You don't get them waxed?

HOLLY: No. Just me and a tweezers.

MAYA: [*Indicating the* **CRYING MAN.**] Check it out. We're not alone.

HOLLY: Oh my God. He's back.

MAYA: Back?

HOLLY: That guy. I've seen him a couple of times up here during lunch.

MAYA: He's crying.

HOLLY: He's always crying.

MAYA: What do you mean?

HOLLY: Every time I see him, he's crying.

MAYA: How many times have you seen him?

HOLLY: I don't know. A few. A bunch.

MAYA: He's really weeping. There's tears streaming down his face.

HOLLY: He usually comes up around one. He cries for a couple of minutes, dries himself up, and then goes back inside.

    [*Pause.*]

MAYA: So you've been watching him.

HOLLY: No! No. I don't . . . No. I haven't been. Watching him.

MAYA: You know what time he comes up here.

HOLLY: I just . . . I noticed. That's all.

MAYA: He works in the building?

HOLLY: I assume so.

MAYA: Look how upset he is.

HOLLY: I know.

MAYA: And he's always like that?

HOLLY: [*With great admiration.*] His sadness is infinite.

    [*Silence.*]

MAYA: He's kind of cute.

HOLLY: I know. [*Silence.*] Somebody must have died. For him to be crying like that. Don't you think?

MAYA: Who?

HOLLY: I don't know. Somebody important.

MAYA: Men cry about weird stuff, though. In my entire life, I never saw my father cry once over anything that mattered.

HOLLY: Look how earnest and miserable he looks. You just want to scoop him up into your arms.

MAYA: One of us should talk to him.

HOLLY: What? Maya, no.

MAYA: Maybe I should try and see what's wrong.

HOLLY: No, please—I'm serious.

MAYA: Why? You have dibs on him or something?

HOLLY: Of course not, I just . . .

MAYA: What, Holly?

HOLLY: Nothing. I just think that someone who comes up here everyday to cry on his lunch break might not be looking for company.

MAYA: Unless it's you, right?

HOLLY: What?

MAYA: If I go over there, he'll probably throw himself off the ledge, right?

HOLLY: I didn't mean— [*The* **CRYING MAN** *exits.*]

MAYA: You know, sometimes I wonder if you're trying to hold me back from meeting someone.

HOLLY: Maya!

MAYA: And now he's gone. Great.

[*Pause.*]

HOLLY: I think it's starting to rain again.

[**MAYA** *helps herself to* **HOLLY***'s yogurt.* **HOLLY** *holds her hand up to the sky to test the weather.*]

❊ ❊ ❊

Lights shift. **HOLLY** *crosses to another part of the stage, where she sits next to* **WARD.** *They are at a movie theater, represented by a row of benches.* **WARD** *eats popcorn.*

HOLLY: Good seats.

WARD: You want any popcorn?

HOLLY: [*Disappointed.*] You got butter.

WARD: Yeah.

HOLLY: No. No thanks.

WARD: Thanks for seeing this, by the way. I know it's not your kind of movie. [*He kisses her on the cheek.*]

HOLLY: Oh, of course honey.

> [*Pause.*]

WARD: I love you.

HOLLY: [*Surprised by this show of affection.*] I love you, too. [*He kisses her again.*] I didn't see the first one, you know.

WARD: Well, the aliens destroy Earth at the end of the first movie, but the main guy is on his way back in time to prevent the attack. Oh, and he's time-traveling with this female astronaut, and they're falling in love sort of, but she's an alien spy, and he doesn't know it yet.

HOLLY: Sounds . . . good. [**MAYA** *enters. She's looking around for a seat.*] Oh my gosh. That's my friend Maya.

WARD: From work?

HOLLY: [*Waving.*] Maya! [**MAYA** *walks over.*]

MAYA: Hey guys. Ward, good to see you again.

WARD: Small world, huh?

HOLLY: Are you alone?

MAYA: What's that supposed to mean?

HOLLY: I just—Maya, all I meant was there's one extra seat here. If you wanted to join us.

MAYA: Oh. OK. Yes I will. Thank you.

HOLLY: I'm not really into these kind of movies.

WARD: She only likes searing lesbian dramas where everyone gets cancer and cries.

HOLLY: Ward!! [**MAYA** *laughs.*]

MAYA: Oh, I heard your car got stolen last week.

WARD: Yeah. It's true.

MAYA: I'm so sorry.

WARD: Don't be sorry. I'm getting a new Porsche.

MAYA: Wow.

WARD: Yeah, Holly wanted me to be more upset about it, but I'm pretty psyched about the new Porsche.

HOLLY: I didn't want you to be more upset.

WARD: Yes you did.

HOLLY: I would never wish for you to be more upset.

WARD: Yes you would.

HOLLY: That's a terrible thing to say.

[*Silence.*]

MAYA: Did you ask Ward if he knows anyone to set me up with?

HOLLY: Oh.

WARD: I didn't hear anything about that.

MAYA: You didn't ask him?

HOLLY: It slipped my mind. Would you excuse me for a moment?

WARD: It's about to start.

HOLLY: I'm just gonna run to the bathroom.

[**HOLLY** *walks to another part of the stage. She begins to cry. The sound of chimes is heard. The* **CRYING MAN** *(from the previous scene) enters, crying. When* **HOLLY** *sees him, she freezes. They look at each other.*]

WARD: You sure got dressed up for the movies.

MAYA: I was supposed to meet someone. For dinner. But he didn't show up.

WARD: Oh. I'm sorry. But now you get to see this movie, right?

MAYA: Yes. With you guys. On my birthday.

WARD: It's your birthday? Happy birthday!

MAYA: Thanks.

❊ ❊ ❊

HOLLY *eats yogurt on the rooftop. She's alone. After a few moments,* **MAYA** *enters.*

MAYA: Oh. Hi.

HOLLY: Hi.

   [*Silence.*]

MAYA: I'm sorry about the other night. Crashing your date like that.

HOLLY: It's OK.

MAYA: What are you doing up here?

HOLLY: Nothing. Just having lunch.

MAYA: Yogurt? [**HOLLY** *produces an apple from her brown paper bag.*]

HOLLY: And an apple.

MAYA: [*Under her breath.*] Not lunch.

HOLLY: Excuse me?

MAYA: You should eat something. For once.

HOLLY: Well. I don't really care what you think. [*Pause.*] I'm sorry. I didn't mean that.

   [*Pause.*]

MAYA: I'm thinking about getting my eyes done.

HOLLY: Your eyes?

MAYA: Yeah. I saw this before-and-after picture in a magazine, and the woman looked a billion times better.

HOLLY: There's nothing wrong with your eyes.

MAYA: And maybe my nose.

HOLLY: You don't need a nose job.

MAYA: Easy for you to say, you're perfect.

HOLLY: Maya.

MAYA: So, where is he?

HOLLY: Who?

MAYA: The crying guy.

HOLLY: I don't know.

MAYA: It's past one.

HOLLY: I haven't seen him lately.

MAYA: You know, I don't think it's right of you. To be doing this.

HOLLY: I'm not doing anything.

MAYA: You already have a boyfriend. You're engaged.

HOLLY: I'm just having lunch, Maya.

MAYA: You're holding a stakeout for the crying guy.

HOLLY: So what?

MAYA: So what?!

HOLLY: I think he's interesting. I'm not doing anything inappropriate.

MAYA: Well, I bet you Ward wouldn't be too happy if he knew what you were doing.

HOLLY: I'm not DOING ANYTHING!

MAYA: If he knew that you were stalking some guy from work? I bet you a hundred dollars, Ward would be furious.

HOLLY: That shows how much you know! Ward doesn't get furious.

[*Silence.* **MAYA** *starts to cry.*]

HOLLY: Oh Maya. Don't cry.

MAYA: You've been nothing but nice to me, and I'm awful. I'm so awful to you.

HOLLY: No, no you're not. [*They hug.*]

MAYA: I don't get along with any of my sisters. Did I tell you that?

HOLLY: No.

MAYA: They all get along with each other. Just not me.

HOLLY: Well, not everybody gets along with their siblings.

MAYA: Four sisters and none of them like me. Not one. I'm horrible.

HOLLY: You're not horrible, Maya.

MAYA: They're all married, of course.

HOLLY: Well, you're the youngest, aren't you?

MAYA: Yes.

HOLLY: So you'll get married, eventually, if that's what you want. And so what if your sisters are all married? I'm sure that some of them are unhappy. [*This cheers* **MAYA** *up.*]

MAYA: You're a good friend, Holly.

    [*Pause.*]

HOLLY: I don't think he's coming today.

MAYA: Who?

HOLLY: The crying man.

MAYA: Oh him.

HOLLY: And besides, it's not like he'd be a good person for you to date. I mean, he's obviously got some emotional problems.

MAYA: Yeah. He's probably a total wreck.

HOLLY: He's probably a nightmare.

MAYA: He's probably gay! [*They laugh.*]

HOLLY: So, should we go back inside?

MAYA: I guess so.

    [*They don't move. Long silence.*]

HOLLY: All right then. Let's go. [**HOLLY** *gets up.* **MAYA** *follows.*]

MAYA: I'll meet you in a sec. I'm just gonna . . . have a cigarette.

HOLLY: You smoke?

MAYA: Uh huh.

HOLLY: I thought you didn't like all the cigarette butts up here.

MAYA: Yeah. Well, I do. I smoke.

    [*Pause.*]

HOLLY: I've never seen you smoke.

MAYA: Yeah, I'm oddly secretive about it. You go ahead. I'll meet you in a few.

HOLLY: Maya! Don't be silly. I'll wait with you. In fact, do you have an extra?

MAYA: What? Cigarette?

HOLLY: Yeah.

MAYA: Um. Do you hear thunder?

❋ ❋ ❋

Lights shift. **HOLLY** *walks to the other side of the stage. Her apartment.*

HOLLY: Ward? Are you home? [*She sits, removes her shoes.*] Ward? [*She looks around the room. When she believes that she is alone, she begins to cry.*]

WARD: [*Offstage.*] I'm in the bathroom! [**HOLLY** *composes herself. After a moment,* **WARD** *enters.*] Sorry, didn't hear you come in. How was your day?

HOLLY: It was . . . all right.

WARD: I drove everywhere today!

HOLLY: Oh. You like the new car?

WARD: I love it.

HOLLY: I'm so happy.

WARD: Yeah, I'm so low to the ground. I feel like I'm a professional racecar driver. And I saw the most hilarious thing on the way home.

HOLLY: Yeah?

WARD: This guy was walking down the street, with his head in his hands. Like this. [*He imitates the* **CRYING MAN.**]

HOLLY: Like he was crying?

WARD: Yeah, so he's walking down the street, not looking where he's going—

HOLLY: Where was he?

WARD: What?

HOLLY: Was it by my work?

WARD: Yeah, actually. About a block from your office. Anyway, he's walking—

HOLLY: Was he wearing a suit?

WARD: Can I finish the story?

HOLLY: Sorry.

WARD: You know what? Forget it. It's not gonna be funny now.

HOLLY: No no. Finish.

WARD: No, it's too much hype. Just forget it.

HOLLY: Ward, what happened?

WARD: Well, he wasn't watching where he was going, and he walked right into a parking meter. Like bang! Right in the nuts.

HOLLY: Oh my God!

WARD: It was pretty hilarious. Maybe you had to be there.

HOLLY: Was he hurt?

WARD: I don't think so. Why, what do you care?

HOLLY: Nothing.

WARD: I'm gonna jump in the shower. You want to go out for dinner?

HOLLY: I was going to cook.

WARD: No, let's go out. I'll even go somewhere ethnic. What about that new Vietnamese you wanted to try?

HOLLY: Oh, OK, yeah. I'd like that.

WARD: I hear they make excellent dog.

HOLLY: Ward!

WARD: I'll be ready in a minute. [*Beat.*] I love you.

HOLLY: [*Surprised.*] Oh! I love you too. [*He exits.*]

WARD: [*Offstage.*] Oh, and keep Thursday free. I found the perfect setup for your friend Maya.

❊ ❊ ❊

Lights shift. **MAYA** *enters, joining* **HOLLY** *at a café table.*

HOLLY: Hi!

MAYA: Hi. Where are the boys?

HOLLY: Oh, they're just parking the car.

MAYA: I'm nervous. I feel like I'm in high school again.

HOLLY: Don't be nervous. Charlie and Ward were in the same fraternity.

MAYA: So he's in finance too? Charlie?

HOLLY: I think so. You look nice.

MAYA: So do you. I love that top.

HOLLY: No, it's too casual.

MAYA: I love it!

HOLLY: Stop.

MAYA: For real.

HOLLY: I paid six dollars for it.

MAYA: Shut up.

HOLLY: I like your shoes.

MAYA: They're knockoffs.

HOLLY: You can't tell. They look amazing.

MAYA: They're killing me.

HOLLY: Mine too.

MAYA: [*Producing a pair of pills from her pocket.*] Advil?

HOLLY: Oh, thank you. [**HOLLY** *and* **MAYA** *click their pills together, as though toasting.*]

MAYA: To blind dates.

HOLLY: I hope it's a match. [*The women take their Advil.* **WARD** *enters with* **CHARLIE.**]

WARD: Ladies. Maya, it's nice to see you again.

HOLLY: Did you get a good spot?

WARD: We did, we did.

CHARLIE: You must be Maya?

MAYA: Yes.

CHARLIE: Charlie. It's so great to finally meet you.

MAYA: Yes.

CHARLIE: Ward told me you work with Holly?

MAYA: Yes.

CHARLIE: That's great. And you guys became friends through work?

MAYA: Yes.

CHARLIE: Great.

WARD: I hadn't seen Charlie in about a hundred years, and then when I was buying the new car last week, who should I bump into but this guy?

CHARLIE: I was getting the same car!

WARD: Small small world.

MAYA: Yes.

CHARLIE: Maya, have you seen their new Porsche?

MAYA: Yes.

WARD: Shit, man. Did you ever think back in college that we'd end up running into each other buying matching Porsches?

CHARLIE: Fuck yeah, bro! [*They high-five.*]

WARD: You should have seen this guy back in the day. He couldn't get a date if his life depended on it.

CHARLIE: Don't say that!

WARD: It's true, you couldn't pay a girl to go out with him, and trust me, I tried.

CHARLIE: Oh man.

WARD: It was one of my official capacities as his big brother. Get him drunk and laid.

HOLLY: Ward!

CHARLIE: You're making me look bad.

WARD: All I mean is, look at him now. Looking swank, top finance job, sweet car. . . . Turned out to be quite a catch. Right, Maya?

MAYA: Yes.

WARD: One time, in school, we took this road trip to Smith—the women's college . . . [*Chimes are heard.* **WARD** *doesn't notice* **HOLLY** *get up from the table. She wanders to the front of the stage, where the* **CRYING MAN** *joins her. They dance a ballet number together.*] So it's me, Charlie, Crocker, Jackson, and Cookie—

CHARLIE: Ryan Cooke. What ever happened to him?

WARD: Beats me. So the five of us pile into Crocker's car, at midnight and speed up to Smith, thinking it's Saturday night. It's a women's college. They're bound to be hurting for men. Well, after numerous U-turns—

CHARLIE: And two speeding tickets!

WARD: I forgot about the speeding tickets! Crocker couldn't drive for shit. Yeah, so after numerous U-turns and two speeding tickets, we pull into Smith, expecting to be greeted by a bevy of desperate lonely women.

CHARLIE: Everyone was asleep.

WARD: It was three in the morning.

> [*The music changes.* **MAYA** *gets up from the table and joins* **HOLLY** *and the* **CRYING MAN.** *The three of them dance an elaborate tango.*]

CHARLIE: Three in the morning! Great, isn't it?

WARD: We wandered around the campus for an hour, and we didn't see a single person out and about.

CHARLIE: Not only was it three in the morning, but apparently, they were right in the middle of final exams. A real ghost town!

WARD: Sometime around four a.m., we realize we don't have anywhere to sleep, and we ought to drive back. But Crocker can't find his car keys! [*The dance evolves into a stylized weeping.*]

CHARLIE: What a disaster that was.

WARD: We had to call a locksmith.

CHARLIE: We waited for an hour.

WARD: And when we finally got back in the car, the keys were sitting in the ignition!

CHARLIE: Oh man. [*They high-five.*] What happened to the women?

WARD: I don't know. Must have gone to the bathroom. What do you think of Maya?

CHARLIE: I like her!

✳ ✳ ✳

Lights shift. **CHARLIE, WARD,** *and the* **CRYING MAN** *exit. The rooftop.*
HOLLY *and* **MAYA** *look around the stage in awkward silence.*

HOLLY: Who are all these women?

MAYA: I don't know.

HOLLY: What are they doing up here?

MAYA: I'm not sure.

HOLLY: I was under the impression that not too many people knew about this rooftop. ·

MAYA: So was I. What time is it?

HOLLY: A little before one. [*Beat.*] Did you tell anyone?

MAYA: Did I tell anyone?

HOLLY: About coming up here. To watch him.

MAYA: You think they're here for the crying guy?

HOLLY: Who did you tell?

MAYA: I didn't tell anyone.

HOLLY: Well, you must have told somebody!

MAYA: Jeez, Holly. Remind me not to get on your bad side.

HOLLY: Sorry. I just—I don't understand what all these women are doing up here.

MAYA: Well, me neither.

HOLLY: This is terrible. They're ruining everything.

MAYA: What do you mean?

HOLLY: All these women! Like pigeons fighting each other for a crumb! If he sees all these women up here, he'll stop coming.

MAYA: Yeah? Well what if he stops coming? Would that be the end of the world?

HOLLY: No. Obviously not. I just—

MAYA: What?

HOLLY: Nothing. [*Silence.*] So, do you think you'll see Charlie again?

MAYA: No!

HOLLY: Really?

MAYA: I don't think so.

HOLLY: He told Ward he liked you.

MAYA: He did?

HOLLY: He thought you were great.

MAYA: Well, why did Ward set me up with his fraternity brother who could never get a girl in college? Does he think I'm desperate?

HOLLY: No! Not at all! That was the past, Maya.

MAYA: Does he think I'm fat?

HOLLY: Of course not.

MAYA: Because I thought I specifically requested an even match.

[*Pause.*]

HOLLY: You didn't think Charlie was an even match?

MAYA: Is that how you think of me?

HOLLY: I like Charlie! I think he's nice.

MAYA: Do you find him attractive?

HOLLY: The only thing that matters is what you think, not what I think.

MAYA: Yeah, right. [**MAYA** *stands up suddenly and addresses the stage.*] He's not coming, so forget it! You can all go back inside now.

❋ ❋ ❋

Lights shift as **MAYA** *exits.* **HOLLY**'s *apartment.*

HOLLY: Ward? Are you home? [*She sits down and removes her shoes.*] Ward? [*Chimes are heard. The* **CRYING MAN** *enters.*] Oh my God. What are you doing here? [*The* **CRYING MAN** *begins to cry.*] You're crying. I mean, of course you are. Can I get you something? A glass of water? A tissue? [*The* **CRYING MAN** *declines.*] I was hoping you'd come. Please, sit down. [*He does. He cries.*]

CRYING MAN: My mother. When I was twelve.

HOLLY: What?

CRYING MAN: I'm sure you want to know the cause of my unhappiness.

HOLLY: Oh, well . . . yes.

CRYING MAN: My mother died, when I was twelve . . .

HOLLY: Oh.

CRYING MAN: . . . My father was in jail . . .

HOLLY: Oh.

CRYING MAN: . . . I was sent to live with my grandparents, who died when I was fifteen. First my grandfather, then a month later my grandmother.

HOLLY: Oh my God.

CRYING MAN: I was sent to live with my aunt. She killed herself. Then I started dating this girl. Her name was Holly.

HOLLY: My name is Holly.

CRYING MAN: I know. She was—and I don't mean this lightly, when you've been in situations like I've been, you know how important it is to have a savior, to lift you out of the mud, and this girl, Holly—I loved her, so much. [*Pause.*] She was murdered.

HOLLY: Oh my God!

CRYING MAN: We were going to get married. She was murdered in her house in the middle of the day, broad daylight.

HOLLY: Your story.

CRYING MAN: I know. It's sad.

HOLLY: Unbelievably sad.

CRYING MAN: That's why I cry. [*Pause.*] So why do you?

HOLLY: Me?

CRYING MAN: What's so sad about your life?

[*Pause.*]

HOLLY: Nothing. My life is . . . great.

CRYING MAN: When you came in, you were talking to someone named Warden?

HOLLY: Oh, not Warden. Ward. We live together. [*Pause.*] He's nothing like you. Everything comes easily to Ward. He has a wonderful job, a wonderful family; he thinks the world is his oyster. And it is. It's always just . . .

happiness, with that . . . perfect smile—it's just happiness.

I have this recurring dream, where Ward and I are in heaven. And Ward sits on his cloud, content and perfect as ever, but I'm sinking through my cloud like it's quicksand—I'm drowning in it. And I call out to him for help, but he just thinks I'm playing. So he laughs. He finds the whole scene funny. And I guess, in a weird way, it is.

CRYING MAN: No it isn't.

HOLLY: No. It isn't. His car was stolen, and he didn't even get angry. He just doesn't understand what it means to be me, to be overwhelmed by everything around you, to feel sadness in your core, uncontrollable longing and yearning and sadness and loneliness. He's just so practical.

I am too. I'm strong and practical. I may not seem it right now, but my family raised me to keep my chin up high. Never show weakness. To take care of the weak, and hide any signs of sadness.

And then there you were. You came here and told me that story, and I felt it too. I felt your story like it was me, and I know that we are . . . kindred. I can show you myself, in my darkest, saddest truth.

WARD: [*Offstage.*] Holly?

HOLLY: It's Ward. He's home.

WARD: [*Entering.*] Hey babe! I just went for a little drive. I thought I heard you talking in here.

HOLLY: Oh.

CRYING MAN: He can't see me. I'm only here in your mind.

WARD: Booger? You alone?

[*Pause.*]

HOLLY: Always.

❊ ❊ ❊

Lights shift. **HOLLY** *and* **WARD** *exit.* **MAYA** *enters tentatively. Chimes are heard.*

MAYA: Excuse me, please don't walk away, all right? I just want to talk to you, and if you walk away, that's really going to hurt my feelings, OK? [*The* **CRYING MAN** *looks at* **MAYA.**]

CRYING MAN: OK.

MAYA: I'm Maya.

CRYING MAN: Nice to meet you. I saw you out here on the rooftop? A little while back?

MAYA: Yeah, I was having lunch with my friend Holly.

CRYING MAN: I didn't notice you were with anyone.

MAYA: You didn't see Holly?

CRYING MAN: No.

MAYA: You didn't see Holly? Perfect-looking Holly?

CRYING MAN: No.

MAYA: She's tall, blonde, pencil-thin? Little matching outfits, short skirts, little silk scarves?

CRYING MAN: No.

MAYA: She's practically stalking you. She comes out here every day just to watch you.

CRYING MAN: I hadn't noticed.

MAYA: But you saw me.

CRYING MAN: I did.

MAYA: Me and not Holly.

CRYING MAN: Yes.

MAYA: Yeah right. [*Pause.*] So—what's up? You come out here every day to cry?

CRYING MAN: [*Crying.*] I don't cry every day.

MAYA: That's what my friend said.

CRYING MAN: Well, she's lying.

MAYA: Yeah, she is sort of a liar. You're crying now though.

CRYING MAN: I have a lot of problems.

MAYA: This may sound crazy to you, but I think you and I might be perfect together.

CRYING MAN: Really?

MAYA: I think we might be a perfect match.

CRYING MAN: I'm very damaged.

MAYA: Good.

CRYING MAN: Good?

MAYA: I haven't been on a successful date in my entire life. I haven't liked a single guy, unless he was already dating one of my friends. I never met a man I wasn't afraid of. I've been mercilessly teased since I was a kid. I have no self-esteem. I say whatever pops into my giant head. And look at you.

CRYING MAN: Me?

MAYA: Crying ball of tears. You're the first man I ever saw who's clearly more insecure and screwed up than I am.

CRYING MAN: Not all of my tears are tears of sadness, you know.

MAYA: They're not?

CRYING MAN: Sometimes they're tears of joy.

MAYA: When?

CRYING MAN: When I'm looking at something of tremendous beauty. Like right now. [**MAYA** *looks behind her.*]

MAYA: Don't make fun of me.

CRYING MAN: I'm not. You're the most beautiful woman I've ever met.

MAYA: Don't lie to me.

CRYING MAN: It's true. You are. [*The* **CRYING MAN** *takes off his suit jacket, and unbuttons his dress shirt, Clark Kent-style to reveal a superhero costume underneath. It features the letter "C" prominently.*]

MAYA: My hero.

CRYING MAN: Maya. More beautiful than Holly. More beautiful than your four sisters. Kind, lovely Maya, whose head is just the right size for her body. Will you marry me?

MAYA: Yes!

❉ ❉ ❉

Lights shift. **MAYA** *and* **HOLLY** *on the rooftop.*

MAYA: What's for lunch today?

HOLLY: Hard-boiled eggs. You want the yolks? I only eat the whites.

MAYA: OK. [**HOLLY** *shares her food.*] Charlie called me. He left a message.

HOLLY: Oh yeah?

MAYA: I haven't called him back though.

HOLLY: Are you going to?

MAYA: I don't know. Weird. [*Pause.*] I got your wedding invitation, by the way.

HOLLY: What?

MAYA: It just came in the mail.

HOLLY: Oh no!

MAYA: Why, what's wrong?

HOLLY: The um . . . I was supposed to see them first. Before the calligrapher sent them out.

MAYA: They look wonderful. It sounds like it's going to be really nice.

HOLLY: I think it will be. Nice.

> [*The* **CRYING MAN** *enters and crosses to his corner. The women nearly jump out of their seats.*]

MAYA: Look who's back!

HOLLY: Oh my God, oh my God!

MAYA: Just when I was starting to give up hope of seeing him again.

HOLLY: He looks good today. I mean, aside from the crying. I like his suit.

MAYA: Yeah. It's a nice suit.

HOLLY: He got a haircut.

MAYA: No, I think he's just combing it different.

HOLLY: I think he got a haircut.

> [*Silence.*]

MAYA: I love him, Holly. Is that crazy? I've never talked to him. [*Pause.*] I'm going to talk to him.

HOLLY: No, you can't! [*She grabs* **MAYA.**]

MAYA: Let go of me.

HOLLY: You can't go over there.

MAYA: Why not?

HOLLY: Because I love him, too.

MAYA: Oh my God, Holly! You're engaged!

HOLLY: I can't help it. I love him. And I saw him first!

MAYA: So?

HOLLY: So, I saw him first! I brought you up here.

MAYA: So? He doesn't belong to you! And you already have Ward! [*The* **CRYING MAN** *stands up, and looks over the ledge.*]

HOLLY: Oh my God, he's going to jump. [*The women rush him.*]

MAYA: No! Get down from there! [*The* **CRYING MAN** *turns around. They pull him towards the center of the rooftop.*]

CRYING MAN: What are you doing?

MAYA: Don't jump! I love you.

CRYING MAN: What?

HOLLY: I love you! And I saw you first!

CRYING MAN: What? What in God's name are you talking about?

HOLLY: We've been coming up here—

MAYA: On our lunch hour—

HOLLY: Hoping to see you again.

MAYA: You look so sad—

HOLLY: You're always crying—

MAYA: We want to help you—

HOLLY: Cheer you up—

MAYA: Find out what's wrong.

CRYING MAN: Excuse me, can you please take your hands off of me?

MAYA: Oh, sorry.

CRYING MAN: Listen.

MAYA: Maya.

HOLLY: Holly.

CRYING MAN: I don't care what your names are! Listen to me! I come up here to get some peace and quiet, OK? Not to be bombarded by two screaming banshees.

    [*Pause.*]

HOLLY: We thought you were going to jump.

MAYA: You looked so sad.

CRYING MAN: Not that it's any of your fucking business, but I'm not sad. All right? I have chronically blocked tear ducts. I don't have emotional problems, OK? The only problem I DO have is nosy women who think they can save me from my miserable existence. It's a medical condition! I can't do anything about it. My allergies make it worse, so I come up here during my lunch break to dry up. I'm sick and tired of being approached about this. Do you have any idea how embarrassing it is for people to think you're crying all the time?

MAYA: I'm so sorry.

HOLLY: We were just trying to help.

CRYING MAN: Well, mind your own business! Stupid cow. [*The* **CRYING MAN** *exits. The women are stunned.*]

HOLLY: He called me a cow.

MAYA: I think he was talking to me.

HOLLY: I feel like crying.

MAYA: It's OK. You can cry in front of me.

HOLLY: Oh don't be silly. Oh my God. I totally lost my head there for a second.

MAYA: Me too.

HOLLY: I told that man I loved him! A total stranger.

MAYA: I know!

    [*Silence. They move closer to the edge.*]

HOLLY: We're really high up.

MAYA: Yeah. I've never been this close to the edge before.

HOLLY: Me neither.

MAYA: The people look so tiny. Like little figurines.

[*Silence. They stare over the ledge.*]

HOLLY: I'd really appreciate it if you never mentioned this to anyone.

MAYA: Of course.

HOLLY: Ward is my rock. He's so dependable, you know?

MAYA: Yes, definitely.

HOLLY: It's just—even when you've got everything you want, even when you're in heaven, it's hard not to feel like you're sinking sometimes.

[*Pause.*]

MAYA: I think I am gonna call Charlie.

HOLLY: I wish you would.

MAYA: And who knows? Maybe it'll work out after all. We could be very happy.

HOLLY: Just like me and Ward.

[*Pause.*]

MAYA: I hope so.

END OF PLAY

Ten-Minute Plays

The Story of
Izanagi and Izanami
KRISTEN WIRSIG

About the Playwright

Kristen Wirsig received a B.A. in English and graduated with distinction from the University of Kansas in May 2005. Her first play, *The Story of Izanagi and Izanami*, debuted at the 2004 KCACTF regional conference in Denver, Colorado. It went on to be performed at the Kennedy Center in Washington D.C., and tied for top honors in the thirty-sixth Annual KCACTF Ten-Minute Play Festival. At college, Kristen enjoyed exploring other genres and saw her poetry published in the *Kiosk, Art and Literary Magazine* and *Kansas City Voices*.

Production History

The Story of Izanagi and Izanami premiered at the KCACTF on April 17, 2004. It was directed by Jessica McLaughlin. The cast included:

HUSBAND ....Larry Herron

WIFE ....Carla McDonald

Characters

HUSBAND (James Daly), a man in his late thirties, dressed in nice, casual clothes.

WIFE (Cassandra Cunningham-Daly), a woman in her late thirties with long, dark hair, dressed in a power-suit.

Setting

In the center of the stage is a bench or armless couch. On the left side of the bench is a small vanity table with makeup paraphernalia on it. On the side of the bench is a small desk with a book on it. The backdrop is painted with three large columns and the middle one is directly behind the bench.

Notes

Until the specified moment, the **HUSBAND** and **WIFE** do not acknowledge each other's presence. During the times that they are directed to stand, they can walk, pace, etc. BUT they cannot cross center stage. They must each remain on his or her own side of the column.

AT RISE: **HUSBAND** *and* **WIFE** *are seated on the bench, the* **HUSBAND** *on the right,* **WIFE** *on the left, as far apart as they can sit and still be on the bench.* **HUSBAND** *is reading from a book about Japan.* **WIFE** *is tweezing her eyebrows.* **HUSBAND** *shuts the book and speaks directly to audience.*

HUSBAND: To begin, the ancient Japanese believed that the universe was formed by creating order out of the chaos. As a result, everything in our world has a fixed order. To upset the proper order of one thing is to risk sending many things back into chaos. At the time of our planet's birth, a god and goddess were sent to dwell here and to be the father and mother of all life on earth. Izanagi and Izanami were their names and they were placed on a tiny island—one on either side of a large pillar that stood in the center of it. They could not see each other from where they stood—unaware of the other's presence . . . [*Stands, paces away a bit.*] I asked Cass to meet me here—today—because . . . because . . .

WIFE: [*Standing, also speaks to audience.*] It's really ironic, what we're doing here, because it's our anniversary, and this—well—this is the courthouse where we were married. Not the most romantic place, but it was the most practical at the time. We just graduated a couple months before—James was an East Asian Studies major and I was in Architecture. An odd couple, I know. We would probably have never even met except we were set up on a blind date our senior year by . . . what's his name . . .

HUSBAND: It's been fifteen years . . . fifteen years. [*Pauses, smiles.*] I remember our first date—we were fixed up by my friend 'Cleat.' I think he felt like I needed all the help I could get. Of course I probably did, compared to him. He never had any trouble getting a date for the weekends—or weeknights, for that matter. I almost told him no. I was pretty much broke, typical poor college student, but Cleat said not to worry about it. He said he didn't know Cass too well—just through a girl he dated, but he had her down for the type that probably wouldn't mind paying for the date herself. Well, I couldn't ask her to do that. Call me old-fashioned if you want, but I just didn't want to get off to that kind of start. So Cleat got us tickets to his football game that Saturday and arranged for us to meet there.

WIFE: So there we were . . . our first date—a packed stadium full of screaming fans. Within minutes we discovered that we had something in common.

HUSBAND and **WIFE:** We both hate football.

WIFE: It was essential to the future of our date that we leave the football game, so I asked him out for drinks.

HUSBAND: When Cass offered to buy me a drink, I didn't want to sound arrogant by turning her down. She was so—different—than other girls I'd dated—in a good way, I mean. She was just so confident. Plus I really wanted to get out of that game. So we went, and it was great. We stayed out until three or four in the morning, just talking. The more I got to know about her, the more amazing she became—so smart and funny and . . . amazing. I remember lying awake after I took her home, and I just knew— she was IT. [*Pause.*] But I still . . . I wish I could have been able to ask HER out for that drink.

WIFE: He and I really hit it off. James was definitely not my usual 'type,' but I liked that. I thought he was a little shy at first, but I realized he was just an easygoing guy, very intelligent and a great listener. What really surprised me was that he didn't mind when I paid—that sure was a change, but I kind of liked that too. So I guess right from the start our relationship was pretty different, and a few months later . . . there we were . . . in front of the courthouse.

HUSBAND: When graduation rolled around I knew she wanted me to propose . . . expected it—pretty much everyone we knew expected it. But I . . . I couldn't. I knew I loved her, I was sure of that—but not of myself. See, I didn't really know what I was doing after graduation. I didn't have anything . . . practical. What I really wanted was to go to Japan, to keep studying Asian cultures there, but how could I ask her to—[*Breaks off.*] How would I take care of her without a real job? It just didn't seem like the right time. Then she got this letter . . .

WIFE: The week before graduation I heard from a contracting firm in Seattle—they wanted me! It was an amazing opportunity. I just couldn't pass it up.

HUSBAND: She said it was...

WIFE: A dream come true. There was just one problem. James still hadn't said the 'm' word. I had no idea what his intentions were. I just didn't feel I could reasonably wait any longer, my life was moving on, full speed ahead. [*Moves back toward bench.*] I just needed to know if it would be with or without him. So . . . I took the initiative and asked. [*She sits, begins applying eye makeup.*]

HUSBAND: Then . . . she asked me. [*He goes to bench and sits, picks up book again and finds his place.*] After Izanagi and Izanami were placed on either side of the pillar on the little island, they soon became curious as to what was on the other side. So Izanagi began circling the pillar to his left and Izanami to her right. At the center, they met and saw each other for the first time. They gazed at one another in silence, but Izanami, unable to contain her deep feeling, said aloud, "Ohh! What a beautiful man!" And Izanagi, in turn, said, "Ohh, what a beautiful woman!" At that moment, Izanagi could not see the unhappy consequences of what they had done, but he knew that a series of events had been set into motion that would soon spin out of their control, into chaos. [*Pause.*] And so he looked into her eyes sadly. [*He turns a little and looks at* **WIFE**. *She is now applying lipstick but still is not aware of him. He speaks to* **WIFE**.] "Izanami," he said, "you are indeed my beloved, but you have wronged me. You know it is for me to speak first. As it is, we shall not please the gods, nor shall we ourselves have joy unless we undo this beginning."

> [*Note: From this point on* **HUSBAND** *is aware of* **WIFE**, *responds to what she says, looks at her, but still cannot cross center stage—to her side.* **WIFE** *continues to be unaware of his presence.*]

WIFE: [*Standing, to audience.*] As soon as we were married, we moved to Seattle to get settled in. I felt a little guilty at first—there was really nothing there for James, but I don't think he knew what he wanted to do anyway. He once mentioned studying in Japan . . . I don't think he was serious. That was the difference between us. He had dreams, I had goals. So following my career was the only practical thing to do.

HUSBAND: [*Standing, not bitterly, to* **WIFE**.] It was the most practical. You were always the sensible one.

WIFE: And he did find a job. At—

HUSBAND and **WIFE:** —Roosevelt High.

WIFE: He started out just in the attendance office, but eventually he worked his way up.

HUSBAND: To substitute history teacher. But it . . . it worked for us. You had your dream job. I had thirteen hundred teenagers who didn't know the Zhou Period from the Mongolian Interlude, and didn't care to, but I wanted to do it. For you. For a while . . .

WIFE: And I loved my job, everything about it—at first. Of course we were—I was—too busy to start a family. I always said "Next year, next year," for years . . .

HUSBAND: But then, one year, it was too late.

WIFE: We decided to try for a baby, but we—we couldn't. We went to a specialist who did some tests and finally told me I had a . . . [*Begins to cry.*]

HUSBAND: The doctor said the tumor was benign, but that he would have to operate anyway, just in case . . .

WIFE: I would never be able to have a child . . . [*She begins applying make-up more heavily, almost erratically as she speaks.*] Of course the only sensible thing for me to do was to return to work, but it suddenly seemed so meaningless, everything about it was empty and cold. Like me. Eventually I hated my job, hated my ROLE. And I—I hated James for not doing anything about it. Couldn't he see I was miserable? Then I hated myself for hating him—as if he ever did anything but follow my lead. . . . And look where I led us. It was never meant to be this way.

HUSBAND: I knew you were miserable . . . I saw. And I did nothing.

For years we dragged on, bitter and resentful, because I was too apathetic to make a decision, to take initiative. Then a couple of months ago I was going through some old boxes and I found one of my books from college. I read this story, an early Japanese myth, and . . . it changed everything. [*Pause.*] So I . . . I've been looking into getting my master's. In Japan. Actually I already found a university in Kyoto. They accepted me and . . . I'm going. Without you if I must.

> [**WIFE** *continues to apply makeup in hard, purposeful strokes and we realize that she is making herself up as a Geisha.*]

WIFE: To return things to their proper order, Izanagi and Izanami had to undo the pattern they had begun. They turned away from each other and walked slowly around the pillar in the direction from which they had come. At the other side they met again.

There was silence, silence that seemed to last for years, and Izanami held her breath as she waited . . . afraid his words would never come, wondering, wondering what he would say, but fearing she already knew.

HUSBAND: Izanagi looked down at her, unable to speak, so great was his love for her. But at last, but at last, he broke the silence. [*Breaking off abruptly, he stands, walks a few paces away and turns and looks at* **WIFE.**] Cass, I wish it hadn't come to this, but I don't know what else to do. I wish . . . I wish there was another way to undo this beginning.

> [**WIFE***'s transformation into a Geisha is complete and she is putting up her hair in chopsticks.* **HUSBAND** *crosses to her side and puts his hand on her shoulder.*]

Cass?

> [*Slowly she turns and rises, but her head is down, he can't see her face.*]

Cass, I—

[*He puts his hand under her chin and raises her face to look into his, he is startled.*]

Oh . . . what a beautiful woman.

[*They look at each other, book slips to the ground. Blackout.*]

END OF PLAY

Stairway to Heaven
GREGORY FLETCHER

About the Playwright

Gregory Fletcher is a native of Dallas. He received a B.A. in Theater from California State University at Northridge, an M.F.A. in Directing from Columbia University, and an M.A. in Playwriting from Boston University. Fletcher's short plays have appeared at Off-Off Broadway's Emerging Artists Theatre, Intar 53, Manhattan Theatre Source, and Greenwich Street Theatre, and regionally at the Boston Playwrights' Theatre, Boston Theatre Marathon, Edward Albee's Last Frontier Theater Conference, Provincetown Fringe Festival, and Provincetown Theatre Company. *Stairway to Heaven* won the 2004 National Ten-Minute Play Award at the Kennedy Center's American College Theatre Festival. Fletcher also the recipient of the KCACTF's 2005 Mark Twain Prize for Comic Playwriting and took second place for the 2005 David Mark Cohen Playwriting Award.

Production History

Stairway to Heaven was workshopped at the 2004 KCACTF regional festival for Region 1 with Ryan Bethke and Julie Miller, directed by Kathy Plourde, and at the National Festival with Kaitlin Yikel and Brian Watkins, directed by Jon Royal. The play premiered at the Manhattan Theatre Source, 2004 Homogenius Festival, with Ari Butler and Allison Goldberg, directed by Janice Goldberg.

Characters

ELISA, 17

GIL, 16. Elisa's brother

Time

The new century, 2000

Setting

The carpeted stairway of a family home

AT RISE: A boy of sixteen, **GIL,** *wearing a dark suit, is lying down on his back. His sister,* **ELISA,** *seventeen years old, also dressed in dark colors and wearing a skirt, starts down the stairs. Her hair is pinned up in the messed-up look.*

ELISA: Get up. [*No response.*] I said, get up. Now!

GIL: So go.

ELISA: Like—I'm in a skirt.

GIL: Like—I'm gonna look? Gross.

ELISA: You're sixteen, of course you'll look.

GIL: In your dreams.

ELISA: Shut up. Why don't you go up to Mom so she can see how wrinkled your suit's getting. You should iron it.

GIL: And you should brush your hair.

ELISA: It's supposed to look like this, you jerk. Move!

GIL: Just go if you're going.

ELISA: If you look, that's sexual harassment, and sexual harassment leads to sexual abuse, and statistics show that one out of five women are sexually abused by a family member—

GIL: I can't believe you're quoting your term paper to me. That is so lame.

ELISA: I got an A plus on that paper. Gil, enough! If you don't move, you are so dead meat!

GIL: Two deaths in one week? Doubt it.

ELISA: Please. Go see Mom.

GIL: I'll see her when she comes down.

ELISA: I don't want her to be alone.

GIL: She's probably dressing, let her be.

ELISA: She's dressed, you're dressed, we're all dressed! Dressed and waiting. [*Sighs.*] And waiting. Go on, at least while I'm making Mom and me a cup of tea.

GIL: Oh, la-de-da, so adult. When did you grow up all of a sudden?

ELISA: When do you think?! [**GIL** *looks away.*] She needs you.

GIL: No, his . . . when I had to go up for his dress shoes, for the funeral home . . . his closet . . . I could . . . you can still . . .

ELISA: Smell him?

GIL: Yeah.

ELISA: Okay, so come down with me, I'll make you your first cup of la-de-da tea. You'll like it.

GIL: No.

ELISA: What?

GIL: Too many...the photos magnets on the refrigerator.

ELISA: Oh. Well, you can wait at the dining room table.

GIL: His chair. Waiting to be pulled out.

ELISA: The living room?

GIL: The recliner. His impression...

ELISA: Still on the cushion, yeah. The backyard? Never mind. The hammock. Even in the garage. His car.

GIL: I could feel him on the steering wheel.

ELISA: Then go in your room, at least you're safe there. I'll call you when it's ready. [**GIL** *doesn't move.*] In your own room?

GIL: Every trophy. Every ribbon. He's there, cheering me on.

ELISA: For someone who's dead, he sure is all around. [*She finally gets it.*] Except here.

GIL: So go. Scram. [**ELISA** *doesn't move.*] Elisa, I don't need your permission to be here.

ELISA: Look, Gil, I know you're upset—we're all upset—but no need to . . . I'm just saying, when things start changing around here—

GIL: Yeah, duh, they already have.

ELISA: I mean it, lose the attitude.

GIL: Stop talking down to me.

ELISA: F you.

GIL: You're using the f word?

ELISA: It was a letter.

GIL: Used in a complete sentence with a subject and verb.

ELISA: I didn't use the word.

GIL: And of all days, I can't believe you.

ELISA: It was a fucking letter.

GIL: Oh my God!

ELISA: I didn't . . . stop, you made me.

GIL: I should fucking wash your mouth out. [*Gasps in shock.*] Oh my God!

ELISA: You watch it!

GIL: I didn't mean it!

GIL and **ELISA:** I don't want Mom to hear that kind of language!

GIL: Jinx, you owe me a Coke!

ELISA: Gil, you're gonna have to grow up. And fast.

GIL: Oh, like you're my authority figure now? My role model?

ELISA: Well, I am the eldest, and it only makes sense now that—

GIL: By a year, big deal. I'm the only man of the house now.

ELISA: Don't think so. It's Mom, dope.

GIL: Wrong equipment. Do I have to explain it to you?

ELISA: You can't even say the word.

GIL: Mom is not the man of the house and neither are you.

ELISA: Yeah, well—

GIL: Yeah, well, what?!

[*They take a breath and calm down.*]

ELISA: If you really want to be the man of the house, then go see Mom. Being the man means putting others first.

GIL: I just want to get this over with. When Howie Levy's dad died, they didn't drag it out with viewings and services. He was in the ground the next day.

ELISA: They don't believe in embalming.

GIL: You don't even know the Levys.

ELISA: They're Jewish. It's a Jewish thing.

GIL: Oh. Well, makes more sense. I think when you die, you should get to be dead.

ELISA: [*Carefully.*] Billy should've been invited.

GIL: Billy—what . . . why . . . I mean, he—he's not that close to Dad.

ELISA: To *you*. Special friends and loved ones . . . to comfort us in time of . . . oh, relax, no reason to clam up.

GIL: I just don't know why you think...I mean, it's...if—

ELISA: You're very close, you gonna deny it? Come on, Gil, when Mom and Dad went away with the church group, I know you guys—

GIL: It was a bath; we were in and out!

ELISA: Morning, noon and night? Please, if you weren't my brother, I'd think it was pretty hot.

GIL: Why do you bring this up like you got some power hold over me? You don't.

ELISA: Because you're gonna . . . you're gonna need someone special, you jerk! To confide in, to cry with, to get through this. And since you don't let me in . . . I can't even think of the last time we shared something important . . . really talked together.

GIL: [*Finally admitting.*] Did Dad know? Me and Billy?

ELISA: Why not? He's totally up on things.

GIL: *Those* things? No way, he's a Republican.

ELISA: Maybe, but only financially. I mean, down deep, he's practically a hippie. He plays Led Zeppelin. Played, whatever. I'm sure he was bound to talk to you about it.

GIL: What he was bound to talk about was how Eddie's too hands-on with you.

ELISA: At least we're out in the open.

GIL: Yeah, too open. Like we haven't all seen?

ELISA: As in Mom and Dad?

GIL: No, as in the entire neighborhood.

ELISA: Liar!

GIL: And he doesn't respect women.

ELISA: What do you know about it?

GIL: I know it's not right. You should respect yourself more.

ELISA: You too! I hear you'll experience a huge relief when you come out of the closet. Like a heavy burden lifts from your shoulders.

GIL: Write a term paper on it, why don't you. You're just too scared not to have a date for the prom.

ELISA: Like you're gonna ask Billy to *your* prom?

GIL: Like you need a boyfriend in order to feel whole?

ELISA: Be proud of who you are.

GIL: Practice what you preach.

ELISA: Preach what you practice!

GIL: Elisa, enough—

ELISA: Homosexual shame is so twentieth century, get with it!

GIL: Hold your voice down.

ELISA: All right. I'll talk to Eddie about it. When you talk.

GIL: That's the last thing Mom needs right now.

ELISA: She can handle it. We can all handle it. As long as you're—you're, you know, playing it safe. Are you? Playing it safe?

GIL: Are you and Eddie . . . playing it safe?

ELISA: Yes, Dad, we are. Are you and Billy? [*No response.*] Well?

GIL: Yes, Dad, we are. We're not stupid, you know.

ELISA: Okay . . . I'm relieved. Good.

GIL: Yeah. Me, too.

ELISA: Cool.

GIL: So.

ELISA: Dad for each other then? On an as-needed basis?

GIL: People would shit if I brought Billy to the prom.

ELISA: That's what people do—they shit. [**GIL** *takes* **ELISA***'s hand.*] You've got Dad's hands, you know. Throw your hand open, palm up.

GIL: [*Opening his hand.*] Weird, huh?

ELISA: Do it again? [**GIL** *opens his hand again.*] Identical. [**ELISA** *takes his hand, and they sit holding hands for a good long moment.*]

GIL: Good. Okay.

ELISA: Okay what?

GIL: [*Standing and buttoning his jacket.*] I'll be up with Mom. How do I look?

ELISA: Like the man of the house.

GIL: Yeah, you too. [**GIL** *smiles and exits up the stairs.* **ELISA** *exits down the stairs.*]

END OF PLAY

Contacts and Representations

Training Wisteria © 2005 by Molly Smith Metzler
    For performance rights and direct script inquiries, please contact
    Molly Smith Metzler c/o Susan Gurman Agency, 865 West End
    Avenue, #15A, New York, NY 10025. Phone: (212) 749–4618
    Fax: (212) 864–5055 www.gurmanagency.com

Lot's Daughters © 2001 by Rebecca Basham
    Rebecca Basham can be reached at rbasham@rider.edu. All performance
    rights for *Lot's Daughters* are controlled exclusively by Samuel French,
    Inc., 45 West 25th Street, New York, NY 10010–2751. Phone: (212)
    206–8990 Fax: (212) 206–1429 www.samuelfrench.com

it is no desert © by Dan Stroeh
    Dan Stroeh can be reached at dan@alarmclocktheatre.org. All
    performance rights for *it is no desert* are controlled exclusively by
    Samuel French, Inc., 45 West 25th Street, New York, NY 10010–2751.
    Phone: (212) 206–8990 Fax: (212) 206–1429 www.samuelfrench.com

Yemaya's Belly © 2003 by Quiara Alegría Hudes
    For performance rights and direct script inquiries, please contact
    Quiara Alegría Hudes c/o Bruce Ostler, Bret Adams, Ltd., 448
    West 44th Street, New York, NY 10036. Phone: (212) 765–5630

Supernova in Hamlet © 1999 by Kristina Leach
    Kristina Leach can be reached at kal813@hotmail.com.

The Man of Infinite Sadness © 2005 by Brian Tanen
    Brian Tanen can be reached at brian_tanen@yahoo.com.

The Story of Izanagi and Izanami © 2003 by Kristen Wirsig
    Kristen Wirsig can be reached at kristenreneemiller@gmail.com,
    or by phoning Mark Miller (913) 909–2301.

Stairway to Heaven © 2004 by Gregory Fletcher
    For more information, go to www.gregoryfletcher.com. The amateur
    and stock performance rights for *Stairway to Heaven* are controlled
    exclusively by the Dramatic Publishing Company, 311 Washington
    Street, Woodstock, IL 60098. Phone: (815) 338–7170
    Fax: (815) 338–8981 www.dramaticpublishing.com

About the Editor

GARY GARRISON is the Artistic Director of and a full-time faculty member in the Department of Dramatic Writing Program at NYU's Tisch School of the Arts. He has produced the last eighteen Festivals of New Works for NYU, working with hundreds of playwrights, directors, and actors. Garrison's plays include *Old Soles, Padding the Wagon, Rug Store Cowboy, Cherry Reds, Gawk, Oh Messiah Me, We Make A Wall, The Big Fat Naked Truth, Scream with Laughter, Smoothness with Cool, Empty Rooms, Does Anybody Want a Miss Cow Bayou?*, and *When a Diva Dreams*. This work has been featured at The Neighborhood Playhouse, Primary Stages, The Directors Company, Manhattan Theatre Source, StageWorks, Fourth Unity, Open Door Theatre, African Globe Theatre Company, Pulse Ensemble Theatre, Expanded Arts, and New York Rep. He is the author of the critically acclaimed *The Playwright's Survival Guide: Keeping the Drama in Your Work and Out of Your Life* (Heinemann Press; second edition was released in October 2005), *Perfect Ten: Writing and Producing the Ten-Minute Play* (Heinemann Press) and co-editor of two volumes of *Monologues for Men by Men* (Heinemann Press), with Michael Wright. He is a faculty member of Playwriting for the Kennedy Center's Summer Playwriting Intensive, the National Chair of Playwriting for the Kennedy Center's American College Theater Festival, and a member of the Dramatists Guild. This year, Garrison was a featured artist at the Last Frontier Theatre Conference in Valdez, Alaska, and chosen the 2005 Outstanding Teacher of Playwriting by the Association of Theatre in Higher Education.

About the Kennedy Center American College Theater Festival (KCACTF)

In 1969, Kennedy Center Founding Chairman Roger L. Stevens created the *Kennedy Center American College Theater Festival* (KCACTF), which is currently the oldest education program of the Center. As college theater departments and student artists showcase their work and receive outside assessment, KCACTF serves as a catalyst for improving the quality of college theater in the United States.

The KCACTF is a year-round program in eight geographic regions in the United States. Each region presents its own festival, where students and teachers can see others work and share ideas. These festivals, held in January and February of each year, showcase the finest regional productions. The five most outstanding productions from the regional festivals are showcased, all expenses paid, at the National Festival, which is held each April at the Kennedy Center in Washington. In addition, regional award-winners and exceptional faculty in playwriting, design, directing, criticism and performance are invited to the Kennedy Center for a week on full fellowship.

KCACTF offers a forum in which to explore the creative process while honoring excellence by recognizing outstanding productions as well as exceptional work by individual student artists. In addition to performance experience, the National Festival includes a wide range of master classes in playwriting, audition techniques, vocal production, movement, stage combat, and Shakespearean verse. There are sessions for all participants ranging from undergraduate students to experienced faculty members. Awards, scholarships, internships and fellowships to prestigious institutions such as Sundance Theatre Lab, the O'Neill Theater Center, and The Shakespeare Theatre, are given in a variety of areas, including playwriting, directing, acting, criticism, and design.

The goals of the Kennedy Center American College Theater Festival are to encourage, recognize, and celebrate the finest and most diverse work produced in university and college theater programs; to provide opportunities for participants to develop their theater skills and insight and achieve professionalism; to improve the quality of college and university theater in America; and to encourage colleges and universities to give distinguished productions of new plays, especially those written by students; the classics, revitalized or newly conceived; and experimental works.